WILLY BRANDT

IN EXILE

ESSAYS REFLECTIONS
AND LETTERS
1933–1947

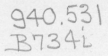

WILLY BRANDT

IN EXILE

ESSAYS REFLECTIONS AND

LETTERS 1933–1947

Translated from the German
by R.W. LAST

Biographical introduction
by TERENCE PRITTIE

OSWALD WOLFF

LONDON

© 1971 for the English edition by
OSWALD WOLFF (PUBLISHERS) LIMITED, LONDON

First published in Germany in 1966 by
KINDLER VERLAG GmbH, Munich,
under the title "Draussen", edited by
Günther Struve

ISBN O 85496 120 8

MADE AND PRINTED IN GREAT BRITAIN BY
THE GARDEN CITY PRESS LIMITED
LETCHWORTH, HERTFORDSHIRE
SG6 1JS

CONTENTS

Foreword to the English Edition

I deliberately chose the short title *Draussen* (Outside) for the German edition of this collection of writings from the dark years between 1933 and 1947. It ought to be made clear that I did not for one moment regard my fate as an exile as a blot on my copybook, but rather as a chance to serve that 'other Germany' which did not resign itself submissively to enslavement but kept watch for the hour of liberation, and indeed fought and made great sacrifices in the struggle for freedom. I do not need to justify my actions to anyone, so what I offer here is an objective account of the past. My fellow citizens can fairly claim the right to know in some detail what manner of man it is whom one of the great parties of our young German democracy has entrusted with leadership. The aim has been to show, without sentimentality or empty words, that during my time 'outside' I did not for one moment cease to regard myself as a German, despite my Norwegian passport, despite the happy circumstance that I found in Scandinavia a second home, to which I shall be bound by ties of loyalty and gratitude to the end of my days. During twelve years of Nazi dictatorship I was worlds apart from the commanders of the prison house that called itself 'Greater Germany', but still felt close to the millions who were driven to their deaths on the front line or who were alone with their fears in the air-raid shelters. Why else would I have resolved to return to that tormented country at a time when all hope seemed lost? Why else would I have chosen Berlin, a city slipping into the clutches of another totalitarian power? The Germans understood my reasons. My election as Chancellor was an act of mutual confidence. It gave me the right to assert that the defeat of Hitler was now finally complete.

There is no doubt that the change of administration in Bonn marks a clear dividing line in the postwar history of Germany—a dividing line, but not a break in continuity. For two decades the fate of the Federal Republic was determined by the Christian Democrat party—in itself a coalition of conservative and liberal elements—which bore the stamp of Konrad Adenauer, who became a father figure to a defeated nation which under his leadership was able to reorganise itself and find its way back to a state of calm and confidence. He gave the Germans on this side of the iron curtain their proper place in the common security system of the western alliance. He opened the door to a close partnership with France, and beyond that, to a reconciliation between the two nations, whose 'traditional emnity' had so often and so unnecessarily shattered the harmony of the continent. His outlook may have been founded on nineteenth-century middle-class attitudes, but at the same time he displayed a keener awareness of the tasks of the future than many younger men. I have no hesitation in naming him as one of the rebuilders of western Europe, and even in times of the most violent disagreement I have never lost my respect for the 'old man of Rhöndorf'. In the early years of the west German state it was not everyone who understood that it was essential for the growing republic to be firmly rooted in the western security system. The fight for the freedom of Berlin had sharpened my awareness of the dangers of a power vacuum in central Europe—and besides, my years 'outside' had taught me to become a European. I became aware before many others that this continent could not be rebuilt on the decayed foundations of the old order of things : the nation state was a thing of the past. None the less I was one of those who took the view at the time that Soviet policy should have been examined in far more depth than was actually the case.

My concept of the new Europe is far more wide-ranging than that of its founding fathers Robert Schumann, de Gasperi and Adenauer. My years in Scandinavia gave me access to the Anglo-Saxon world. I never doubted that Great Britain would draw closer and closer to the continent, the more the basic community of the six stabilised and consolidated itself. But the will towards unity could not be allowed to be blocked by a process of continental isolationism. A political community—whether made up of independent states or a confederation—is unthinkable without Great Britain or our Scandinavian neighbours. That demands of Britain that she should renounce the insularity of her past greatness.

My impassioned attack on Vansittart's plans for Germany which is to be found in these pages is a clear enough demonstration of the significance I gave to Britain's presence on the continent when the time had come to think beyond victory and defeat to the nature of the coming peace. After 1945 many wise men in London stuck rigidly to the view that it was Great Britain's task to remain steadfastly and for all time as a bridge between Europe and the United States. Indeed she has a bridging role to play—and this is underestimated by no one for whom history is a living force in the present (and the present history in the making)—namely, as one of the strongest pillars of the treaty system which spans the Atlantic, the ocean which Thomas Mann, the most notable son of my home city of Lübeck, had recognised even during the First World War as the new Mediterranean. If you like, Mann had thereby anticipated J. F. Kennedy's formula of the interdependence which holds America and a united Europe together.

The vital forward thrust of Europe seemed to have faded with the passing of Konrad Adenauer from the political scene. The change of power, for which the way had been prepared by the 'grand coalition' of autumn 1966 and the changed situation in Paris did however release new European energies. To all those whose ultimate objective is a political community (which means more than an amalgam of separate national interests), it was essential that the dialogue with Great Britain should be renewed unconditionally. The Hague conference in December 1969 opened the door. I played my part in bringing this about. The revitalisation of the community spirit in western Europe and partnership with the United States encouraged us to enter into discussions with Moscow and eastern Europe, culminating in the signing of the treaty with the Soviet Union and in parallel agreements with Poland and other Warsaw Pact countries; and these agreements move us one stage further towards a secure peace.

That too is a natural consequence of the concept of the new Europe, which was determined by the re-entry of Germany into the councils of the great powers—a consequence which the first Chancellor and his party did not venture to draw. The Anglo-Saxon world, and particularly Great Britain, remained foreign to Adenauer. He found it difficult to free himself from the mental attitudes of his Rhineland Catholic background, although he was able to think more into the future than many of his friends and supporters, even on those lines which under the heading of *Ostpolitik* have come to be taken for granted in international discussion.

I come from a north German Protestant background; my youth was spent under the influence of the Social Democratic socialist movement. This may also explain my broader and less inhibited initiatives towards a European policy.

In conclusion : Konrad Adenauer was a man of the 'inner emigration'. Stripped of his official position by Nazi officials, he withdrew into the protective cocoon of a strictly private existence, in order to await calmly and earnestly the catastrophe which he knew would come. The Terror drove me to leave the country. My only choice was 'external' emigration. I took that choice, and I have never regretted it, because it offered me not only the chance to learn but also the chance to resist. So it is logical that the office of German Chancellor should be filled first by a representative of the 'inner emigration' and then of the 'external emigration', the latter being a man who saw Germany's years of darkness from 'outside'. Thus the pattern and continuity in the history of the second German republic is revealed : it is in truth the history of the Europeanisation of Germany. And at the same time of the Europeanisation of Europe.

The majority of my fellow countrymen have accepted my view that a nationalist cannot be a good German. I recognise my position as Chancellor as one offering the challenge of reconciling Germany with her neighbours and with herself. At last the time has come for Germans to be at peace with themselves—so that the world at large can be at peace with Germany.

Willy Brandt.

Translator's Note

The present translation follows the German text as edited by Günther Struve, with the exception of some cuts aimed at removing material of limited interest and tightening up the narrative. Struve points out that he offers the reader a relatively small but representative selection of Brandt's voluminous writings over the period 1933–1947. He stresses that it has been his aim to provide an honest picture of Brandt's political development in those years, and that he has strenuously sought to avoid selecting only those passages in which Brandt's evaluation and projection of a given situation have turned out to be correct.

Thus this book offers a unique insight into the growth to political maturity of a man whose impact on the European and international scene is increasing almost daily. Perhaps the most fascinating aspect of the text is the way in which Brandt, despite the ravages of Nazism and the heated passions it aroused, was able to keep a cool head politically and to develop undeterred his conviction that internationalism alone is the key to social justice and world peace for the future.

Brandt himself has provided introductions to each of the chapters, which are divided not chronologically, but according to subject-matter. 'Extracts are marked off by double spaces in the text, and the sources indicated by marginal numbers which refer to the list of sources at the end of the book.'

I wish to express my gratitude to those who have assisted me in the work of translation, and in particular to my publisher, Mrs. Ilse Wolff, for expert research work; to the Director of the Centre for Computer Studies at Hull University for permission to make use of the facilities there in the computer-assisted preparatory work on the index; to Miss Diana Smith, without whose swift and skilful typing the manuscript would have been much delayed; and finally to my wife Pat for checking through the typescript and proofs.

R. W. Last.

Biographical Introduction

There is a convention that, when writing about a politician, one should describe him in 'political' terms, reduce his life to a balance-sheet of achievement and failure, and at the end of it all produce a mathematically exact sum of his story. By this sort of process, one could even decide whether Adenauer did as much for Germany as Bismarck, or whether Winston Churchill was a greater man than Julius Caesar.

Fortunately, this convention need not apply to the still living. They defy political autopsy. They remain creatures of instinct and impulse, a part of the world in which we are all living. But, then, contemporary biography is frowned upon, because it is popularly supposed that it has to be written with an ulterior motive—to glorify or to denigrate. This is certainly wrong. For a truthful picture of a man, even if obviously incomplete, can be of more value when he is alive than when he is dead, pointing his purpose, making him understandable when it is very important indeed that he should be understood.

For that reason, I gladly agreed to introduce the writings-in-exile of Willy Brandt, the Chancellor of the Federal German Republic, which constitute an important historical document and illuminate a vital period in the development of a man who has, and always has had a purpose.

Willy Brandt was born, in December 1913, illegitimate. His mother's name was Frahm; he never knew his father's. Illegitimacy was probably more of a spur to him than anything else, a spur to make his own way in life, relying completely on himself, forming his own views and philosophy of life. He grew up poor, with a deeply ingrained belief in human freedom and dignity, and social justice. When Hitler came to power he was only nineteen, at an impressionable age in a period of German history when it was easy to be impressed by the manifestations of returning German power. German youth, growing up under this stigma of military defeat, a tough peace and a label of war-guilt which none of them really felt was justified, was mainly easy game for the Nazis. Already a thoughtful and convinced socialist, Brandt could never have become a Nazi. But he could easily have joined the serried but surreptitious ranks of the 'non-Nazis', who found it convenient to conform while not believing, to serve the Nazi machine while keeping one's reservations to oneself. This, after all, was the creed—if one can use such a word—of probably two thirds of the German people. It was, quite simply, based on self-preservation.

The first, and one of the greatest of Willy Brandt's achievements was that he went into active opposition. He fought the Nazis in the streets even before they came to power, at a time when there was the greatest chance of stopping them. In order to continue his opposition, he went into exile, first in Denmark and then in Norway. This meant giving up home, friends and country. This was when he took the name of Willy Brandt, as a part of his new start in life. Thirty years later he explained that there never was the slightest reason for him to have felt any sense of personal or political shame—he used the memorable phrase, 'I have nothing to hide'. He served the socialist cause in Scandinavia, worked as a journalist on the republican side in the Spanish Civil War, returned clandestinely and at the risk of his life as a member of the Social Democratic 'underground' in pre-war Berlin.

Brandt put on Norwegian uniform which saved him from the danger of being discovered by the Gestapo. He never took part in active fighting. A German PoW camp proved to be the best hiding place. Before being discovered as a German refugee Brandt managed to escape to Sweden.

During the war he carried on further, dangerous work for the anti-Nazi underground and returned when the war was over to his former country as a Norwegian citizen and press attaché with the rank of major. He took the second momentous decision of his life in 1947, when he sought and was allowed to resume German citizenship. I have personal memories of the shy young man who lodged with other Allied officers in West Berlin's Hotel am Zoo in the early days after the end of the war. It was probably the sight of Germany's abasement, shame and bitter need which induced him to become a German again. He had no need to do so; he could have had a comfortable, secure and successful career as a Norwegian. Unlike other German emigrés who came home after 1945, Willy Brandt had been completely successful in identifying himself with the country of his adoption and in being accepted by its people. He chose to become a German again in Germany's darkest hour. The last man in the world to talk about himself, he did this because he wanted to serve his country and his people.

My next memories of him are as a rising star in the ranks of the Social Democratic party. He made his home in Berlin. Like Jakob Kaiser of the Christian Democratic Union and Ernst Reuter of his own party, he believed that it was in Berlin that the real struggle for Germany's future had to be fought. He served as a member of the party's executive through the 1948–49 Blockade, was elected a year later to the Berlin City Parliament, and became one of the closest confidants of the Governing Mayor, Ernst Reuter. The Social Democrats became entrenched as the strongest party in the old capital; Willy Brandt was one of their most forceful and practical younger members.

His political apprenticeship was a long one. One reason for this was the character and idiosyncrasies of the party's chairman, Kurt Schumacher. A highly oratorical ideologist, Schumacher picked lieutenants who served him unquestioningly and veneratingly. To him, Willy Brandt's strongly practical bent was inimical; he would not have made the right kind of disciple, for he was more inclined to reflection than to revolutionary fervour. He also opposed Schumacher's bitter attacks against Chancellor Adenauer's policy to integrate West Germany and West Berlin into the framework of a European and Atlantic community. Even at this early stage in German postwar history, Brandt was aware of the fact that there was virtually no hope of reconstituting the German state. Thus he inclined to Adenauer's strategy of strengthening and consolidating democracy in West Germany. Schumacher died in 1952, but under his political testament a solid 'bloc' of his followers remained in control of the Social Democratic party. Doctrinaire policies remained in vogue, and condemned the party to the role of what looked like being eternal opposition. Brandt made his way up the political ladder only with the greatest difficulty. It was only in 1955 that he became President, or Speaker of the West Berlin City Parliament. As a result of patient and passionate party work he won the post of Governing Mayor of the city in 1957, the most important post in Germany outside the federal administration in Bonn. He held that post for nearly ten years.

During those years Brandt gained a unique reputation for staunchness in the face of threats and danger, and for devotion to duty. He worked with easy informality but immense determination, winning the hearts of the Berliners and showing great courage in moments of crisis. There were plenty of these for Berlin, with a violent Soviet propaganda campaign in 1959 and 1960 after the Krushchev ultimatum, and the building of the infamous Berlin Wall in 1961. Psychologically, if not physically, Berlin remained in a state of siege as daunting as the 1948–49 Blockade, and in one sense even more depressing. It seemed likely to go on for ever, and the long years of strain are only now beginning to have a cumulative effect on the morale of the normally perky, self-assured Berliner. Brandt's personal contribution to Berlin has been incalculable; it continued even after he became the Social Democratic party chairman and its candidate for the Chancellorship in the Federal elections.

German democracy owes Willy Brandt another, almost equally important debt, for his part in reviewing and revising the basic policies of the Social Democratic party. Until 1959 this party, the only true guardian of German democracy before the Nazis came to power, stood next to no chance of winning political power in Bonn. It remained committed to outworn Marxist tenets, uneasily accepting the doctrine of class warfare, still paying lip-service to the anti-religious jargon of a vanished age. After 1945 Marxism became an ugly word, and the Red Flag a symbol of Soviet oppression and imperialism. The Social Democratic party badly needed a new image, and it was given one at the 1959 Bad Godesberg party conference. A man of instinctive moderation and a patriot who believed in serving the interests of the whole community, Willy Brandt played a big part in securing acceptance of the free-market economy and private ownership of the means of production, and the ending of the tradition of hostility towards established religion. The Social Democrats, he realised, had to win over at least a part of the middle class, and in doing so could afford to sacrifice cracker-mottoes but not basic principles. His calculation was correct; the 'new' Social Democratic party was in 1969 entrusted, for the first time since 1945, with the leadership of the Federal government. And Brandt became the first post-war Social Democratic Chancellor.

Brandt had already served for three years as Foreign Minister in the grand coalition in which his party was junior partner. As Chancellor he outlined his aims as being the following: co-ordinating social reform, helping to secure peace in the world, promoting east-west détente in Europe, working for the unity of the German people as a democratic community and for the unification of Europe as an effective force in the world, able to carry the burdens and to use the possibilities of true partnership with the United States and to open the door to realistic discussions with Moscow and Germany's Eastern neighbours including the German Democratic Republic. These are forthright, positive aims which can only be applauded.

In the field of east-west relations in particular, Willy Brandt went to work in a manner which contrasted with the ultra-cautious approach of previous West German governments. He opened talks with the Soviet Union, Poland and even the East German Republic. One uses the word 'even', since it has been an article of faith with previous governments that no sort of recognition could be accorded to Ulbricht's puppet régime in East Berlin and that the Federal government in Bonn was the sole legal representative of the whole German people. Brandt, with his supremely practical habits of mind, decided to jettison dogmas, which may indeed have had their uses in their day, but which had become outworn by time and by the political processes taking place in eastern Europe.

He wanted talks with the Soviet Union because, unfortunately, there can be no final solution of the German Question without Soviet approval. He wanted talks with Poland, because the hostility maintained by Poland towards Bonn is unnatural and unnecessary, and because this Polish hostility stimulates and supports the far more aggressive attitude maintained by the east German régime. Finally, Brandt was prepared to establish contact with the east German leaders in order to take the first, small steps towards lowering tension between the two German states. What is important to remember about this policy of 'small steps' is that there was no real alternative. To hold the east Germans at arm's length is to cement the division of Germany. But Brandt, a complete realist in this as in other respects, knew that he could not expect quick results. Tremendous patience is needed—something that the outside world has understood only imperfectly.

Brandt is a good European; he is heart and soul for the expansion of the Common Market by admitting Britain and other applicants, and for the deepening of its aims. He is a good socialist, believing implicitly in social justice. He is, above all, a good German, representing his country's interests with courage and common sense. The German people no doubt needed Konrad Adenauer, the father figure, in the first phase of their post-war history. They needed patriarchal guidance and direction while seeking to reverse the disastrous course of German history and make a fresh start, as a democratic community with firm friends in the democratic world. In Willy Brandt the German people have a natural successor to Adenauer, a man who is of the people and for the people. Practical, confident and still relatively young, he has a big contribution to make to the consolidation of the Federal Republic. He has contributed much already.

Terence Prittie.

I

After the War—What Next?

I

After the War—What Next?

INTRODUCTION

8 April 1940: the first copy of my book War Aims of the Great Powers and the New Europe *is lying on the writing desk of my Oslo office, 12 Storgaten. It will never find a reader nor have to face the reviewers. For 8 April 1940 is the eve of the German invasion of Norway. Soon the Gestapo will be raiding the Tiden publishing house. But not without tragi-comic incidents, as I was to find out later: when they discovered books by a certain Maxim Gorki, they demanded to know his address . . .*

At that time I was twenty-six and had been living for close on seven years in Oslo. Alongside my work as a journalist and on the educational side of the Labour party, I was full-time secretary—mainly involved with press relations—to the Norwegian People's Aid. This humanitarian organisation, which had developed out of Norwegian-Spanish Aid, drew its main support from the trade unions. In the winter of 1939–40 we were sending gifts of money and material to Finland. At the same time a start was being made on the development of a welfare and medical organisation for relief work within Norway itself.

I was naturally involved in the work of German emigré groups and the discussions of the German opposition. At that period they were mainly concerned with the fundamental issues raised by the outbreak of war in September 1939. Hitler's Germany had won a swift military victory over Poland. The western front was quiet. To the east, the pact between Ribbentrop and Molotov was in force. I was convinced that this was only the quiet before the storm. As I was to realise later, there was much I had been wrong about in the early years. But I had been right in my judgement of the nature of the crisis which the Nazi phenomenon would create. Shortly after my arrival in Norway in 1933 I had written: 'The victory of Fascism in Germany brings with it a marked increase in the danger of war, even if the Fascist leaders themselves are afraid of war.'

In the political parlance of the day 'Fascism' was a collective term for a rightwing totalitarian radicalism implacably opposed to democracy, trade unionism, liberalism and intellectual freedom.

In the years since 1933 I had been present at many discussions of the 'war question', many of which were depressing, some even nightmarish. But that April day in 1940 brought home to me just how confusing and deceptive wishful thinking can be. When the paper reported at midday that a strong German naval force was passing through the Straits of Denmark, and when this was followed up that same evening by confirmed reports of troop transports, it did not take much imagination to predict the events of the coming night and the following day. In the evening, at a gathering of German and Austrian refugees in the community centre I said as much—letting my reason guide me—, namely, that no one should be surprised if German planes were to appear over Oslo the next day. But at home I said to the one person who meant most to me—this time following my wishful thinking—that there was no cause for alarm, and any air raid warning in the night would certainly be no more than a test alert.

In the early hours of the morning I received a sobering telephone call. There was no more doubt about it. The invasion had begun. A few hours later some leading Norwegian politicians took me out of Oslo in their car: I was in flight again.

In the years after 1933 the main preoccupation of the German opposition was: After Hitler—what next? From 1 September 1939 they were all asking: After the war—what next?

From the very first day I followed European and international discussions on war and peace aims with the closest attention, wrote articles and speeches on the subject and finally composed that book whose first copy was lying on my writing desk on the eve of the occupation of Norway.

In the next few years the question of war and peace aims was never far from my mind. During my years in Stockholm (1940–45) I expressed my views on the subject in newspapers, periodicals and to student gatherings. In an international study group, about which I shall have more to say later, I took part in fascinating discussions on this issue, and we published painstakingly drawn-up policy statements. I was soon striving to analyse the problem more systematically and in greater depth. Thus I wrote in the foreword to the book After Victory, published at the beginning of 1944 in Stockholm and Helsinki, that it had actually started life 'as a by-product of a wider preoccupation with post-war problems' and it had not been my intention 'to add yet another sample to the sum total of private plans for saving the world'.

A really thorough-going and systematic study remained no more *than a pious hope, as my involvement in politics and the need to earn my living as a journalist on a daily paper left me no spare time. In the case of other projects, for example my attempt at a* History of the Youth Internationale, *irreplaceable manuscripts went astray as a result of the occupation of Norway.*

In this book you will not hear about the troubles of a young man who fell out with the German state at the height of its power and returned to Germany when it was defeated. Nor will you hear about the German refugees' fight for existence when Hitler was in power. After a difficult start, my own material circumstances were more favourable than those of many others. I escaped threats on my person and life by a mixture of luck and judgement. There are two points I should like to make clear at this juncture:

Firstly, I have done my best never to fall victim to an over-restricted examination of questions of the day. And I have equally sought to avoid those passions and exaggerations which every war brings in its train and which Nazi excesses could not help but bring to the fore. I strove to think beyond the events of the war and to add my voice to those of others for the establishment of a realistic and just peace.

Secondly, I was a young German who had left his home at the age of nineteen, was deprived of citizenship by the government of his country in 1938, and who as a stateless person in 1940 gratefully accepted Norwegian citizenship—someone, then, who when writing about peace aims, had more than just one homeland dear to his heart, and who regarded himself as a European. That is why the foreword to After Victory *contains the words:*

'I feel bound to Norway by a thousand ties, but I have never lost faith in Germany—that other Germany. I am working towards the elimination of Nazism and its adherents in every country, that both the Norwegian and German nations might live. During those years I twice lost a homeland. I worked to regain two homelands—a free Norway and a democratic Germany. The day will surely come when the hatred inevitable in war is overcome. Some day a Europe in which Europeans can live together in harmony will surely become a reality.'

WAR, PEACE AND A DEMOCRATIC FUTURE FOR GERMANY (1)

When the troops came back from the trenches to their starving wives and children in 1918, all they wanted was an end to all wars... In spite of this a new world conflict has broken out in the space of a single generation, a conflict that threatens to engulf the entire world.

. . . The peoples of many lands, victims of the new war, asked themselves what the cause of this struggle between the great powers was and why they were really fighting. But a straightforward answer rarely came . . .

In contrast to the 1914–18 war, the governments of 1939 felt themselves constrained to talk openly about the aims of the war. Much remained unsaid, and no one knows how much of what was said was true. But the fact that even in the first stages of the war governments were mobilising all the resources of modern propaganda methods to compete with one another as the most loyal supporters of international law, of a just peace and a positive new order after the war, demonstrates that they were more concerned for the men in the front line and to the rear and for the broad mass of the population than they had been on the last occasion. And in the gloomy situation after the outbreak of a new world war this ray of light is of great significance : namely, that ordinary people were not caught in the grip of war psychosis and fanatical chauvinism but were demanding ever more insistently to know where all this misery was leading them and how the necessary conditions for a secure and lasting peace might be created. Of course, the shifting patterns and aims of the war could bring about changes in the mood of the people. A ray of light in the first stages of a war can all too easily be engulfed in the blackness of worldwide conflict. But no power on earth will be able to prevent people from asking the question or stop them from trying harder and harder to look beyond the surface symptoms in an attempt to come face to face with the root causes of this European and international crisis . . .

The question of war and peace aims was already the object of scrutiny before the outbreak of war. And in the first months of the war it was subjected to repeated further examination. This demonstrates that people understood more than at any time in the past that their attitudes should be determined, not by the fact of war, but by its aims and the nature of a renewed peace . . .

There was no need for an absolute ruler in medieval times to utter a single word about the aims of a war. It was up to him to determine what the war was for, when it should start and when it should come to an end. In spite of everything, this is no longer the case. The active concern about war and peace aims which engages every single nation and the concessions governments are obliged to make to that concern demonstrate that the democratic spirit is more deeply embedded in the peoples of Europe than many would have thought possible after the tragic experiences of recent years. The democratic train of thought is reinforced with every discussion of the aims of the war, and the fight against the forces of medievalism which still persist in our day is carried a stage further. But discussion of war and peace aims must break out of the narrow and petty terms of reference which are a legacy of the past. An earnest quest for the causes of the war, the real motivation of nations, a sober evaluation of historical memories and experiences, a factual exposé of the needs and interests of the population : all these things lead inevitably to a critical analysis of long-standing social conditions which can no longer face up to the demands of the present age.

Peace, when it comes, will not only be a product of articles in newspapers, books and public debate. It will be determined by the social balance of power at the end of the war. But in the meantime this balance of power has yet to evolve. Public debate is just one of the factors paving the way to the social foundations for the coming peace . . .

There are few people in Europe today who believe that we simply need to return to things as they were when this war started or the last one finished. The wheel of history cannot be set in reverse motion across a long span of time without serious consequences. For the way into the past leads to renewed war. The future of humanity depends on tangible success in conquering the barbarity of the Thirty Years' War.

. . . All nations and all peoples, the whole world and mankind itself desire a lasting peace founded on mutual trust and justice. They need a true peace among the nations which can resolve matters of dispute from a supranational, European and international stand-point. Such a peace will not be presented to us by a handful of great men. For the 'great' men who have shouldered the task of acting on behalf of the people have led them into the miseries of war. Peace among the nations is not just a matter of peace *for* all men, but equally of peace *through* all men. We cannot leave it to dictators to hold out the promise of a 'new Europe', nor to new Woodrow Wilsons incapable of realising the 'new world' of which they speak.

Conditions for the new peace must be established in each country individually. For it is there that the issue is resolved whether people support those forces which are championing historical progress, or whether they ally themselves to those working for the destruction of Europe and the triumph of barbarity. Allied with the struggle for a new peace is that against the forces of reaction and suppression in every land. It is such efforts towards a new national community that will form the basis for a new Europe and a new world.

Stockholm, 27 December 1941

Dear Arne,[1]

...Even if I did think that Germany should be carved up and humiliated in every possible way—and of course I don't take that view at all—I should still not be expressing my views on the subject here and now. It is far more prudent to say little about peace aims than to throw out seemingly constructive occupation plans. In other words, I take the view that Churchill's attitude is more tenable than that of Trygve Lie.

According to what I have heard, Martin [Tranmäl][2] has already expressed a view shared by all friends in the party here in Stockholm [the reference is to Norwegian friends in the party]. I have deliberately refrained from becoming closely involved in these discussions, as it could be taken that my origins might distort my judgement. But it has been a real experience for me to see just how many reasonable people coming from 'home' [Norway] are far less anti-German than I would have thought possible in times like these. You are directly influenced by Britain, a country which is in the war, and naturally that colours your discussions. We on the other hand are not entirely unaffected by the atmosphere in neutral Sweden. Still we do keep a little in touch with the mood in Germany to the modest extent to which it is possible to gain any impression of what is going on there. But we also have a pretty keen finger on the pulse of the attitudes held on the 'home front' [Norway]. Even a year ago when I was 'home', I was most surprised when talking to numbers of my best friends about their projection of the way things would go in occupied Norway. For my part I advanced the view that Norway could claim the right to disarm occupation troops and to arrest and put on trial members of the Gestapo and others who had committed crimes against Norwegian life and other vital interests. On the other hand I was of the opinion that the Norwegian side should show its goodwill by sending the occupation troops home as humanely as possible, naturally without allowing them to take with them anything which was not theirs. The reply I received to all this was : 'There is no need for you to make things any worse than they are. When the time comes, the German soldiers will surely assist in bringing their Gestapo and SS and their own officers to account. And that will create an entirely new set of circumstances.'

A little while ago a meeting of the regional committee of our most active young friends in the party was held. The man who gave an introduction to the political position and who is probably the most significant among those responsible for the establishment of the youth movement today, stated with the greatest emphasis that Germany must be granted a just peace. Understandably one of the delegates opposed this view. It would have been unnatural if all present had taken the same view of German actions in Norway. It was however a sign of considerable maturity that the vast majority of delegates from all parts of the country considered the question in a sober and commonsense manner. The same holds good for nearly all our people coming here. And this should be much more representative of our views than the attitudes struck by the large number of fledgling activists and jingoists.

... Most of what we said earlier about Nazism on the one hand and the position of Germany within the new European order on the other still holds good. Naturally Germany must bear the chief responsibility for the present war, but even today I do not feel inclined to admit that Germany is the sole guilty party. Others should bear their share of the responsibility for Hitler's rise to power in the last years of peace and for allowing him to create his war machine. Of course the Germans are responsible for letting Hitler come to power, but other nations are equally responsible for the policies of Chamberlain and Co. which operated to Hitler's advantage. If it were the case, as many people maintain, that the German people consist entirely of Nazis, then Hitler would have no need of terror, the Gestapo and concentration camps to keep him in power. There must be no doubt that the weak-kneed policy of the western powers is one of the most decisive contributory factors to the absence of an active political opposition in present-day Germany. People have lost faith in the existence of any power strong enough to halt Nazism. This is underlined by statements from German soldiers in Norway, themselves opponents of Nazism. Others point out that a German collapse would make things even more difficult for them than they are, and that it would be the German worker who would bear the main brunt of peace in a defeated Germany. By appealing to fear, Hitler continues to exercise a strong influence even among certain sections of the German workers. So it is on this very point that Nazi propaganda must be attacked and the view taken, firstly, that the basic principle of self-determination for the people will also hold good for a democratic Germany; and secondly, whilst Germany should contribute to the reconstruction of Europe, she should not be starved to death but should be given a real chance of developing within the framework of a broader international organisation.

There is talk about the need for educating the Germans to behave in a reasonable and civilised manner. It is clear that strenuous efforts and much patience will be required to overcome getting on for 200 years of Prussian militarism, but the right conditions can only be established when a genuinely democratic revolution takes place. Such a revolution will defeat 'Prussia'. But I have no faith in an education programme assisted by English and other Allied officers ... And in Germany this would cause a repetition on a vast scale of the same kind of national opposition movement which is to be seen today in occupied territories everywhere. England should also understand that a policy of humiliation and occupation in Germany would be the surest way of forcing the Germans into a firm alliance with Bolshevism. In spite of my respect for the Russians' courageous conduct of the war, I cannot regard the spread of Bolshevist domination across the whole map of eastern and central Europe including Germany as a desirable prospect.

I believe that people are often wrong in their assessment of the likelihood of revolution in Germany in the context of what you call the poisoning of German youth. I have no intention of minimising the impact on the growing generation of nine years of Nazi domination. On the other hand, I was talking in the concentration camp a year ago to a substantial number of quite young soldiers, and these are the very people with no political roots. But they were not really Nazis. It could rather be said that they have become totally apolitical. Politics in their eyes had become one of those things which 'they' deal with, that is, the party, the Gestapo and the rest on whom they had no influence at all. Young people are mostly concerned with their own personal problems. They told me about their desire to marry when they returned home, about their work and so on, but they did not say very much about Nazism. That is something stuck on to the outside. I am fully aware of how depressing it can be to have to deal with a people shorn of all interest in politics. But it is still not beyond the bounds of possibility that they will begin to move in the right direction, just as soon as the foundations of the ruling power begin to crack and when people see for themselves that they were wrong after all in their belief that Nazism was invincible ...

Stockholm, 11 February 1942

Dear Arne,

... We are agreed that we must count on a democratic future for Germany as a working hypothesis. Even Stalin has proclaimed that Germans and Nazis are not necessarily one and the same. Nobody could object to the declaration he made on this subject in his order of the day for 23 January. It is only a pity that the English have not come round to a similar declaration, best of all before Stalin. A statement from London means far more to large sections of the German population than one from Moscow. But it is still not too late.

You point to the fact that a democratic revolution in Germany would hasten the whole process of recovery. It is clear that this would make it much easier to overcome the violent hatred and not wholly unfounded suspicion directed against all that bears the name German, although the real culprits are the imperialistic, militaristic and Nazi forces in German society—forces which in the course of nine years of Nazi domination have demanded almost as many sacrifices and martyrs among the German people as among the nations who are now being trampled underfoot by the Prussian jackboot. But if Germany really does desire a democratic future, then other countries must so shape their present policies that the forces of democracy and freedom in Germany are lent all possible support.

On the basis of our socialist position and on general democratic demands for justice we cannot defend the view of those who dispute Germany's right to a democratic future. In addition to the guarantee of the Atlantic Charter that equal provision should be made for industrial reconstruction in the defeated nations, we need a firm declaration that when Nazi dictatorship is overthrown the German people will be granted in principle the same right to self-determination as other nations. Slogans and threats to the contrary—understandable as they might be after the violent actions of the German Nazis—are grist to Goebbels' mill. Therefore there should be no talk of partitioning Germany. If the Austrians express the view in a plebiscite that they want to be part of Germany, then their wishes should be respected. You do concede that it would be advantageous if democratic forces in Germany were strengthened. But must we therefore not speak out in support of this line even when the present balance of power situation seems to exclude the possibility?

... To be sure, the occupation of Germany is not a question of principle. Such an occupation can become necessary or even desirable for the development of democracy. But it can take on a quite different character. Even then it can become unavoidable and we might be unable to oppose it. In spite of this, we as socialists and democrats should never forget and never cease repeating that such an occupation of a foreign country will be an evil that must be overcome and run down with all despatch. In any event it cannot be a long-term solution ...

... The war and peace aims of the Axis powers have become (2) meaningless. Italy has already surrendered. Germany is going to lose the war. The first aim of the Allies is to achieve a military victory. But history has demonstrated that a war can be won on the battlefield and still lost politically. A real victory is not achieved until guarantees have been secured against a repetition of the events which led to war. It must be the aim of the Allies to establish conditions in which World War Three would be an impossibility.

... It must be the prime object of the new peace to create an international organisation of justice in the spirit of the Atlantic Charter. If individual countries supported such an organisation in the right spirit of collaboration, it would give the population of the whole world something which it has long desired and to which it can lay strong claim : freedom from want and freedom from fear.

(3)   It is widely held that a 'cooling-off period' of between two and five years must follow the end of the war. Such a procedure has many advantages. The wounds of war can heal over, the worst material want can be overcome and international hatred can simmer down before work on the peace treaties has been concluded. It would indeed be less than satisfactory to have dealings with governments—on whichever side of the conference table they may be sitting—which are unrepresentative. Anyone who has the right to speak in the name of his country will refrain from taking a firm line before the country concerned has regained stability after the initial period of upheaval.

This postponement of a definitive peace conference also allows more time for expert investigation. On the last occasion humbug and improvisation had to be made to do on many points. Then there is no need to weight the actual peace treaty so much with the question of responsibility that the conquered nations are discriminated against and debarred from the international community.

I get the distinct impression that if it is difficult to conduct a war of coalition, it will be even harder for a coalition of states which differ so greatly one from the other to win the peace. An Allied victory is a necessary condition for peace, but it has long been no guarantee that peace will be realistic, just and lasting.

In the long term, an international security system cannot be policed by the victorious powers alone. However, the way events have turned out, they must be the ones to make a start. Co-operation among the great powers in the Allied camp is decisive. International discussion has repeatedly been returning to the point that, in the event of a breakdown in the alliance between the Soviet Union and the Anglo-

Saxon powers, the world might drift towards a new war. It would be too naive to consider rearmament by the 'Axis powers' as the only possible future threat to peace. When Vice President Wallace very candidly referred to the danger of a Third World War early in 1943, he was thinking precisely of the situation which will inevitably arise if stable co-operation between the great powers now fighting a common enemy proves impossible.

For peaceful co-operation, not just spiritual disarmament, but also spiritual rearmament is essential.

POSTWAR RECONSTRUCTION, NOT REVENGE

With the exception of isolated hints by spokesmen of certain occupied countries, demands for compulsory reparations were not raised until August 1943. It was not in the interests of the English and Americans to push this too much into the foreground. *The Economist* was expressing a fairly widely held view in Anglo-American circles when it asserted shortly after the outbreak of war that the reparations issue had been sorely mishandled in Versailles and that politicians should be on their guard against repeating the same blunders. Lord Vansittart was still writing in the autumn of 1943 that strictly speaking it was the economic sections of the treaty of Versailles which were the most difficult to defend.

For the rest, two main points kept recurring in Anglo-American discussions : it was regarded as just and fitting that the demand be made that property of economic value and *objets d'art* stolen from occupied territories should be restored. On the other hand, in the light of the experiences of the inter-war period, the view was advanced that it simply was not worth the effort to burden the defeated nations with enormous war reparations. This distinction was underlined by Hambro among others in *How to Win the Peace*.

It became clear to many that world economic reconstruction must necessarily be an international undertaking. A defeated country cannot be exploited to achieve this end at cut prices. This basic principle naturally in no way excludes the possibility of imposing special responsibilities on defeated nations in the context of European reconstruction or of allowing them to undertake them themselves— as representatives of the German democratic Labour Movement in exile have stated.

Past experience highlights another aspect of the problem. In Versailles, Germany was burdened with reparations because she was deemed responsible for the war. These took on the character of punitive measures. This time the question of who was responsible for the outbreak of war is far less a matter of dispute than it was then. But the question still remains whether those who have to pay up are really responsible. Even if we take the view that all Germans, including those who have been in concentration camps, are responsible for the policies of Nazism, that still does not solve the problem of whether such responsibility can justifiably be visited upon their children and the generations yet unborn.

It is not inappropriate that German industry should be prevailed upon to deliver a reasonable proportion of the reconstruction needs of devastated territories. But this presupposes that German industry will be placed in a position to meet such demands. Many people want a defeated and demilitarised Grmany to be 'industrially disarmed' as well. Such a line is clearly irreconcilable with demands that Germany should supply vast quantities of materials. It is senseless to want to 'disindustrialise' a country and at the same time to expect her industries to deliver the goods.

A special problem is posed by the large-scale plunder and destruction of objects of artistic and cultural value by the Nazis. It will certainly be possible to recover and return the bulk of confiscated *objets d'art*. But in many countries, Poland and Czechoslovakia among others, such a vast amount of damage has been done that it is difficult to make even approximate amends. No amount of financial compensation can properly outweigh the injustices wrought in those countries. Apart from *objets d'art* there is the question of equipment in laboratories and similar establishments. The demand has been made that destroyed equipment should be made good to a certain extent by surrender of equipment in equivalent institutions in Germany. But here too we shall need an internationally agreed plan to incorporate the suggested compensation for material loss into a broader scheme of reconstruction.

If this basic principle is rigorously observed it will mean that reparations will play only a secondary role. In so far as they are resorted to at all, they should not take the form of punitive measures, but should rather be incorporated into a common European policy of reconstruction. However important economic correctives may be, the main emphasis must lie on the positive side : namely, exploitation of the steep increase in the productive potential of industry and agriculture. Then it will not take so many years to cancel out the material damage of the war.

NATIONAL FRONTIERS AND THE PROSPECT OF FEDERATION.   (1)

None of the projects for the improvement of relations between east European countries touches on the important issue of future relations between Germany and her eastern neighbours. There are many arguments in favour of a federal union between Germany and these countries. The whole of this central and east European group have strong common economic interests ... Trade conditions would be rendered substantially more favourable if Germany and her European neighbours to the east could be brought together in a federal organisation. This would facilitate the solution of the minorities problem. Common provisions in national constitutions throughout the whole federation would not give individual countries cause to use or abuse 'their' minorities on the other side of the frontier.

National Socialism has sought to advance itself by trampling underfoot the freedom and independence of its neighbours. A democratic federation in central Europe can only become a reality if it is not dominated by an imperialistic Germany. The Slav races will never willingly agree to a federal system so long as they have grounds to fear that they will be the object of exploitation by German imperialism.

... Today the economic life of Europe is compartmentalised by tariff barriers, import restrictions, trade disputes and the war economy. Disunion and economic conflict have stood in the way of a developing prosperity which would reflect the state of modern science and technology. Agreement in economic affairs could bring about enormous growth in common productive effort and in the results of human labour. Even the minorities question would take on a totally different complexion.

... The plan for a federal system in central Europe was discussed along with other matters in a pamphlet published jointly in the summer of 1939 by leading German and Austrian socialists (*The Coming World War*). The authors of this pamphlet set out from the view that an eventual uprising against Nazism would initially have to take the form of a democratic revolution ... Relations between the new Germany and neighbouring nations must be decided with two main points in mind : (1) liquidation of German imperialism and acceptance of the right of self-determination for all the subject nations, (2) the defence of Germany herself, and equal right of self-determination for the German people.

Not unnaturally, demands for punishment of those responsible for   (3) crimes in Nazi-devastated countries have kept pace with the increasing extent of those crimes. Nations which have suffered Nazi occupation demand that the criminals should be punished for their misdeeds. Not to do so would infringe an elementary demand of justice. And that would only lead to nations taking the law into their own hands and would cause the international atmosphere to remain poisoned for longer than is absolutely necessary.

First comes the problem of Quislings. Dealing with them is an internal matter for each of the liberated nations. In international usage a war criminal is usually one who has transgressed against international law by means of terror, maltreatment, murder or other acts of violence. But within those terms of reference, the accomplices in the principal crime, namely that of causing the outbreak of war, are not necessarily going to be brought to justice. But the view can surely be taken that leading Nazi politicians bear an equal responsibility for the actual crimes committed in the course of the war and the occupation of individual countries.

The Atlantic Declaration lays down what is generally regarded as the right to self-determination for all nations. It is perhaps no accident that the actual formula established after the First World War as the central principle for the new order in Europe—with very dubious results—has been avoided.

In the first place this principle was never rigorously observed, but was undermined wherever the supposed interests of the victorious powers demanded it. Secondly, the nationality problem was dealt with in isolation, resulting in thousands of miles of new frontiers and this meant the erection of new barriers to freedom of movement, trade and industrial development.

But the boundaries question cannot be brushed aside. And it is in the very nature of the situation that eastern Europe stands in the forefront of this issue. Even on the last occasion the greatest difficulties were encountered because of a lack of a clear common identity between states and nations. The Soviet Union now appears on the scene as a new factor and has made clear her interest in improved strategic frontiers to the west.

The Russian attitude is based to some extent on the fact that annexation of the former eastern territories of Poland should be regarded as final . . . Disagreement on this matter was one of the factors which caused the Russian and Polish governments to break off diplomatic relations in April 1943. And the dispute became critical right at the beginning of 1944 when the Red Army was approaching and very soon overran former Polish territories.

In January 1944 the Russians made known their readiness to adjust the boundary in accordance with the line proposed between 1919–20 by the then British Foreign Minister Lord Curzon and accepted in principle by the Allied great powers. Such a modification would have the effect of returning to Poland those territories with an overwhelmingly Polish population, principally the Bialystock area.

... The Russians are able to point to the promises of Wilson and the Allies that an independent Polish state would be set up consisting of territories with an indisputably Polish population. But that still does not get round the fact that the previous Polish military dictatorship was in no position to resolve national and social problems.

Their method of burning Ukrainian villages to the ground was no less disgraceful than the obliteration of Lidice and the firing of many Polish villages by the German Nazis.

As far as Czechoslovakia is concerned, the Munich agreement is void, and the rise of a new republic can by and large be based upon the same territorial area as that possessed before partition. No responsible Czech has made any territorial claims since that time. Quite the opposite : directing his words at the great powers, Foreign Minister Jan Masaryk stated at the end of 1943 that the Czechs wanted no more than restoration of the 1938 frontiers. What is meant by the 1938 frontiers is that the Sudetenland should belong to Czechoslovakia and also that the Poles must hand back the Teschen district and the Hungarians the territories which they had annexed.

It is true that at an early stage of the war Czech plans were drawn up to expel one million Sudeten Germans, to disenfranchise the rest and transport them further away from the border area. But such plans could hardly have been an expression of the views of the Czech government. At any rate Dr. Ripka, a member of the government, made it clear in October 1943 that all nationalities—including the Germans—would have parity of treatment under the new Czechoslovakian republic. He added that no one innocent of any crimes against the republic had any cause for fear.

The three million Sudeten Germans mainly living in one clearly defined region naturally have a different outlook from other racial groups or minorities living in very mixed regions. It is a well-known fact that the Sudeten Germans were far from satisfied with their status under the Czechoslovakian republic. And it is obvious that there are considerable difficulties attendant on a rapprochement between Sudeten wishes and the interests of the Czechoslovakian state on any terms, and indeed all the more so when the Czechs are intent on regarding a large proportion of the Sudeten Germans as accomplices in the Nazi crimes.

Sudeten German Social Democrats in exile under the leadership of Wenzel Jaksch take the view that Germany annexed their territories by violent means no different from those employed against Austria. They are of the belief that the nationality question in Czechoslovakia is best resolved by a federal system on the Swiss model. This would involve a fairly extensive degree of autonomy for Sudeten German territories.

The Poles have suffered more than any other nation under German occupation. They have a right to the re-establishment of their state and national security. But the question remains whether security can be achieved simply by a reversal of German expansionist policy.

It is doubtful whether Poland would be any better off with a much larger territorial area, as this could well lead to a renewal of the conflicts of the inter-war period. It would be a grave enough encroachment for Poland to annexe territory in East Prussia and Danzig where there are three million German inhabitants. It would be even more problematical to bring into effect the 'full programme' which would involve territories with nine million inhabitants—that is, as much as the populations of Norway and Sweden put together.

The case of Germany and Poland is a prime example of the necessity for 'loosening up' frontiers by supranational agreements. Against this is the fact that for a certain period—fortunately not for all time—it will be difficult to balance the attitudes of a democratic Poland and an anti-Nazi Germany.

The question of the Polish frontiers is also closely related to the shape of a future Polish government. If a régime is set up which is to a greater or lesser extent under the influence of the Soviet Union, this would mean on the one hand that the question of the boundaries to the east would no longer be raised on the Polish side. The other result would be that the western frontiers of Poland would depend as much on German-Soviet as on German-Polish relations.

As far as Germany is concerned, Allied discussions have mainly held to the boundaries of the Weimar Republic. But many suggestions have been advanced for a reduction of German territory. We have already touched upon Polish demands in this respect. Naturally there is no disputing the fact that Alsace-Lorraine must be returned to France. Various interpretations have been placed on earlier French plans to strengthen the strategic and industrial position of France and Belgium by transferring German territory on the west bank of the Rhine to these two countries or by establishing a separate state in the Rhineland. But it is significant that such suggestions, as far as is known, have not been advanced by responsible people on the French side. It came to be known in February 1944 that the French representative in agreement with the governments of Holland, Belgium and Luxembourg had informed the Allied great powers that they had no intention of taking over territories bordering on their own.

In the border discussions there are two main opposing trends. On the one hand the view is gaining ground that the old concept of national sovereignty must be revised. On the other side nationalist sentiments have been greatly intensified by the war and the occupation. Nationalism has been an important constructive factor in the fight against Nazism. But in the work of European reconstruction it can develop into an extremely destructive force.

. . . Intermixed as the various national groups are, particularly in central Europe, it is impossible to draw up boundaries which are fair to all. And the question of minorities cannot be swept under the carpet. However much present boundaries are altered there will always be substantial minorities left living on the wrong side of the frontier. So the real question is one of securing the rights of minorities.

Dictatorships resort to compulsory resettlement. The inhabitants of southern Tirol have no voice regarding the land which their forefathers have tilled for centuries. The Germans living in the Baltic countries were summoned 'home to the Reich'. Millions of Poles were compulsorily resettled. Such compulsory resettlement is not determined by the interests of the racial group in question but by power politics and deals among the great powers. Such a solution is neither just nor democratic.

. . . The members of a national minority should not be treated as second-rate citizens just because they are in a minority. They must have equal civil rights and their cultural needs must be taken into account.

... The most natural solution of such problems would evolve within the framework of a European federation. The constitution of a United States of Europe would be in a position to offer equal constitutional rights to all citizens—regardless of language, race or religion. Common agencies could be set up for the whole federation to serve the national and cultural needs of the various population groups. A federal system in central Europe would largely be able to resolve this issue, even if a broader federation covering the whole of Europe cannot yet become a reality.

... Only a solution of the European problem which brings the nations together is capable of sweeping aside the old conflict between the national security interests of a country and the economic, social and cultural development of Europe as a whole ... The realignment of national sovereignty in accordance with common European interests does not necessarily imply any threat to the freedom and independence of individual nations. The demand for European unity embraces the need to reach out beyond the primitive attitude that one individual can only preserve his own security in conflict with others. If it is recognised that every nation has a right to exist and to its own special interests, then a far stabler state of of international security can be attained.

Three main issues require particular attention in relation to the discussions which have so far been conducted on the economic aspects of a European federation.

In the first place many people are well aware that a lasting peace is not possible unless economic problems are also solved at the same time. In the second place it is recognised that the war economy as an emergency measure may have served a useful purpose. (But we know what is really needed : economic planning, the planning of the economic pattern of individual states and economic relationships between peoples.) If the aim is to be 'disarmament' in the economic sphere, larger economic units must be established than those represented by the existing national states. Such a development can come about step by step with a view to a European and later a worldwide economic union. Thirdly, it is becoming increasingly evident that the struggle is one on behalf of mankind and that the state and economic institutions are at their service—and not the other way round. This recognition should be a strong argument in favour of linking the coming peace with an economic structure which takes true account of the vital interests of the nations.

International law must be renewed and widened in scope. Membership of an international organisation presupposes the obligation to comply with international law and justice. But that is no guarantee against violation of the law. The real problem is that there is no valid law. The task is still the same as when Kant highlighted it 150 years ago : the achievement of a constitution for all citizens of the world or at the very least justice among the nations on the basis of a commonly formulated international law. Or in the words of the inaugural address of the first Socialist Internationale in 1864, when Marx wrote that the simple laws of morality and justice which determine relationships between the individuals must also be regarded as the highest law in relationships between nations.

Many European and American democrats hold the view that in future a distinction will have to be drawn between cultural and political entities. If the Alsatians are good Frenchmen, as the present war has demonstrated once again, although they speak their own German dialect, and if the German Swiss despite their close relationship to German culture think Swiss—why should it be impossible for a Sudeten German to become a good Czechoslovakian, although he continues to preserve his own cultural and national characteristics? Certainly Hitler's watchword that all Germans should be united in a single nation had a great attraction but this did not cause the outbreak of war. The reasons for international conflict lie deeper. And Hitler's power of attraction was by no means restricted to native German speakers outside the boundaries of Germany. Austrian Social Democrats, for example, were less inclined to lend an ear to the siren song from Berlin than certain Lords and Labour pacifists.

One task which must be faced whatever happens is the question of compensation for the injustices brought about by Nazi resettlement of population groups. Reservations of principle and practice need not weigh so heavily that any form of minority resettlement is out of the question. But anyone who believes that the minority issue can be solved simply by setting up states with 'pure' nationality frontiers is on the wrong tack entirely.

For this reason it is important to establish satisfactory guarantees for the national rights of minorities. If minorities are given equal status, this assumes that they will be loyal to the state of which they are citizens. And putting it the other way round, equality of treatment is a necessary condition for such loyalty.

ARMS CONTROLS

Even after this war two important factors cannot be left unconsidered. Disarming the defeated nations affords no guarantee that conflicts cannot arise among those countries which maintain their military alliances. If such a conflict situation crystallises, it will be in the interests of the parties involved to draw on to their side the states which were originally disarmed together. That means it will be in their interest to let these states achieve renewed military power. If the pattern of sovereign states is to be further developed, each will inevitably strive to attain status by means of military strength. Long-term occupation is a theoretical possibility in preventing this law from operating among the defeated nations. Such a long-term occupation however presupposes an enduring community of interest among the occupying powers. There is no certainty that such will be the case. This is why it is so important to move towards a prompt settlement of the disarmament issue.

Several questions arise in connection with the practical execution of the challenge of disarmament. Disarmament can be set a time limit; in this case the destruction of present war materials would be regarded as the prime objective. But it can also develop into long-term demilitarisation and this assumes a veto on the production of weapons and control of such stipulations. Further, the question arises of how and where the dividing line should be drawn between forces for internal order or border guards of the countries concerned and armed forces falling within the terms of disarmament agreements.

THE WESTERN ALLIES AND THE NEW EUROPE

It is doubtful whether the idea of union between France and Britain will be taken up again after the war. None the less, close co-operation between the two countries is a strong possibility. A declaration from the French National Committee in October 1943 states that Great Britain is a cornerstone of French foreign policy. On the other hand conditions appear favourable for co-operation between the Soviet Union and a new French popular front régime. Of equal importance is the prospect that France will place greater value on a solution which is European in scale, in view of her position as a subordinate partner among the major Allied powers.

This means that Britain, whether she wants to or not, will be compelled to take a stronger interest in European affairs. The conditions of her previous balance of power policy no longer obtain. Britain must share with the Soviet Union the chief responsibility for European policy in the immediate postwar period, where attention will naturally be focused on eastern and southern Europe. The Americans will probably be more concerned with that half of mankind living in the underdeveloped parts of the world—China, India, South America and Africa—than with the quarter living in Europe.

But it would be intolerable for America to withdraw from Éurope. In spite of everything, she and Britain have strong common interests on this very question of European issues.

DEMOCRACY AND HUMAN RIGHTS AFTER THE WAR

There are many indications that this war will have a totally different complexion when it comes to an armistice. Shortsighted tendencies towards nationalism, great power mentality and imperialism make themselves more strongly felt in the final stages of a war. They could become so dominant that the democratic objectives of the war would be forgotten. Roosevelt's promises for the future have become more cautious. Wallace no longer wants to speak as a statesman but as a private individual. Even the programmatic utterances of Herbert Morrison do not express the views of the British government. The representatives of the Soviet Union speak in a language strongly coloured by the hard realities of big power politics.

When Eden was asked in the Commons in the middle of February 1944 whether Article Two of the Atlantic Declaration—according to which changes in territorial area should only be recognised if they are in accordance with the freely expressed wishes of the peoples concerned—was valid for enemy countries, his reply was a firm 'no'. On 22 February Churchill declared on the same subject that enemy countries had no right of appeal to the Atlantic Charter. A respected Swedish weekly claimed to have evidence to the effect that the common declaration of the Allies 'should naturally never be applied to the enemies of the Allies'. The periodical continues by stating that it would not be surprising 'if Germany were compelled to hand back all her conquests'. As if that had even been in question!

Article Two of the Atlantic Declaration on territorial relationships was naturally not conceived in terms of possible boundary disputes between Holland and Belgium or between the USA and Mexico. But in the Article on economic policy defeated nations are specifically mentioned. Enemy countries are also named in connection with the demand for disarmament. Thus it cannot be claimed that these Articles are invalid in the case of enemy countries. Of course it is quite a different matter that the 'enemy countries' are not parties to the contract and therefore have no claims in law with respect to the Atlantic Declaration.

A reaction less favourable for the Allies to the statements of Eden and Churchill was not long in coming. In Italy the Americans had the greatest difficulty in preventing a symbolic general strike. In Germany the view that they were confronted with enemies whose aim was total destruction gained ground even in circles which had long resisted Nazi pressures and infiltration.

In the free world too these statements which could spell the annulment of the Atlantic Declaration were not accepted without question. It is clear that the unbroken succession of atrocities in the German conduct of the war on the one hand and the lack of co-ordinated planning among the winning powers on the other have placed serious obstacles in the way of a constructive and democratic outcome. The fight for a democratic outcome to the war against the the Nazis will be tougher than many have believed. But democracy still has hidden reserves. When it really comes to the point, the shifts of emphasis in big power politics will perhaps prove to be of less significance than the fundamental social changes and the rethinking of values which have taken place during the war.

Democratic attitudes may be temporarily suspended. But the key issue for the postwar period is and remains whether it will prove possible to come to real grips with the aims proclaimed at the beginning of the war. This means, firstly, the re-establishment and reinforcement of basic human rights and the rule of law; secondly, the transference of the principles of freedom and equality from the political to the economic sphere; and thirdly, bringing the rules governing international coexistence into line with those guiding the internal relations of every civilised community.

The people fighting in occupied Europe have demonstrated time and again that there are values higher in their eyes than fleeting material gain. To them freedom is more than an empty word. The urge towards freedom has created a spirit of militant humanism. The war of machines has underlined the importance of human enterprise. It is up to the new democracy to capitalise on this militant humanism. But it alone is not enough. Freedom must be underpinned and broadened. Democracy cannot be rationed. It must operate in all areas of social life and in relationships between peoples and states.

The Atlantic Declaration and the four freedoms indicate how the concepts of freedom and equality may be broadened. They establish that the claim to freedom must be coupled with a demand for security. The American New Dealers have sketched a new Bill of Rights . . .

Most important among the new demands which individuals are making of the state are the right to useful and rewarding work for all who are capable of work; the right to food, clothing and a roof over their heads; the right to education with equal opportunities for all; the right to protection against disease, poverty, in old age and in times of hardship. A state which grants such rights to its population, which serves the well-being of the many and not just the privileged few; which mobilises the work force, science and all the resources of productive achievement; which plans production to raise the standard of living among the population—such a state is one worthy of our greatest efforts and sacrifices.

Attitudes such as these have already become widespread. In many countries, views which used to be the object of violent dispute are now taken more or less for granted. Socialists meet individuals from other camps in common recognition of the fact that the special rights of the individual have to give way only when it is necessary in order to be able to grant economic and social security to the highest possible number of people. The discussion does not turn so much on attacking or defending rights of property, as on the question of how best to exploit productive potential, or how to achieve the greatest productivity for the benefit of society as a whole.

Democratic socialists and liberal-minded radical socialists alike have a common interest in creating a planned economy which at the same time preserves the freedom of the individual. The same standpoint has been reached by a variety of routes : namely, that planning must be regarded as a means rather than an end in itself. Cost effectiveness is important, but not all-important. Planning should serve to strengthen freedom by granting the people a larger measure of security. It may only be allowed to infringe upon individual rights in very exceptional circumstances. Like the civil service, economic planning is there on behalf of the people, and not the other way round.

Planning has been employed to advance the ends of reaction, dictatorship and the bloodiest brand of imperialism. But this is no evidence that planning necessarily brings loss of freedom in its train. A planned economy in a democracy is not the same thing as total collectivism . . .

The great challenge of our generation is to achieve a new synthesis of collectivism and liberalism. Human rights must continue to be maintained whilst at the same time industrial progress is achieved within the context of a planned economy. The same problem exists on an international level : without international security no true national freedom is possible. International law must be given teeth. The special privileges of nations must be subordinated to common international interests.

The future of democracy depends on the measure of success in achieving this national and international synthesis. The greater the success the less bloodshed there will be in the future.

(4)   FRENCH ATTITUDES

... It was known in advance that Vichy would be removed from power as soon as the Germans had been forced to withdrawn from French territory. Now it is known that even the authority of General de Gaulle does not go unchallenged. First in Normandy and later in Paris de Gaulle was received by an enthusiastic population. To them he represented a policy of uncompromising resistance.

When the outlook was at its bleakest, de Gaulle stated that France had lost a battle, but not the war. In the beginning he did not have a large measure of support when he challenged Frenchmen to continue the struggle on the side of Britain.

... De Gaulle not only had great difficulty in achieving a broader basis of support among the population of the home country, he also had to fight for recognition among the big Allied powers. Relations between the USA and the provisional régime did not become settled until after the invasion had begun. All these are facts familiar to the informed Frenchman. The leaders of the various resistance groups have all joined forces with de Gaulle. But they support him as a symbol and not as a leader.

Too little is known about de Gaulle's attitude to the problem of reconstruction. But it is known that he has a good chance of remaining at the head of the Fourth Republic, if he maintains the democratic republican line developed by the advisory assembly in Algiers and the most influential organisations on the home front. But if de Gaulle dropped this approach his position would become precarious. The Swedish correspondents who visited parts of liberated France established that he was not regarded as the obvious leader and that the French did not wish to become caught up in any situation resembling dictatorship ...

On the foreign affairs front the French are certainly in agreement with de Gaulle's demands that France should have a voice in the vital Allied decisions. Just as the populations of other occupied countries , the French have recognised the importance of international collaboration. Understandably hatred of the Germans goes deep. But the Swedish correspondents were able to report that an astonishing number of Frenchmen were underlining the importance of co-operation with the populations in the present enemy territories.

The general secretary of the Socialist party said at a congress in Paris that extending the hand of friendship to the German people and helping to prevent circumstances which might breed a new Hitler was all conditional on the eradication of the 'spirit of Prussianism'. Whatever might be thought of such an attitude, it is still impressive that this kind of view can find support a mere fortnight after the liberation of Paris. It demonstrates that France has retained her identity in a period of self-renewal.

PEACE AND THE NEW WORLD POWERS (5)

There is peace on earth once more. Our destroyed and shamed corner of the globe can be reconstructed again. But there are still many obstacles to reconstruction. Many millions are undernourished and have no roof over their heads. Starvation and epidemics are dangers yet to be averted. Economic misery stands in the way of political and cultural reconstruction. Even Nazism has to be finally overcome. As a régime it has been destroyed. As a spiritual pestilence we regrettably find it or a related mentality persisting in the minds of many people. No one should expect Europe to recover overnight. A thoroughgoing process of healing is needed.

But many positive forces have been released by the war and the destruction of Nazism. Conditions have been established in which individuals and nations have a chance to live together in harmony. With the end of Nazism the strongest bulwark of national suicide lies in ruins. In the fight for freedom new forces were aroused which are now active in the reshaping of national life in individual countries. It is true that these developments are not taking place at a uniform rate in all countries. But everywhere a strong drive towards freedom can be observed. Everywhere new approaches are coming to the fore which seek to achieve greater prosperity and a richer cultural life through planned exploitation of material and technological resources.

Europe does not hold the same position in the world as before. As great powers, Germany and Italy are finished. France rejoices in undiminished recognition of her role as a great power. The shape of Europe is largely determined by the Soviet Union and Great Britain, that is, by two world powers whose interests are not restricted to Europe alone. But America too is resolved to make her influence felt in Europe. This time she has no intention of withdrawing into isolationism. In many respects the path of American progress has led her into different directions from the majority of European countries. Whilst Europeans are engaged in seeking by all manner of means to reconcile political freedom with the collective planning of economic life, the overwhelming majority of Americans continue to stake their faith on private possession as the ultimate principle. The still very widespread notion that the American population consists exclusively of cowboys, film stars, gangsters and racketeers is too ridiculous for words. America can point to scientific and industrial achievements which can measure up to those of any other nation; she has carried out reforms in her own way from which Europe has a great deal to learn.

The end of the war has brought out the Soviet Union alongside the USA as a decisive world power. Of all nations she has made the greatest sacrifices in human terms. She has staked her entire national existence in a manner which has called forth general admiration and considerably reinforced her international standing. The Soviet Union is no longer surrounded by mistrust, and great hopes are placed upon her.

The other nations today are largely willing to learn from the Russian experience in planned construction. Like all other countries the Soviet Union too doubtless desires to carry out her reconstruction and further development under the banner of international collaboration.

Britain, like all other countries, has suffered considerable economic losses in the war. But the war has assisted the breakthrough of new forces. The British people were prepared to follow Churchill as the superior war leader. They were not prepared to trust Churchill the Conservative party leader with the leadership of peacetime politics. The elections which took place in July 1945 brought the Labour party into the Commons with a strong majority. The Labour party is firmly resolved to carry out internal reconstruction on the basis of a planned economy and, in harmony with the objectives of the United Nations, to work internationally for collective security on democratic principles.

At present Germany lies like a political vacuum between east and west. But there too serious efforts must be made to introduce democ-

racy with the support of present anti-Nazi forces and in accordance
with the decrees issued by the victorious powers.

Europe is in a state of radical change. Everywhere demands
are being made for a greater degree of freedom and justice. In some
countries these demands have tended to spill over into economic
and social life as well. In others the process of social upheaval itself
has come to the fore, but even there it is closely bound up with
demands for the progressive development of political freedom. Naturally these changes are not going unchallenged, and there will be
many setbacks before Europe has assumed her new shape. But there
will be no lack of evidence that international collaboration is essential in order to fashion the new peace in accordance with the true
interests of all nations.

Stockholm, 14 August 1945

Dear J.,[3]

... I am quite certainly not a German nationalist, and for years
have made a stand against those who believe that everything depends
on the maintenance of old boundaries. But I consider that in its
present form the settlement reached in the east is absurd. It is quite
possible that there will be no altering the conditions now created.
But that does not mean simply saying that's that and there's nothing
more we can do about it. I believe an attempt should still be made
to work towards a modification of resolutions up until the time of
the peace conference.

... That heavy burdens would be placed upon Germany was to be
expected in the order of events. But the occupying powers still recognise the necessity for the maintenance of some degree of economic
unity.

... An expanded population in a reduced territorial area cannot
keep itself alive on handicraft and farming. The last word has certainly not been said on the resolutions as published. Our only tenable
position is one of co-operation on the present basis. But we must
preserve a degree of independence which will permit us to continue
working towards rationalisation in the economic sphere as well.

POTSDAM, THE OCCUPATION AND THE NEW GERMANY

Stockholm, 26 August 1945

Dear both,[4]

We have had various conversations about the Potsdam agreements.

On the side of the CP—which has also taken up a very aggressive attitude to you two—everything is shown through rose-coloured spectacles. On the other hand there are those who are protesting with all their might and main and crying doom. Both are wrong. As far as politics are concerned, there is no doubt that Potsdam represents a step forward by contrast with the previous state of affairs. But I have definite reservations about the settlement of frontiers to the east, which in my view goes much too far, so that the attempt should be made to achieve at least some modifications. From an economic point of view there is much that is positive in the Potsdam agreements. That there would be heavy reparations was clear in advance. But here too some things have been taken to extremes, and these will probably prove impracticable. It is up to the forces of democracy inside Germany to determine how far it will be possible to go in modifying the Potsdam terms.

(6)   The Soviet Union, America and England together with France have taken over the administration of those territories which up to a few months ago constituted the German Reich. According to the four-power agreement ratified at the beginning of July, the German state has ceased to exist . . .

None of the occupying powers has so far put forward a programme for a definitive solution of the German question, although they are all in no doubt that 'total' occupation cannot be a long-term solution.

The Russians have declared that occupation does not mean annexation and that they are opposed to a partition of Germany. The question of whether and within what boundaries a German state should be set up again is a matter for later consideration. At the moment common administration of German territories is not a matter of urgency. The Allied control commission has certain co-ordinating functions. For the rest the four zones are administered independently; but it can be assumed that the western zones have a broadly similar approach to the structure of the administrative system.

All four occupying powers demand reparations and the acceptance of other responsibilities which have resulted from the war guilt of the Nazi régime. On the other hand they are all concerned to prevent chaos and starvation. In the east as in the west the occupation officials have striven from the outset to win over the Germans to work on their side. In the two 'main zones' work is in progress on rebuilding the unions.

These are some of the common characteristics of Allied occupation policy. On the other hand, as far as the clearly apparent divergences are concerned, these are partly the result of different physical circumstances. The Russian zone comprises one half of German territory. 15 to 20 million people live there. The supply situation is serious but not catastrophic. In the other half of Germany there are just under 45 million people. There they are on the brink of starvation. The housing situation is desperate.

Another fundamental difference is that the Russian officials set to work according to a plan which is not unnaturally based on the social conditions obtaining in the Soviet Union and the economic experiences gained during the hard years of work on their own plan. In Russian policy towards Germany, military, political and economic factors were co-ordinated in advance. The situation is different in the western zones. There the power lies chiefly in the hands of military officials. Generals can be good politicians but it is not invariably the case. Political issues in this part of Germany are the object of lively discussion in the countries administering the occupation. There are several conflicting attitudes to the shaping of economic policy in occupied Germany.

Most striking is the contrast between the veto on fraternisation on the part of the western Allies and the collaboration propaganda on the Russian side. But we must be on our guard against overstating the position. Western Allied restrictions have already been eased. And they are not going to be kept in force for an extended period. General Eisenhower has himself announced a change of approach towards the population. This is clearly essential in order to give German democracy the chance to develop and to prevent the emergence of an anti-Allied front. Marshal Zhukov has spoken about a veto on fraternisation in force in his zone. But that does not prevent football matches between Russian and German teams taking place. And above all it does not prevent that clear distinction being drawn between Nazis and other Germans which Stalin had established right at the beginning of the war in newspaper, radio and poster propaganda.

At the present time it is not yet possible to compare conditions in the various zones. But it is clear that the Russians are giving top priority to providing relief for the population in both economic and social spheres.

By and large, the western Allies still tend to regard all Germans as Nazis to be severely purged of the master race mentality. Many people have fallen victim to a new brand of racialism. And indiscriminate threats of punishment have achieved the opposite to what should be in the common interest of the Allies and the German anti-Nazis.

In the eastern zone the formation of anti-Nazi parties has been permitted. Among the western Allies this is still forbidden. The unions are limited in number and are not allowed to involve themselves with political questions. Anti-Nazi committees have been broken up in various towns and mayors who have worked on such committees dismissed. However, English and American press commentators very rightly point out that the final overthrow of Nazism can be achieved only by allowing a democratic movement to develop inside Germany. If they are encouraged instead of suppressed, we shall soon discover that a total denazification of civil servants is possible and that the state governments which are set up can be given a much broader basis than can be effected by representatives of this or that middle-class party.

It would be wrong to try to draw final conclusions from the experiences of the first few weeks. Allied occupation policy will doubtless undergo decisive chances in the course of the coming few months. The forces of German anti-Nazism which really do exist will make their presence more strongly felt. The differing lines of development in the various zones do not make their task any the easier. And yet they will have to hold fast to the fact that a solution can only be attained by a positive approach, not by strengthening centrifugal tendencies but by bringing east and west together in the interests of the German population and Europe as a whole. Occupation officials will on the other hand be faced with the continuing problem of how to achieve the final defeat of Nazism and prevent complete economic collapse.

There is only one answer: the evolution of democratic forces and the development of a plan carried out in the interests of the people. To this end the socialist movement is needed.

'My view of the question of alignment with east or west is that Germany will not rise up again nor attain self-sufficiency if she cannot find agreement with both sides, and for this reason those who throw in their lot with just one of the powers are pursuing a policy doomed in advance. It is clear that there can be no neutrality in questions of democracy for the socialist movement, but it ought to go without saying that it must preserve independence in the face of the big factors in the international power game.'

Germany is no longer a great power. At the present moment she does not even possess the shadow of national sovereignty. It is not yet certain whether the German people will come through the present crisis without being torn apart. Already German territory has been reduced. That is not necessarily a tragedy. It would be tragic if anti-Nazism in Germany actually contributed to the final collapse.

The anti-Nazis can prove that they did not incur guilt by war crimes and crimes against humanity. But they would be deserted by all men of good will if they did not confess their share of the responsibility for Nazism—apart from the fact that they cannot escape the consequences of Nazi war and murder policies. Those Germans who seek to argue away or excuse what happened are doing their fellow countrymen a considerable disservice. It is of course untrue that Germany alone was responsible for the war : the conflict could have been prevented if the shortsighted policies of other governments had not given succour to Nazism. But that in no way minimises the great responsibility which the German people must bear. Anyone who seriously desires a democratic future must make a clean break with the past . . .

It does not follow that German democrats who have chosen the path of honourable collaboration need sacrifice their own aims and interests. They do not have to surrender their right to protest against misunderstanding and misrepresentation. But at the same time they should recognise that the best way of refuting nonsensical contentions is to create a new pattern of relationships. German anti-Nazism has chosen the path of collaboration, but this is not synonymous with a lack of principles, self-humiliation and servility. People who seriously desire the establishment of a free Germany living in peace with her neighbours will not rest content with a subordinate role. After the unconditional surrender of the régime they cannot support unconditional appeasement. They cannot promise meekly to put their signature to every piece of paper placed before them. Their desire to co-operate rests on recognition of an overriding common interest . . .

. . . But how is it possible to conceive of a German policy which is neither geared to 'revenge' nor aimed at collaboration with the Soviet Union on a basis of mutual trust? That is not the same as one-sided 'alignment with the east'. But it is equally irreconcilable with one-sided 'alignment with the west'. Hitler's Germany was crushed by a coalition of the Allied great powers. Germany is now under their occupation. A unified state can only emerge from this crisis if the work of reconstruction is carried out in friendly collaboration with 'both east and west'. Any one-sided solution represents an attempt to alter the balance in favour of one partner. Each such attempt arouses the mistrust of the other partner. And that helps to stabilise zonal frontiers and turn Germany into a colonial territory. If the worst came to the worst, the line of the Elbe could become the catalyst of a new military conflict many times worse than the one we have just experienced.

I am very well aware that a lot of people abroad take an extremely sceptical attitude to attempts at reuniting Germany across the zonal boundaries. Such attempts are regarded as a potential new threat to peace. If they are undertaken by trustworthy anti-Nazi forces with the right approach in foreign policy, then they can become something quite different, namely a decisive contribution towards securing peace. But it is certainly not a particularly secure or satisfactory solution if colonies of the great powers are situated right in the middle of the continent of Europe. As long as this state of affairs persists, there will be no basis for any real policy for Europe. But it is in the common interests of the peoples of Europe that their continent should once again become something other than various 'spheres of influence'. However difficult things may appear at present, the common interests of the European democrats and German anti-Nazis should not be overlooked.

There is an absence of mutual trust. It cannot be forced into being. This is not the least reason why events within Germany have an international political significance. German anti-Nazism still has strong internal enemies. Nationalism has not yet been overcome. The fight against the ideology of the master race, against racial fantasies, the militaristic tradition and lust for revenge has only just begun. This poison must be drained out of the 'corporate body' of Germany. The Allies are actively dealing with this problem. But this is really up to the Germans themselves. They must defeat the enemy within not only for the sake of their own future, but also because there will be no future for them at all if they fail to gain the trust of others . . .

It is somewhat more difficult when we turn to the frontier issues. The Nazi annexations are a simple enough matter. But it cannot be expected that the German anti-Nazis will offer German territories with a German population in a kind of international auction. On the other hand a new basis for negotiation has been created by the course of the war and the absence of a clear internal resistance. Hitler— and in large measure forces at work even before him—sparked off a chain-reaction which resulted in changed frontiers and population resettlement. Boundaries are not sacred. Unfavourable territorial solutions cannot be the only yardstick in judging the order which will come out of the Second World War. It is to be hoped that the wounds of compulsory resettlement will heal over. German democrats will have to take up the watchword of the Danes after 1864 : 'What we have lost outside shall be regained from within!' The future of Germany will not be secured by a lust for revenge and quixotic foreign policies, but by means of resolute, effective reconstruction on the internal fronts—social, economic and cultural. But there is a frontier even among the frontiers. Reducing territory is one thing, partition is another. All those who commit themselves to co-operation with all their neighbours in a spirit of mutual trust, not least with the French, Czechs and Poles, are not therefore obliged to take a passive attitude towards separatist subversive activity. I am personally convinced that Germany cannot exist without the Ruhr . . .

There should be no demands that ignominious subjection of the anti-Nazis should follow on unconditional surrender by the Nazis. On the contrary it is in the interests of Europe no less than Germany that any movement to break the German spirit should be stopped in its tracks. What must be done is to give the young European-minded generation growing up in Germany today a new ideal which they can work towards. German Europeans and world citizens have not had much luck in the past. That is no reason for them to give up now. The thread of freedom which runs through German history must be spun further. German opponents of Nazism did not go to their deaths primarily on patriotic grounds but for what they regarded as international and human aims. Individual Germans can perhaps make some contribution, however small, to the spiritual and political renewal of our age. Perhaps such contributions will only become more numerous and impressive when the way is cleared for self-determination and reconstruction—and not just in the material sphere.

The Nazis sought to Germanise Europe after their own fashion. Now the task is to Europeanise Germany. This cannot be done by partition nor by playing one group of Germans off against another. The problem of Germany and Europe can be resolved only by a rapprochement between east and west—and the territories in between. It can be resolved only on the basis of freedom and democracy.

Notes

1. The historian Professor Arne Ording, at the time adviser on foreign affairs to the Norwegian government in exile in London.

2. At the time Trygve Lie was Foreign Minister of the Norwegian government in exile. After the war he became UN General Secretary. Brandt is here referring to differences between himself and Lie on the treatment of Germany after the war. In his book *Med England i ildlinjen* (*With*

England in the firing line—Oslo, 1956), p. 308 f., Lie points to these differences between himself and Martin Tranmäl's Oslo circle, mentioning Brandt by name. Tranmäl was for many years a leading figure in the Norwegian socialist movement. Lie writes: 'But I took the view that they were going too far in seemingly thinking more about Germany and winning the war than about the interests of Norway.'

3. Jacob Walcher, a member of the 'rightwing' KPD opposition, took a leading position in the SAP in 1932 and from 1933 to 1939 controlled SAP activities outside Germany from Paris. He returned to Germany at the beginning of 1947, joined the SED, but a few years later was stripped of all offices.

4. To August and Irmgard Enderle, who at the time had already returned to Germany. Both were SAP members, who spent the Nazi period in Stockholm and came back to join the SPD. From 1947, August Enderle was chief editor of the DGB newspaper *Der Bund*, later of the periodical *Die Quelle*. Chairman of the German union of journalists in the DGB, he died in 1959.

II

The Opposition in Conflict

II

The Opposition in Conflict

INTRODUCTION

In April 1933 a fisherman from Travemünde brought me across the Baltic to Rödbyhavn, not without some risk to himself. In Copenhagen I spent a few days with the worker poet Oscar Hansen. Then I went on by sea to Oslo. In my wallet I had 100 Reichsmark. In my briefcase I had a few shirts and the first volume of Das Kapital—*but that never succeeded in turning me into an orthodox Marxist.*

Why had I left Lübeck, where I was apprenticed to a firm of shipbrokers at the beginning of 1932 after matriculating at the Johanneum? I was escaping the problems which at that time surrounded arrest on political grounds and which might well have had dire local consequences. Besides, my closer political friends in Berlin had given me the task of establishing one of the bases for our work abroad in Oslo after the man first picked for the job had been arrested on the island of Fehmarn when attempting to leave the country.

'Closer political friends'—that means in this context the underground national leadership of the SAP. Like many other young Social Democrats I had joined this organisation at the end of 1931 after it had broken off from the official Social Democrats to form a leftwing opposition. It was a break which to us represented a strong protest against ailing, impotent and appeasing policies. Smaller groups aligned themselves with this movement, which had command of substantial organisations in Saxony and Silesia: for example, at the beginning of 1932 a section of the 'rightwing' Communists who a few years earlier had been expelled from the KPD. From the outset there were disputes about the line we should take, and after the National Socialists came to power the two most prominent founder members, Reichtag deputies Max Seydewitz and Kurt Rosenfeld, proclaimed the dissolution of the SAP. But the bulk of the party membership had other views.

Disillusionment amongst many supporters of the two big socialist parties seemed to bear us out. The moment we went underground our group played a part out of all proportion to our diminutive num-

bers. On *12 March 1933 I took part in an underground national conference in Dresden, and on my way there gained my first fleeting glimpse of the great city of Berlin. The majority of the delegates at the meeting—which was overflowing with a spirit of militancy— nursed no illusions that the Nazis could be thrown from power overnight.*

Although itself a product of a party split, the SAP made the 'unified front' one of its principal policies. I too was convinced at the time that Social Democrats, Communists and groups in between were in the last analysis members of one and the same socialist movement and that if the whole movement erected a unified barricade against Nazism it could not help but succeed in blocking its progress.

After the victory of Nazism it was evident that left-wing socialist criticisms of the 'reformist' mistakes of the SPD and the 'ultra rightwing' errors of the KPD were largely justified. Not without a degree of self-righteousness and an inflated self-opinion the SAP evolved the arrogant theory that they constituted the core of the 'new' party of the German left. This leftwing socialism was also interpreted in current party jargon as 'genuinely Communist'. 'Genuinely' sought to express two things: on the one hand association with the theoretical starting point of the modern socialist movement (the Communist Manifesto of Marx and Engels), on the other hand dissociation from the practice of Communists who castigate all those of different views as 'Social Fascists', and also from the undemocratic conduct of the KPD organisation in its dependence on Moscow.

At the risk of confusing the present-day, chiefly young reader, I must draw attention to the fact that we regarded the Soviet Union at the time as an ally of the socialist movement. Notwithstanding much criticism of details and many reservations in matters of principle, the Soviet Union appeared not only as the object of Nazi aggression—and thereby as an ally of the German opposition and of the western powers in the Second World War—but also, despite her shortcomings, which were the subject of avid discussion, as a state which was the embodiment of socialist principles. This view was widespread among the ranks of the Social Democrats and also among non-partisan intellectuals.

Opposition Communists as well as the leadership of the SAP were moreover inclined to fall in love with their role as 'genuine' friends of the Soviet Union. At any rate the young member of a group in between found a political platform which gave much cause for thought. It took me a few years to grow out of the narrow dogmat-

ism and sectarian characteristics of my own group. Because I used to refer to practical necessities and to my Scandinavian experiences, I had already antagonised some of my older friends.

But there is no doubt that in my early twenties—in the belief that I knew more than I actually did—I allowed myself to stray not a little into political dilettantism, which I did not entirely rid myself of in my early years in Norway. But it is true that in the Norwegian language my political style shook off the dross much more quickly than in my German correspondence with friends from home . . .

A certain lack of maturity in the German opposition abroad was not only the outcome of those characteristics among my closer political friends which caused other people to speak of emigré groups with bitter humour as 'lower forms of life' which 'reproduce themselves by internal division'. Measured against the necessities of the age, the inadequacies of the various groups revealed themselves more than anywhere in their inability to co-operate in creating an at least partly representative image of the German opposition. None the less it should not be forgotten that the Germans in exile had a particularly rough time. They bore the burden of a defeat without a fight, often living in the most difficult financial circumstances, and for a long time foreign democracies were more inclined to respect or fear Hitler than to listen to the warnings, let alone the demands, of Hitler's German opponents.

It would be a mistake to allow the inadequacies of German political refugees during the Nazi period to devalue or underrate their useful—and in my view meritorious—activities. These were largely given due credit in the years after 1945 and contributed to the demolition of the wall of repugnance and mistrust which encircled Germany.

These activities included the dissemination of information about Nazism and the other Germany which was indeed not always welcome. And also there were sensational campaigns like those which earned Carl von Ossietzky the Nobel Peace Prize in 1936. Or attempts to obtain the release of friends standing trial in Germany. In this respect there were occasional successes in exercising a welcome moderating influence with the help of jurists from Norway and other countries, for example, when members of the SAP national leadership were sentenced at the end of 1934; and also unpublicised and modest assistance for people who were arrested and their families.

Contact with friends in Germany was kept alive by illegal correspondence, couriers and the underground distribution of pamphlets. Meetings on the frontier, as for example those I frequently had

*in Denmark with political friends from North Germany, always
made a powerful impact on me. Contacts with ports played a special
role for us in Scandinavia and brought me into contact with Edo
Fimmen, the legendary General Secretary of the International
Transport Workers' Federation.*

*I spent the second half of the year 1936 in Berlin. I lodged with
a delightful lady, Frau Hamel, at 20 Kurfürstendamm, disguised as
the Norwegian student Gunnar Gaasland and holding a passport in
this name. I had been asked to place myself at the disposal of our
Berlin resistance organisation, and I did not regret the opportunity
of experiencing at first hand the realities of life in the 'Third
Reich'. But I will not disguise the fact that I was not unafraid when
travelling on the night train from Paris to Berlin or before that
when I had crossed to Warnemünde from Gedser. Our work in
Berlin remained severely limited in its practical impact although it
did extend among several hundred political friends.*

*I had previously been somewhat nervous of the big city, but now
I warmed to it. I encountered splendid loyalty and in many Berliners, to whom I was naturally unable to reveal my true identity,
an unforced readiness to help and that characteristic Berlin 'big
heart and big mouth' which even the Nazi bosses had not been able
to suppress. Naturally I had to live very simply, but it was fun
finding out where to eat well in the middle of the day for next to
nothing. I profited greatly by mornings spent in the Prussian state
library and many evenings at the Philharmonic.*

*At the end of 1936 I travelled from Berlin via Prague to Brünn
where I met up with Otto Bauer, the leading light of the old
Austrian Social Democrats. With exceptional co-operation from the
Sudeten German Social Democrats he had made it possible for us to
hold a conference in Mährisch-Ostrau at which representatives
from home and in exile took part. On security grounds it was given
out as the 'Kattowitz congress'. Not the least of the issues discussed
there—as at many later gatherings—was that of unity. The 7th
Comintern congress in 1935 had dropped their extreme leftwing
line, had spoken out in favour of collaboration with the Social
Democrats, and even gone further to recommend the formation of
'popular fronts' with leftwing middle-class elements. In France the
splits in the unions were patched over. After a leftwing election
victory early in 1936 the Blum government was set up with the conditional support of the Communists. In Spain the popular front made
strong progress and militant rightwingers sparked off civil war.*

*The Germans in exile were also seeking to establish a popular
front. Among the opponents of Hitler at home there were many*

who took the view that all differences of opinion must be suspended in the interests of a united opposition. 'Outside' there were numerous Social Democrats, above all in France, but also 'middle-class' personalities prepared for limited co-operation with the KPD. But the executive of the SPD in exile which had been in Prague up to 1938 consistently opposed any such collaboration.

My own group reaffirmed its support for a unified front of Social Democrats and Communists and took the view that a 'revolutionary but independent' unity party could develop at a later stage. The question of the popular front was much disputed. When a German popular front committee was formed in 1936 there soon developed unedifying quarrels with KPD representatives who were trying to lead this plan by the nose. During my stay in Berlin my name appeared beneath the declaration of the German popular front which had been worked out and published in Paris. So I did not 'sign it together with Ulbricht', but my friends made use of my name which they were entitled to do according to the terms of the time. But I must add that I would have signed the paper myself if it had been placed before me.

I have never met Walter Ulbricht. I have encountered other leading German Communists, among them men who later fell out of favour with the party, but also men like Hermann Matern, Herbert Warnke, Karl Mewis who were to figure prominently in the other part of Germany after the war. The only central popular front gathering in which I participated took place in the autumn of 1938 in the Hotel Lutetia, the subsequent Paris headquarters of the Gestapo. It was in many ways a macabre event since it lacked inner veracity as well as clarity and strength. I shall never forget the chairman Heinrich Mann saying to me, his youngest Lübeck fellow countryman, with tears in his eyes: 'We may well never see the seven towers of our old city again'.

That was after the Munich agreement which handed the Sudetenland to Hitler on a plate. Not at this meeting but around the same time I met up with Rudolf Breitscheid in Paris, the chairman and foreign affairs spokesman of the Social Democrat party in the old Reichstag. He was an impressive figure, although he had become very cynical; later he was delivered over to the Gestapo by the Vichy and met his death in Buchenwald. I also met Paul Hertz, former chief executive of the Reichstag party and later Economic Secretary in Berlin. He had parted company with the executive of the SPD in exile and numbered among those refugees in France who succeeded by various adventurous routes in finding refuge in the USA during the war.

Unfortunate experiences with Communists contributed to the realisation in 1938–39 of the ambition to bring together various socialist groups into a study group. This turn of events came at a convenient time for me, for my own political development had led me to a more practical and realistic approach and a clearer understanding of the fundamental value of democracy. In 1939 I publicly put forward an interpretation (in the Oslo Arbeiderbladet*) of socialism as 'extended democracy'.*

In Paris this collaboration was called 'socialist concentration'. Actively involved were the underground Austrian Social Democrats, who called themselves the RS (Revolutionary Socialists). Into our Oslo study group we drew Czechoslovakian as well as Austrian friends.

After the war, membership of opposition groups was recognised in the reconstituted German Social Democrats as equivalent to continuous party membership. My friends and I had joined the Social Democrats while still in Sweden.

In London during the war Erich Ollenhauer had once more brought the independent socialist groups together with the supporters of the old leadership. I had visited this man of great moderation who had done so much for Germany in Paris in 1938, and in 1939 we had met in Oslo.

During the war it naturally became more and more difficult to keep contact with underground groups in Germany. We had some success in Sweden, among other means through sailors who called at German ports. Contact with the central resistance circles in Berlin was of a quite different order. It was particularly important for me to be able to enter into renewed contact with Julius Leber who had meant much to me in my youth in Lübeck, and with whom I had fallen out politically during the splitting up of the SAP and who now let me know in what ways I could help a new German government.

Up to the summer of 1944 I was in spite of everything not fully clear as to what forces were behind the July plot or became involved in it. After the abortive attack on Hitler the opportunity of liberation from within, however limited, had been lost. The new German democracy also had to suffer the loss of many leading figures and the absence of personalities of the quality of Julius Leber.

Between 1943–44 I had still not been able to imagine in my exile in Sweden that Germany would experience total collapse. This only really becomes clear to me again when I read over what I had noted down at the time about the German opposition. We simply assumed that the new state would be brought into being by

*a popular uprising against the present authorities. That was well
wide of the mark. It would have been far better for us if we had
not been so mistaken.*

THE VICTORY OF NAZISM AND THE THREAT OF WAR   (1)

What was regarded within the socialist movement as an impossibility only a few weeks ago has now become a fact : German
Fascism has triumphed.

The German workers were told that 'Germany is not Italy' and
this catchphrase strengthened them in the belief that their organisations, ballot papers and demonstrations were invincible. They believed that the 'brownshirts' would never achieve what Mussolini's
blackshirts had achieved, in other words, the crushing of the
working classes.

It is true, Germany is not Italy! Hitler seized power far more
swiftly; he rode more comfortably in the saddle than Mussolini,
who was obliged to fight embittered resistance on the part of the
Italian workers. Hitler achieved as much in the course of weeks as
Mussolini did in years. This has also disproved the ingenuous theory
that Fascism is a southern phenomenon, a result of the fiery Italian
temperament, and that Fascism might well be victorious in an
agrarian community but would never come to power in a modern
industrialised state like Germany.

Fascism has its roots neither in the temperament of a people nor
in the characteristics of the national economy. It is rather an
international phenomenon in the decline of any capitalist state.

But the victory of Fascism would never have been possible if the   (2)
German socialist movement had not failed.

The proud organisations of the German socialist movement collapsed. Without resistance. Not only did their illusions collapse but
also the whole vast election machinery. That is the bitter reality
which no amount of false optimism can sweep aside.

The collapse is the result of a policy extending back over many
years.

But the issues facing Fascism in Germany will be of a quite
different order from those that confronted the Italian brand. Everything points to the fact that dictatorship will not be a matter of
weeks and months but years.

The victory of Fascism in Germany heightens differences with neighbouring states. It is also a dangerous source of friction with the Soviet Union . . .

There are centres of unrest everywhere, and world war threatens. Certainly Hitler does not want war. He would like to wage a war of big words to keep his frenzied supporters happy. Fascism will not survive the violent shocks that war brings in its train. He knows that war will spell his own ruin. But we know that the logic of events is more powerful than the desires of the Nazi leaders. Hitler's Germany is fundamentally isolated in her foreign policy. Internal economic difficulties swept her into a position of world power. Von Papen has already declared that the battlefield means for man what motherhood means for woman. That is the same old tune as the one to which Germany marched into world war in 1914. The victory of German Fascism signifies a fundamental heightening of the danger of war even if the Fascist leaders are afraid of it.

(3)   German Fascism which came to power in recent weeks in order to rescue its ailing master is basically a youth movement.

The crisis has hit German youth with particular severity. Their unemployment benefit had first been decreased and then stopped altogether. The young hang around in the streets when their education is finished. The rest is all one great question mark. On top of this there are the usual conflicts with the environment, with the family, and a spiritual vacuum.

Middle-class youth in particular has had a great deal to endure. It has to suffer doubly under this crisis, both as a body of young people and as a class which has slipped down to the level of the proletariat. Among them Fascism reaped its richest harvest. These young people were dissatisfied with 'the system', and this dissatisfaction tipped over into rebellion. At bottom they were revolutionary.

A movement with so much martial spirit, with uniforms, parades and revolutionary slogans—such a movement had great powers of attraction on young clerical workers, farm workers, university and secondary school students and to a lesser extent on working class youth.

The German university population, some of whom had already studied with empty stomachs in unheated rooms, can see no future before them at all. They study in the knowledge that they will end up signing on at the labour exchange. But then a movement comes along offering them work and bread, a chance to live, and employment for all who use their brains or hands. So they naturally fall in with this movement. There is something else, a blossoming of the spirit, particularly noticeable in the secondary schools and universities : conservatism lies in ruins and liberalism is bankrupt. The liberal mind suffers the same fate as middle-class democracy. Discipline and standards of conduct had crumpled and collapsed in the absence of firm principles. Here too Fascism had a power of attraction with its myth of the Third Reich.

(4)

The majority of young people are now in the Fascist camp. They started off with revolutionary sentiments and ended up in the counter-revolutionary camp. The day of awakening will come when the soldiers of young Germany recognise in the heat of their nationalist ardour that they have let all their aspirations culminate in barbarity. Then there will be an awakening . . .

Until then the most enlightened of the young German workers will fight on under the most arduous conditions for a political change of heart among the German working class and particularly among young people.

TASKS OF THE UNDERGROUND OPPOSITION

Underground work demands the greatest sacrifices from all who participate in it. Certainly operations are far more carefully organised than they were at the beginning. But in spite of this every week brings its new sacrifices. From the socialist youth league alone several hundred comrades are in concentration camps and prisons, but the league still numbers some thousands of comrades in all parts of Germany. In the 'cells' training work is undertaken and practical tasks in various fields discussed. Socialist youth journals are published regularly, and so too is special material for training work as well as for activities in the various districts and organisations. Besides this, pamphlets for the young are distributed when the occasion warrants it.

It is difficult to get an overall picture of what this work means. Every member of the youth movement must be prepared to stake his life in the battle . . .

The whole of the youth underground work is a battle against militarism, because the whole of Nazi youth policy is geared to preparing them for war . . .

Today it can be clearly seen that in the not too distant future the Hitler régime will have only two options : economic bankruptcy or a new war. Whichever happens, the underground battle is of vital importance.

1. German Fascism is approaching the end of its fourth year of

power. After the destruction of the socialist movement and every other form of opposition it is concentrating all its efforts on the planned preparation of war and on carving up the world anew.

2. The war problem is highlighted by the existence of the Soviet Union on the one hand and on the other the reactionary Fascist big powers, with Nazi Germany at their head, surging irresistably towards the inevitable explosion.

If it should come to the point at which certain capitalist powers at the outbreak of war are in alliance with the USSR, then the war in these countries will take on a double character. Revolutionary socialists in these countries must not lose sight of this fact. They must never give up the struggle against their own bourgeoisie.

3. The development of the USSR is a mass of contradictions. In spite of gigantic defence efforts, economic construction has made enormous progress. At the same time we have suffered shattering reverses in the political order and almost unimaginable social changes. None the less the USSR is the country without capitalists. What we in Germany must do is to present the facts as they are in our efforts to combat the Fascist propaganda war against the USSR, which has even found an echo among class-conscious workers.

4. The changes which have been wrought in the camp of the international socialist movement make it essential for us to revise the policies which we drew up in 1933. We must take the initiative by committing ourselves to the efforts of the revolutionary parties towards unity.

5. The developments which have taken place have also broached the issue of a popular front on an international level. In spite of many errors which must be admitted, we should affirm the policy of a popular front in principle.

6. We should not turn ourselves into one more of the many parties in the Bolshevist wing of the socialist movement. The SAP must put itself into the front rank where the task is to work out the best guidelines for the policies of revolutionary socialism on a basis of internal discussion within the socialist movement.

7. We must work from the assumption that the current régime will shortly be confronted with two options : economic collapse or, as a way out of this, war.

8. The main centre of our work is inside the Reich. That demands among other things better and more thorough coverage of all German issues in the press, and the establishment of a central point for collating all the experiences gained in underground work.

9. We must exploit the legal possibilities of the régime—in factories, the labour service and the armed forces.

10. The party leadership should be supplemented by representatives of the most important districts in the Reich.

Never forget that for the ordinary man in the street life is not (5) made up of 'isms' but of food, sleep, football, canaries, allotments and other pleasurable pursuits. Do not forget either that it was Lenin who recommended that agitation in the factories should be initiated by demands for 'water for making tea'. We must learn not to keep on about high politics all the time but work our way up to it by means of the appropriate 'water for making tea'.

Next to work in the factories, work among the young people represents the most important area of our activities among the mass of the population. In the Hitler Youth the 'radical' expressions of its leadership offer valuable points of contact.

... We as Marxists are bound by the duty to examine in all (6) earnestness the complex role of the subjective factor, the responsiveness of the individual himself.[1] Bound up with this is the generation problem. Fascist ideology partly rests on the fact that—according to Rosenberg—the centuries-old conflict between father and son, the tensions between revolutionary and conservative ensure 'the constant creation of new forms of life in ever-changing movement'. The Fascists have put this into practice by exploiting the revolt of the adolescent against the parental home, school and everything that represents authority. They have channelled youthful discontent against the representatives of a senile, crisis-torn establishment. The socialists were held responsible for the present situation, and considering the fossilised and largely corrupt state of their movement, this is hardly surprising; nor was it surprising to find 'Marxism' compromised and dismissed by the Fascist demagogues as part and parcel of the 'old crowd'.—*Fascism did not create the generation problem, it exploited it to its own ends* ...

This age-old contrast between young and old, although variable in intensity, can scarcely be called in question. It is so to speak a socio-biological antithesis. We are all to familiar with the conflicts in the parental home, at school, with the foreman and older colleagues at work, with that selfsame 'old crowd', which has actually or supposedly obstructed the young in their drive towards acceptance and independence. But none of that lies at the heart of the generation problem.

I understand by generation a group of people who have together been exposed to lasting impressions at decisive points in their formative years... There are no hard and fast boundaries between generations, but gradations of unequal length and intensity which arise as a result of disturbing phenomena in the development of a society. If the gradation of generations has played a lesser part in the past or largely disappeared altogether by virtue of the class divisions in society, then the *particularly volatile state of society today* has bestowed a stronger and far more uniform imprint upon the young generation of our time. The present state of society *renders the introduction of the generation conflict a supremely important weapon in social struggles...*

In conclusion: *the state of the present younger generation is characterised by the fact that the vast majority of young people are deprived of the chance to develop to real independence, to the setting up of secure family units, etc.; that only a tiny group has a real chance in life under Fascist capitalism; and that the actual prospect of Fascist capitalism, namely war, threatens to destroy the entire younger generation.*

... We have not learned to talk to the broad mass of the younger generation anywhere near enough, and we have been far from an awareness of their actual problems. Under the Reich one age group after another is growing up knowing next to nothing about the socialist movement in the time before Hitler or hearing about it only through the distorting mirror of Fascist propaganda.

These young people will no longer be able to understand us if we confront them in our old shape. We must evolve a new shape if we want to establish contact with them, and we must discover a new language through which we can make ourselves understood by them.

The problem of a new language has been considered before. But we are not dealing here with one of the great riddles of existence. *How are we to talk? Just like the young people to whom we are turning talk, as simply and directly as they do.*

Fascism holds out before the young the carrot of a 'great future' in a 'powerful state' with 'fame and honour'. It is up to us to reveal what this ideological vain promise to the young of a 'great future' actually involves, to set against the crisis-torn, war-heavy creed of Fascism the ideal of a socialist state which will secure for the entire working population of the young an existence worthy of mankind...

We must recognise the socialist element in National Socialism. I do not take the view of those who hold that such aspects of National Socialism were 'dreamed up only to deceive the workers'. It is rather the case that National Socialism ideology is something of a rag-bag, that it has learned how to turn the vital social aspirations and revolutionary urges of the broad mass of the people to its own ends. We must recognise the socialist yearning in the broad mass of German youth for what it is. It is a yearning towards a future in which there is work for all, in which the chance to get on will be open to workers in industry, to clerical workers, farm labourers, technologists and intellectuals alike, in which the individual can think in terms of setting up a happy home and starting a family. I can already hear the objections of those who see concessions to reaction in what I have written. But do let us get away from the habit of categorising people, let us examine their real desires and aspirations instead.

SOCIALISM DIVIDED AND THE ADVANCE OF HITLER (7)

We are all too inclined to discuss and discuss until we are blue in the face without recognising the necessity for *concentrating our attention* on the crucial issues, nor have we learned to act in accordance with the spirit of our conclusions, even if they have not removed every doubt from our minds. Today I should like first *to draw some conclusions from our unity policy to date.*

Nowadays it is no longer fashionable to idealise the split between the SPD and SAP in October 1931. Just as many of the gatherings taking place within the SAP would have better been left within the SPD or the splinter groups, so there were highly influential groups remaining in the SPD who should by rights have been on our side. For reasons which it is inappropriate to discuss here, the rift at that time was essentially limited to a secession by the impatient radicalised youth wing. Differences in the German reformist socialist movement had gone a stage further in 1931. The overwhelming majority of industrial workers were under the control of the Social Democrats. To win them over would be decisive. Although some groups were absorbed into the KPD and although sympathy for the USSR in the underground movement inside Germany had grown by leaps and bounds, we must still clearly recognise that the work force which had formerly been organised on a Social Democrat basis did not feel it belonged to one of the other organisations, although it did not identify itself with the pre-1933 party line or the Prague Sopade office either. We can affirm with some confi-

dence that this state of affairs will persist until a change in political
conditions inside Germany has taken place, and even beyond that.
We have not succeeded in attracting these Social Democrats and
we must recognise that we shall not succeed either as the SAP. It is
not enough for us to turn all our attention to the prospect of a
unity party, it is up to us to make this prospect a reality, to define
our position more exactly. And the establishment of this position,
in accordance with the structure of the German movement, must be
made independently of the means we employ to set up the
strongest possible contacts with the Social Democrat workers. Further, I would state that, seen from an international standpoint, our
place must be with that part of the west European movement which
is not controlled by the Comintern. For Germany this means :
among the progressive elements of the German Social Democrats.

We must also never lose sight of our goal of amalgamation with
active Social Democrats. The CP will react sourly to any such
development. But that cannot frighten us. By the same token the
Sopade office will have every reason to be nervous. But we have
nothing to lose from this objective. Or rather, our ability to amal-
gamate is dependent upon the extent to which we ourselves are
united. The SAP dare not hold back any longer. We must also be
clear in our minds that we cannot dictate all the terms. We must
distinguish between central and secondary factors and judge issues
from the standpoint of practical politics.

(8)　　On the fifth anniversary of the Nazi seizure of power we should
naturally have far preferred to be writing its obituary, the history
of the collapse of Nazi domination. But if we are talking about
collapse, what we should be announcing is the collapse of illusions.
... The might of Nazism will only be broken when illusions are
shattered. What we must seek to do above all is to understand
German Nazism. In this respect the German opposition has not
been particularly productive ... And the rest of the world has also
had some little difficulty in digesting the fact of Nazism.

National Socialism set up its monopoly of party machine and
propaganda at a very rapid pace. Even in 1933 it was able to
advance as far in as many months as the Italians took years. The
monopoly of the ruling party was only broken in a few places :
heavy industry succeeded in carrying on as master in its own house,
the reactionary and largely monarchist officer corps preserved a
certain degree of independence and the church has been able to
hold its own up to now.

Essentially the National Socialists suffer no other gods before them. They demand totality.

The strength of Nazism lies in the centralisation of all the forces of the economy, of politics and propaganda ... Nazism succeeded by suppressing all human freedom, by evolving a reign of terror which will never be able to acquit itself before the court of history, and by cultural barbarism. There is a burning desire among the German people for the rights of freedom. The true value of freedom is only realised when it has been lost.

Those who reckoned with a rapid collapse of Hitler's rule had misunderstood the true nature of the National Socialist mass movement. The real strength of the Fascist reaction lies in the fact that it can count on the support of an activist mass movement.

... Objectively speaking, National Socialism should be the watchdog of reaction and capitalism (and it has been), but subjectively speaking the stand taken by the masses who supported it was revolutionary and anti-capitalist in outlook. This is an illustration of the revolutionary atmosphere of the age.

The character of the grass roots has led Nazism into difficult internal crises. The worst was overcome on 30 June 1934. The régime was given a new basis of support among the masses. This chiefly consisted of those who owed their livelihood to the régime. But even among some of these people and among the young the ideas of 'German socialism' live on.

These ideas—we might just as well call them illusions—can never be replaced by reactionary alternatives. Hitler's system has acted pitilessly against the special interests of capitalism, it has insisted upon 'common interest before self-interest', and demanded more and more sacrifices on behalf of 'the nation'. And essentially this was an appeal to the concept of solidarity, to vague socialist notions, not simply to nationalist sentiments.

Even our illusions about the Nazi economy have been shattered. Many people had the concepts of liberal capitalism so ingrained in them that they were incapable of comprehending the changed situation. It was also astonishing that the Nazi economy was able to keep its head above water in spite of the ever-growing burden of internal debts. At the same time a certain amount of confusion has arisen over whether Nazi 'planned policy' might have something to do with socialism. And it must be admitted that there are good grounds for confusion. The Nazis not only opposed the demands of specific capitalist groups, suspended freedom of investment and concentrated surplus profit where they needed it, but in 1936 they went so far as to threaten capitalists with the death penalty if they allowed a flight of capital abroad.

The Nazi 'mediator', who has come to power with the support of crisis-torn German capitalism, has achieved some measure of independence. He shares his power with heavy industry and the army High Command.

Perhaps the most dangerous aspect of our illusions was the belief that the Nazi régime would be politically isolated. In reality Germany's power position has become stronger. Actual power interests have proven more substantial than political ideologies.

Hitler's offensive foreign policy has been able to achieve the desired results because it mostly got what it demanded. If Weimar had gained only half the concessions that have been made to Hitler's Germany, National Socialism would probably never have seized power.

By and large, Hitler has lived off his political victories abroad. Preparations for war are represented as measures to preserve the peace. Broad areas of the German population, who in other respects were far from content, were kindly disposed towards Hitler for restoring Germany's 'national honour' and overcoming the 'shame of Versailles'. National issues can indeed turn into burning political realities. Hitler understood how to exploit these questions and turn them into concrete realities. But individual instances point to the fact that he has overstepped the mark. It seems that he is losing ground in this very area. If that is so, then his greatest strength could turn out to be his greatest weakness.

There is no point in indulging in speculation on the durability of Hitler's rule. The German authorities today are sitting pretty firmly in the saddle.

It will probably need external changes, for example an economic crisis or a war. But even then it will only be possible to overcome the Hitler régime if it is confronted with a force which is not only strong but which can also present a positive and constructive alternative.

(9)   The victory of Germany in Munich rested as much as earlier conquests on elements of myth. National Socialism has repeatedly demonstrated its outstanding ability to exploit the manifold weaknesses and conflicts in capitalist Europe.

The tempo of the offensive was however equally dictated by internal conditions. The depression on the German stock exchange, operations against Jewish property and new taxation plans all bore witness to the increasing economic difficulties of the summer.

The military foundations for the action against Czechoslovakia were laid by the gigantic mobilisation operation which began in August and which around the time of the Nuremberg party rally had brought together 1½ million soldiers in the various manoeuvre units. The general staff used the opportunity to iron out the weak spots which had come to light during the march into Austria. If it had come to the point of military conflict then, Germany would have suffered a great fiasco. The weakest points were troop transport and victualling. The totalitarian state put into effect total mobilisation. Germany resembled one vast army camp.

Alongside the military preparations, propaganda preparations were being completed. But in this respect the National Socialists were far from strong. Uncertainty and unrest among the population intensified, and the grass roots of National Socialism became weaker than they had ever been since the defeat of the socialist organisations. An exposé of the situation inside Germany is extremely important in destroying the legend that it was a combination of the strength and internal unity of Germany which made victory in Munich possible, and in putting us on our guard against the front of superiority which dictatorships present in their propaganda.

During the summer months rising discontent was evident among the middle classes as well as among agricultural workers. They were reacting against the economic difficulties and against the new burden of taxation. There was little popular support for the persecution of the Jews. And in parallel with the crescendo of propaganda and the increasing scope of the mobilisation, fear of war rose daily.

The picture which can be drawn on the basis of reports by reliable foreign correspondents and direct reports from Germany shows that only a tiny majority of the German people were psychologically prepared for war . . .

We must be on our guard against overstatement. Anti-Nazi feeling has been voiced in various places, but it is extremely difficult to arrive at a reliable overall picture when dealing with a dictatorship without freedom of the press or freedom of expression. It is certainly the case that the propaganda campaign against Czechoslokavia ultimately wakened a response among a substantial proportion of the population who were reacting against preparations for war but who had no means of forming an objective assessment of the situation. But the resultant total impression has been that Germany was in such a poor state of military and ideological readiness that sober-minded observers in Berlin were of the opinion that it would be most doubtful whether the authorities would really be able to 'save the situation' by embarking on a war which would inevitably lead to catastrophe.

Hitler has been in no doubt about the power pattern in Europe. Probably he was equally clear about internal difficulties. What is politically impressive about his presence is the exploitation of this awareness, so that he was able to transform weakness into strength. The authorities in Berlin were well aware that ruling circles in England and France had feared the ultimate consequences of a German defeat... Hitler's political strength resides in his realisation that power was the decisive factor in politics and also his recognition that the European establishment was afraid of social upheaval.

National Socialism gained renewed strength within Germany after the Munich 'peace'. Hitler's prestige was further increased. After all the internal disunity, the resolution of the crisis had the effect of offering renewed proof of the irresistible might of the Führer. The attitude of the western powers had a depressing and demoralising impact on those Germans opposed to Nazism. But German socialism will survive this defeat too.

In Germany there are few who believe that peace was secured in Munich. The onward march of National Socialism in recent months has further contributed to underline this view. Jewish pogroms on a previously unimagined scale employing medieval methods—with the exception of the confiscation of Jewish property to the national treasury—were designed among other things to raise morale in National Socialist circles. But when the Hitler Youth and SS were employed in persecution, the ordinary population did not respond favourably and in many places voiced the contempt they felt towards a régime which resorted to such methods. The continuing external political demands by the régime in the direction of new colonies and new boundaries also strengthened the conviction that the German authorities could not be counted upon to steer a peaceful course. Germany is certainly not satisfied; on the contrary, she has simply gained renewed appetite.

In any case Germany has achieved a short-term solution of the difficulties into which militaristic and capitalist planned policies had led the country. The new successes have offered a breathing space but solved nothing. The basic social conflicts still persist. The new victories also create an increasing number of internal conflicts in that part of central Europe under Nazi domination.

The way in which National Socialism has increased its hold on the German people is a clear illustration of the interconnectedness of home and foreign policy. In the autumn the German opposition was for a brief space on the verge of becoming a practical political force. After Munich it suffered a further setback, and it will lose even more ground if the co-operation between Germany and Britain were to form the basis of an extended reactionary period. The German opposition can now take the opportunity to draw certain lessons from recent events. One of these lessons should be that it can find its true role only on the basis of social developments inside Germany and that it will not conquer on the morrow with the help of foreign arms.

In the first half of September a gathering of political friends took (10) place which directed its attention towards the present situation and the tasks before us. There follows a short summary of the more important conclusions from these discussions in depth :

1. Nazi German imperialism must bear the full responsibility for the outbreak of the present war. However, the root cause is to be found in those far-reaching conflicts resulting from the imperialistic peace imposed at the end of the last world war and which have now crystallised out in the form of a confrontation between Germany and England.

After 'Munich' a decisive change of direction has become evident in British policy. The attempt to ward off and where possible to contain Fascist Germany's expansionist aspirations in the east was a failure. From this point date efforts towards the establishment of a British system of alliances in eastern Europe and the preparation of the military forces of the western powers. England was only able to give up this line at the cost of rejection of German hegemony on the continent which would be followed by renewed attacks on direct British interests. For this reason, and because of the mood of the broad mass of their populations, the western powers have stood firm by their obligations towards Poland. The conflict which has thus arisen cannot help but take on a European character and shows every sign of turning into a new world war. The view that the western powers are not 'taking the war seriously' and are ready to give up after the defeat of Poland is wholly untenable. After the western powers have made up their minds to take up arms in the Polish cause, it would be suicidal for them to stop proceedings at this stage.

Although imperialist conflicts lie at the root of the war, and although the present situation is dominated by the confrontation between Germany and England, it is not a carbon copy of 1914. The front which stands opposed to Hitler's Germany also contains numerous non-imperialist elements. Our attitude to the war is based now as ever on the necessity for the defeat of Hitler.

2. The Hitler machine has evidently assumed that, after signing the pact with the Soviet Union, the subjection of Poland would be feasible without war. After this hope proved groundless and the prospect of a war on two fronts became a reality, German strategists were faced with the task of dealing with Poland as swiftly as possible. In spite of the military successes in the first week of the war it must still be reckoned that Polish resistance has not yet been broken by a long chalk. In projecting future military developments, it must be assumed that German superiority will be successful in subjugating Poland within a few months.

Even if Hitler's Germany were to succeed in throwing the main body of its troops to the west, the western powers would be superior from practically every point of view—economically, at sea, in the quality and morale of their forces, heavy weapons, the Maginot line, whilst maintaining at least a balance of strength against the Luftwaffe. Supplementary support will in all probability be provided through the economic and material resources of the USA. Seen from this angle, a conflict between Hitler's Germany on the one hand and the western powers on the other should surely result in the ultimate defeat of Hitler's Germany.

Italy will hardly be able to maintain her present position. She will either have to offer guarantees to the western powers that she will not actually enter the war on the German side, or she will be exposed to an attack by the western powers and in all probability be defeated. Turkey and the Balkans will then stand firm at the side of the western powers, whilst an Italian defeat would inevitably bring grave consequences for Germany in its train.

In the new situation Japan will clearly seek to arrive at an accommodation with Britain and the USA and to disengage herself from her Chinese adventure. After that there arises the possibility of a confrontation with the Soviet Union.

The Soviet attitude after the outbreak of war remains inscrutable. Whilst there are various reports that deliveries of materials to Germany have already begun, it seems unlikely that the treaty of friendship will be extended into a military pact.

And even if it did come to the point of a military pact and a joint leadership of the war by Hitler and Stalin, this would not be a decisive factor in determining the outcome in the west. However, it is much more probable that the next stage of the war will see a conflict between Germany and Russia.

For the immediate future, British hopes of a relatively swift success in forcing a change of government in Germany must clearly be taken into account. When these hopes fade the struggle will be continued even more bitterly than before. We can conclude that, given the present balance of power, there is little serious likelihood of Hitler's Germany having a chance of winning the war.

3. The reversal in Soviet foreign policy had clearly already begun shortly after 'Munich'. Taking the attitudes of the English and French governments into consideration, a swing towards neutrality was also an understandable possibility, even though indefensible in the light of Russian policy and propaganda in recent years. But the facts of the situation are that the position taken up by the Stalinist régime is not one of neutrality but of direct aid to Hitler-Fascism. The pact between Stalin and Hitler was the direct prelude to the German invasion of Poland and Russian deliveries facilitated Hitler's conduct of the war.

Just as Soviet Russian foreign policy a year or so ago was exclusively determined by the self-interest of the USSR—as Stalin understood it—so the new change has taken place heedless of the interests of the international socialist movement and the fight against Fascism. The Stalinist régime has—although perhaps only temporarily—allied itself with our arch enemies and therefore excluded itself from the ranks of the international socialist movement. We have now to examine closely what possible internal conditions and changes in the USSR form the background to this reversal in foreign policy.

Stalin was anxious to keep out of the European war, perhaps fancifully speculating on a subsequent Russian intervention in Europe. But it must be considered likely that the expansionist thrust of German imperialism against Russian territory is still a real threat and that after a period of co-operation a new conflict will arise between the two powers. Then the USSR will be more isolated than ever and because of her present policies the Stalinist régime will be faced with the first serious threat to her continued existence. Reversals in Russian foreign policy have swept the ground away from under the previous policy of the Comintern parties. The confusion in the Communist ranks must be resolved, and the inevitable result will be a break with the Comintern and the Stalinist régime. There can be no association between revolutionary socialists and the apologists of Stalinist policy or the official organs of Russian foreign policy. This is a particularly severe blow for the German opposition. But this blow too must be overcome and the conviction strengthened that the work of liberating German workers is their task and theirs alone.

(11)   PROBLEMS OF EXILE

In the whole period since the defeat of the socialist movement and the need to flee from Germany, lively discussions on the issues raised by the war have taken place among politicians in exile. Those who have fallen victim to the victorious National Socialists have frequently been incapable of properly assessing the new problems which presented themselves. Representatives of a movement which was destroyed without a struggle will always have difficulty in discussing their views in a balanced manner. But the members of this movement were at any rate far quicker than many others to recognise the connection between the break-through of National Socialism in Germany and its aggressive foreign policy which, they said, would lead to war. Agitation against the National Socialists has often been oversimplified, but in all those years attention has rightly been drawn to this connection between National Socialism and the danger of war. The work which German socialists carried on after the defeat of 1933 in underground groups and in exile was throughout the whole period a fight against a policy based on war.

Thus German socialists were not taken by surprise at the developments in foreign policy which have taken place. Those who were living in the Third Reich and stood firm by their socialist views— whether or not they belonged to an underground group—became increasingly convinced that National Socialist policy would result in war. They could also hope that this war would lead to the collapse of the present régime. But at the same time they knew that war would affect the German people as a whole, and it was by no means certain that socialism and democracy would emerge victorious after a destructive conflict between the great powers. On the other hand they were aware that there was no point in hoping for a revolution inside Germany, as long as those in power advanced from one victory to another. But should they still permit themselves to hope that it would come to war, and the sooner the better? It was this question which tortured the consciences of many socialists. They understood the horrors war would bring but saw no means of warding off this danger by action from inside Germany.

The same conundrum faced the Germans in exile. In those groups which had least contact with the homeland and where they were in an advanced stage of political disintegration, there had already been some canvassing in the direction of wishing a war to come at an early point in time. The argument went that there was nothing to lose, and everything to gain. But it must be stressed that this attitude consistently met with firm resistance on the part of responsible socialists. Throughout recent years German socialists have agitated against the Nazis. But they have not agitated for a war against Germany. They have said and written that Nazi expansion must be checked. And information received from friends inside Germany clearly demonstrated that the policy of appeasement which the western powers pursued up until early last year was continually eroding internal opposition to the National Socialist régime. Their view was that a firm stand would secure peace and strengthen those forces in Germany which were committed against a policy of war. The policy of the great powers, however, operated in the opposite direction and, quite understandably, they paid no heed to what the Germans in exile had to say.

In many ways the war has completely altered the situation. Its first result was that one of the German opposition groups, the Communists, stood down. Up until the end of August the German section of the Comintern was pushing out propaganda to the effect that if it came to the point, war should be waged against Germany, whilst simultaneously continuing to promise that a revolution in Germany was only a matter of time. Then the pact between Germany and Russia came and that silenced the German section of the Comintern. Profound disappointment was felt by those Communists who were left in Germany, and among those in exile confusion, whilst a few party secretaries actually managed to defend not only the pact which had made war against Poland possible for the German régime, but also the new Russian line which banished the word Fascism from the dictionary and off-loaded all the blame on to the western powers, the neutrals and—believe it or not—the German socialist movement.

And then after all the war caused the western powers to become interested in achieving co-operation with at least some of the Germans in exile. New problems confronted the various groups : was it right to collaborate with other powers in the fight against the Nazi régime? How far could such a possible collaboration be taken? What demands should German socialists raise on their own account in the new situation? It can scarcely be said that the groups who today speak in the name of the German socialist movement present a united front. Some of them represent old levels of the organisation, others have become spokesmen of new groups which have formed since they went underground.

The various initiatives towards the unification of the socialist groups have never really borne fruit. In spite of this the tendency towards unity is considerably stronger than it was immediately after their defeat in 1933. Discussions do not keep revolving about the question of who was responsible for the collapse as much as they used to, but about a future new revival of the socialist movement, of democracy and of socialist policies. Among those emigrés who have little contact with an active movement there will always be a tendency towards the formation of separate groups. But today there are fewer different groups than previously. And the new policy lines which are being formulated can count on a greater response than the disputes of recent years among the various directions in the movement, because these viewpoints are in touch with the realities of the situation and also because they are drawn up by people who in these changed circumstances should have a greater chance than ever before of making an impact on the political life of their country once again.

(12)   THE SOVIET UNION AND THE BETRAYAL OF SOCIALISM

It is becoming increasingly clearer that a change in the European situation is on the way in the direction of an extension of the present theatres of war. The war is beginning to grow out of its initial diplomatic phase.

This initial phase has up to now operated in two sectors : first, in the period of the 'Blitzkrieg' overthrow of Poland and the common German and Russian peace offensive; and secondly, in the developments which culminated in the Russian invasion of Finland.

From the outset we have rated the chances of success of the 'peace offensive' as nil. In so doing we were fully aware of the fact that those in power in Germany were vitally concerned to avoid a great trial of strength and to continue to pursue the old strategy of a war on several fronts; further, that there were influential circles as high up as the leadership of industry and political leadership which wished to carry on the policy of Munich. Nor had it escaped our attention that pacifists and parts of the socialist movement together with neutral powers supported this 'peace party' and were able to draw on the support of the unmistakable yearning for peace among wide areas of the population. In our evaluation of the European situation we must not overlook the fact that the outbreak of war was not caused by a constellation of chance circumstances nor by misunderstandings, but by fundamental imperialist conflicts of interest between Hitler's Germany and the western powers. That isolated groups among the captains of industry in France and Britain gave preference to other means of representing their interests changed nothing.

Only when Russian policy towards the subjection of her border states culminated in the invasion of Finland did the 'peace offensive' stand a more reasonable chance—but in a quite different fashion from that imagined by Stalin and Molotov. However ridiculous it might seem, much points to the fact that Nazi diplomacy egged the Russians on to military action against Finland. The Russian war on Finland could not help but bring about a decisive crisis point in the confrontation between Russia and Britain. And so the conditions became ripe for drawing the Russians into a binding pact with Germany. At the same time interest was switched from the quiet main front to the active secondary front and the German authorities were able to maintain their diplomatic and propaganda pressure on neutrals and on the defeatist elements on the opposite side.

Two theatres of war remain side by side : the western front which has been 'all quiet', and the Finnish front, where in the meantime tens of thousands of Russian workers and peasants paid with their lives for the insane policies of Stalin. The attentive and critical observer will not fail to notice that since the beginning of December there have been pressures at work everywhere seeking to turn the Finnish front into the main theatre of war. Stalin was branded as World Enemy Number One in place of Hitler. The League of Nations suddenly took on a youthful vigour once more after years of the most pitiable senility. The betrayers of Abyssinia, China, Spain and Czechoslovakia all of a sudden remembered the basic principles of collective security.

The Soviet government justified itself by claiming that it was forced to act in order to secure Russian frontiers, but this reveals itself more and more, in so far as it is more than a twist of propaganda, as a crucial error of judgement. It was this action by Stalin which engendered and intensified that generally hostile mood against Russia which would never have arisen in the present power situation if Russia had remained even tolerably neutral.

From the outset we have most rigorously opposed the Russian invasion of Finland and expressed our solidarity with the Finnish socialist movement in its fight to ward off the invader. But at the same time we have not altered our basic position in this war. In our eyes Hitler and his régime have been and remain the principal enemy. It is from this basic premise that we socialists in Germany, Austria and Czechoslovakia derive our attitudes to the war between Germany and the western powers. And it has also conditioned our attitude to the Stalinist policy of pact-making with Hitler, and not the other way round.

Since December there have been determined efforts towards a resolution of the differences between Germany and England. But they seem to us to have precious little prospect of success. If our supposition turns out to be correct then all the signs are that the alliance between Germany and Russia will be consolidated and that fighting on the diplomatic front line will soon come to an end in the west as well. During the first period of the war Russia succeeded in consolidating her power position. Since the subjection of Poland, Germany has had hardly any successes worth mentioning. Since the outbreak of war in Finland the Russian position has considerably weakened, and the failures of the 'Red Army' have painfully demonstrated the consequences of Stalin's policies over the last decade. Weaknesses on both sides during the initial phase of the war have driven Germany and Russia closer into each other's arms. Both of them regard the overthrow of the British Empire as a cause well worth fighting for; and in this respect it remains to be seen whether it will prove possible to involve Japan as well in the struggle towards this objective.

As early as last November Holland and Belgium found themselves compelled to reply to the German plans for an offensive by general mobilisation, and the same process was repeated in the middle of January. Whilst the Scandinavian countries were intent on preserving their neutrality even after the outbreak of the Russian-Finnish war, they have found themselves exposed to increasingly serious threats from Russia and Germany, not simply in the form of newspaper articles, but also in unambiguous diplomatic notes. In south-east Europe, Italy—aided and abetted by England— took the lead in strengthening the resolve to maintain the *status quo*. In this way three sectors are marked out in which the expected expansion of the war might be supposed to concentrate. It will be a shorter step from here to the unleashing of all the weapons of destruction which modern war technology has at its command, than from the outbreak of war until the conclusion of the initial diplomatic phase.

The first months of the war have disproved countless theories and prognoses. For the fronts have not become more clear-cut, on the contrary, they have become more confused than ever. The socialist movement has been further weakened and suffered renewed setbacks during these first war months—principally as a result of Russian policy. The prospect of a progressive outcome to the war has become even more remote. There is nothing to justify our supposition that no further shifts of position or regroupings would be possible when the fronts had been opened up. But on the other hand there is every reason to believe that the great collision between the war powers will create upheavals and liberate forces which it will be beyond the ability of those in power today to control.

Russian policy in the last year has transformed the entire inter- (13)
national situation. The pact with Germany was responsible for the invasion of Poland and the declaration of war against Germany by the western powers. It rescued the Third Reich from a hopeless predicament. Russia's involvement in the war sealed the fate of Poland. The war against Finland has posed a whole series of new problems which may well have a decisive impact on future developments.

The attitude of the socialist movement towards the Soviet Union today must be considered against this background. Relations have changed almost beyond recognition. It is hardly a novel situation to find the leaders of the Soviet Union in a state of outright war against the socialist movement. It has happened before. But today the whole movement is obliged to stand up and fight and draw a clear dividing line between itself and the Soviet Union. It is not the socialist movement but the Soviet Union which has changed. It is not the socialist movement but the Soviet Union which has entered a pact of friendship with Nazism. It is the Soviet Union which stabbed Poland in the back and initiated the war against Finland. It is the Russian leaders who are saying that it is 'the work of madmen to wage war in order to destroy Hitlerism', that their friendship with Nazism is 'sealed by blood' and that the real villains are democracy and the socialist movement.

If nothing else has happened, it is the policies of the Russians themselves which have removed the basis of our former attitude towards them. A new situation has arisen, and this new situation calls for much thought if we are to understand it aright. The attitude of the movement must be brought into line with the new turn of events. And the way reactionaries have exploited Russian policy against socialism and the socialist movement underlines the necessity for a swift, thorough and decisive re-evaluation of the situation.

Stalin's policy has helped to strengthen reactionary anti-socialist and anti-working-class forces throughout the world. And not only because it has increased the power of Nazism.

... Socialists must not make judgements on the basis of abstract principles. They cannot demand of a state which calls itself socialist that it should wage war at a moment's notice for the sake of ideals.

Nor can it reproach such a state for maintaining regular com-
munication with other states, regardless of their system of government. But this is not the matter in question. Behind a smokescreen
of peaceful policies the Soviet Union has been an accessory to setting the world war in train. And under the guise of seeking to
regularise her relations with Germany she has entered into a treaty
of friendship with those forces which throughout the last few years
have represented the principal threat to freedom, democracy and
socialism in Europe. Under the pretext of seeking to 'liberate' the
Finnish people the Soviet Union has set out to plunder them.

By such policies the Soviet Union has become a comrade-in-arms
of Nazism and has excluded herself from membership of the anti-
Nazi front. Above and beyond this she has herself employed Nazi
techniques in setting out to attack a peaceful and democratic
neighbour. The Soviet Union has become an agent of reaction in
international politics. The socialist movement must fight her as
it must every reactionary.

The socialist movement has no cause to regret the attitude which
it previously took to developments inside Russia. Its attitude must
be regarded in its historical context. There is certainly the frequent
inclination to idealise conditions there, but it is clear that in many
respects the roots of the policy which we see before us today can be
traced back to the starting point, the ideas of the revolution and
the way in which they were implemented . . .

The 1917 revolution and subsequent developments created the
basic *conditions* for reshaping Russia as a socialist state. But this
does not mean that socialism *was actually created* in the Soviet
Union. The Stalinists even try to make us believe that the socialist
revolution has not only taken place but that a 'classless society' has
actually been established.

Without freedom and democracy socialism is unthinkable. But
we have seen a hardening of dictatorship in the Soviet Union in
recent years. The curtailment of democratic rights, which were at
first thought of as a temporary measure, was maintained, extended
and hardened into a bureaucratic dictatorship . . .

The socialist must make an effort to understand developments
in the Soviet Union. And he must never surrender the view that
any change in conditions inside Russia must ultimately be the affair
of the Russian people themselves.

No 'crusade against Bolshevism' will be able to liberate the forces
of socialism which now lie in chains. On the contrary, the crusaders
of reaction plan to take Russian society in its present state of
transition and restore capitalism, replacing Stalinism by another

brand of dictatorship. The socialist movement takes the view that liberation of the forces of democracy and socialism in Europe will create the essential conditions to enable progressive forces in Russia to rid the country of its bureaucratic and state capitalist dictatorship. Therefore the struggle for freedom and independence inside small nations remains even today the best and indeed the only means of assistance which we can offer to the workers and peasants of Russia.

NATURE AND TASKS OF THE GERMAN OPPOSITION   (14)

The second imperialist World War is at the same time a war whose outcome will determine the social order for the future. It is not simply a matter of choice between a new order created by Fascism or a straightforward reversion to pre-Fascist conditions. If these were the alternatives then Fascism would have the upper hand. Because of the impact of Germany's military successes, Fascist borrowings from socialist concepts (economic planning, supranational European order, etc.) have caused us to overlook the crucial factor. And that is that the essential condition for a new social order in the immediate future is and remains the overthrow of Fascism. As the war progresses, the necessity for restructuring the social order will become increasingly apparent. The nations will want to know why they are fighting. The old socialist movement was incapable of indicating a way out of the crisis, of evolving an effective resistance against Fascism, of preventing war or, after the outbreak of war, of influencing its course.

When faced with the challenge of a second World War, what remained of the socialist movement crumbled to dust...

There is certainly no question of war fever inside Germany. On the other hand there is no question either of any serious challenge to the present régime.

What the forces of national and socialist opposition will actually achieve depends on the situation at the end of the war. We have no influence on the development of power relationships outside Germany. What we can plan to do is to be active, where there are no direct power conflicts, in bringing together social and national upheaval factors in central Europe. Today more than ever it is vital that we should never lose sight of the fact that a realistic and lasting new pattern for Europe can be achieved only on a federal basis and that national issues can be resolved only on the basis of socialism.

The old parties and groupings have lost their *raison d'être*.

Naturally traditional relationships which still offer some kind of support to the individual cannot and should not simply be torn apart. But the only sensible course today is to bring together people who are prepared to co-operate in specific fields and who possess the necessary human qualities. The structuring of new forms of organisation can comfortably be held over to a later date.

(15)   The question of which forces in the opposition inside Germany will be able to make their mark on developments in the immediate future is becoming an increasingly real and important issue. Any attempt to resolve it, even indirectly, suffers from the disadvantage that even with a number of contacts and careful study of conditions in Germany it is possible to gain only a relatively limited view of the situation.

In the first place, this issue concerns the situation within the army and the relationships between army and party leaders. It must be borne in mind that Goebbels has contrived with great skill and by all manner of means to spread every kind of misrepresentation. The following factors are of particular importance for the situation as it stands :

1. There is no question of a united or even a clear majority opposition among the officer corps. Reports from Norway, from the Reich and other territories make it clear that a greater number of the officer corps than is generally supposed identify themselves with the Nazi leaders and are loyal to them. This is especially the case among those younger officers who owe their career largely to their membership of the party.

2. On the other hand it can be stated without qualification that opposition movements among the officer corps have gained considerable ground in the recent past. The principal reasons for this are opposition to the strategic measures of the Führer's headquarters and reaction against the broadening of the power base of the SS. Because of 'Vansittartist' tendencies in Allied foreign policy, and internal political moves in the direction of social revolution, fear of the consequences of a German defeat is an inhibiting factor.

3. Even though a considerable number of German officers today are opposed to the hard-core Nazis, it does not follow that they are prepared to translate thought into action. The feeling that the Gestapo and the Waffen-SS are in a position to nip any initiative from the army in the bud effectively cripples opposition. At the same time the hope is gaining ground that the longer the war continues the better Germany's chances might become. There is specu-

THE OPPOSITION IN CONFLICT

lation here about real or supposed differences of opinion in the Allied camp and the belief is that a possible heightening of these differences might result in better peace terms. This whole discussion is being conducted in the knowledge that Germany can no longer win the war.

4. Among those who are striving towards a postponement of the ultimate conclusion of the war there are some who hope for a separate peace with the Soviet Union, whilst others believe it possible to make terms with the western powers. Apart from officers of the old school, members of the former category also include the so-called national-Bolshevist circle, which even numbers some NSDAP members among its adherents. These people place the main emphasis on recognition of Germany's national interests. Some are also not a little influenced by the hope of an act of revenge against the west at some time in the future. The other category comprises a conservative opposition among some industrialists and also members of the opposition movement within the church.

5. The army leadership has recently achieved a greater degree of independence from Hitler and his associates. Downgrading the civilian party bureaucracy has led to a parallel strengthening of the influence of both the SS and the army. The foreign political office of the army command has been reinforced. The latest decisions on the eastern front have in essence been taken without regard to Hitler's prestige policies.

6. The increased independence of the army leaders does not however mean that there is any kind of consensus among them. Nor is there any one individual who is, so to speak, a natural for the role of Badoglio. People are also aware that a new situation will arise if the hard-core Nazis and SS fight to the finish. Halder and Manstein have both been named as leaders of a possible military coup but it is most significant that this has come about without their co-operation.

7. The example of Norway is typical. Falkenhorst belongs to the group of generals who are not party members. For a long time he has been aware that the war can no longer be won and is trying, however timidly, to bring into the open the differences between himself and Terboven and Rediess. In spite of this it must be stated that Falkenhorst himself is not an active member of the opposition. It is younger men who are active, and some of them are certainly close to Falkenhorst. But it can be assumed that these younger— Christian, conservative and anti-Nazi nationalist—groups of officers will attempt to push men like Falkenhorst to the fore in a crisis, because they have hopes of thereby securing a greater degree of

unity among the armed forces. That could also be the case with Halder, Manstein and others.

8. In discussions of what is taking place in the German army, people often wrongly think only in terms of the officer class and ignore what is happening among the other ranks and what their reactions in a crisis might be. For the simple reason that even now so many officers are Nazis, there are strong indications that a large number of soldiers will not be prepared to continue to submit to discipline. They will acknowledge the people they trust, and the groundwork for this has been already laid by increased underground activity among the progressive section of the military.

9. But one fundamental distinction must be recognised. There are numerous reports confirming the fact that even now morale among troops on the eastern front is relatively better than among those at home or in the occupied territories. Part of the reason for this is the spontaneous *esprit de corps* generated by the enormous sacrifices and challenges to which all those on the eastern front have been exposed. And this applies equally to a not insignificant number of officers.

10. Nevertheless it remains to be said that no evaluation which fails to place due emphasis on the role of the ordinary soldier in the coming revolution can possibly be viable. Reports to hand from the occupied territories to the north and west taken together indicate that, alongside general expressions of dissatisfaction, there are also signs of more serious initiatives in the direction of premeditated anti-Nazi activity (in underground groups and writings).

The following points can serve to illustrate the situation as it exists within the Nazi camp itself :

1. Because the main power centre has shifted on to the side of the Gestapo and SS, discontent has increased throughout the civilian party bureaucracy and the civil service which is organised along Nazi lines. Among the general party membership there is strong evidence of 'party fatigue' which is being fought by meeting after meeting and even by threats of violence.

2. The conservative element in the party, which is often popularly termed the Göring wing but which finds its principal support among industrialists, is increasingly seeking to dissociate itself from the 'radical' leadership of the party and in many cases is even attempting to enter into closer contact with corresponding elements in the army. In these circles there is talk to the effect that Göring is the only man able to play the part of a German Badoglio, as he can count on support in the party and also in the civil service, army and in industry. But naturally we should not discount the possibility

that Göring will do all he can to save his skin, but it is true at the same time that rumours about his opposition leanings were in the first instance deliberately put out by the party leadership. In addition, Göring would be in no position to check the further advance of revolution inside Germany.

3. The 'socialist' and 'national-Bolshevist' wings of the party are hardly likely to be forces to be reckoned with. There are no indications that Strasser or people like him would be able to step into Hitler's shoes. The party is so hated and its internal disintegration will be so complete on the day of defeat that there is scarcely any possibility that it will be able to regroup. The remains of the party will gather themselves around Himmler and the SS and they will all go under together.

There are clear signs of a revival among both the conservative and liberal opposition. In this context the following points are the most important:

1. That part of industry which is not wedded to the Nazis for better or worse, together with representatives of business, shipping, etc., place great hopes on an American occupation. There are reports about concrete measures promised under the occupation and great efforts to revive or re-establish contacts abroad.

2. With the support of some groups among the *petit bourgeois*, certain areas of the middle class and the officer corps, the monarchists have stepped up their activities.

3. The urban middle class who formerly counted as one of the social mainstays of Nazism, are today among the most disillusioned. The social influence of this class has however been decisively weakened by the measures of the Hitler régime.

4. Opposition among scientists and higher management has risen steeply. True, these people are neither so united nor active in their opposition as in Italy, but they will play a key role when defeat comes. They are strongly disposed towards a planned economy on a democratic basis.

5. A variety of instances are pointing to increased resistance on the part of the student population. All German universities have their underground groups. These groups are broadly libertarian and democratic in outlook, although they do not present a uniform front nor are their attitudes particularly clear-cut.

6. At this juncture it should be stressed that it would indeed be a fundamental error to regard all those young Germans who grew up under the Hitler régime as a solid pro-Fascist bloc. On the contrary it has proved the case time and again that neither the schools nor the labour service have been able to turn young people into hard-

core Nazis. The conflict between the generations has operated against the Nazis and a substantial proportion of young people in Germany are critical of Fascism. The most dangerous Nazis are to be found among those age-groups which were on Hitler's side in his years of struggle towards power. It should equally not be overlooked that the majority of the young have no political instincts, and this is going to place great difficulties in the way of their political engagement after the fall of Hitler.

Opposition within the church is naturally of the utmost importance, above all to the extent to which it expresses the discontent among the country population :

1. The main emphasis here is on the side of the Catholic church. It compromised itself in 1940 when the conference of bishops in Fulda spoke out in favour of the Nazi war, whilst at the same time a considerable proportion of the rank and file clergy were also supporting the Hitler régime. But the situation has changed since then. Men like Galen and Faulhaber are taking a lead today, and Catholic services and processions in many places are increasingly taking on the unmistakable character of demonstrations against the régime.

2. In the Protestant opposition the role of Niemöller has frequently been overestimated. As a symbol he does however have a certain significance. More important in fact are the men surrounding Wurm, the bishop of Württemberg.

3. Links between active opposition circles in the Catholic and Protestant churches have been strengthened. There is in fact a common high-level leadership in the clerical opposition. The church has also had an easier ride than any other organised group in that she has been able to maintain a countrywide semi-official organisation without too much difficulty.

4. Contacts between the clerical opposition and corresponding circles abroad are better than those of any other body. Influenced by members of the clerical opposition, central co-ordinating committees have been set up in recent months in the Reich and also regional committees, in which church representatives come together with representatives of the officer corps, of industry and also with Social Democrats, trade unionists and Communists. As things are, it must be considered likely that the church opposition will play a leading part when defeat comes. In the first place it is better organised than anyone else. And nowhere is this more so than in the south of Germany where the Catholics are very strong.

The most neglected part of the German opposition is the one which history will reveal as the most important and progressive, namely the workers. The following points may serve to summarise their significance :

1. The underground activities of the workers' parties which had already suffered repeated blows under the Gestapo were struck again in the course of the war. On top of this, many of their key men were arrested. Hitler's successes effectively crippled underground work. But since last winter there has undoubtedly been a revival among underground groups, even though on a limited scale. The task of liaison has largely been passed on to women and girls. Young trade union officials who have succeeded in avoiding recruitment are among the main pillars of these underground political activities. Since last year it has also been noticeable how contacts between underground groups in Germany and their comrades in the army have been strengthened.

2. It is however extremely difficult to arrive at a comprehensive picture of the underground political movement as a whole. After the defeat most of the unknowns among the young underground workers will not be of sufficient stature to take a leading role. The formation of new parties will be a pretty confused business. On the other hand it is well known that the main body of the older workers, among them not a few old trade union officials and shop stewards, have been able to hold their own in the factories. In recent years they have largely been passive, but they have been able to maintain their natural basis of trust in the factories, and after the war will be able to play a very important part, especially because the factories will have to form the broad basis of a new administration.

3. The relationship between German and foreign labour in many industries has improved, and there are reports that common underground groups have been formed. In spite of this foreign workers acting on their own account will inevitably create disunity. What they want more than anything is to return home. But present and future contacts will still be able to have some mollifying effect upon any unfortunate situations that may arise.

4. It is very difficult to pass judgement on the balance of political affiliations among the work force. The Nazis can now count on only a few per cent. The majority of workers are vaguely dissatisfied but politically inactive because of their long working hours or for a variety of other reasons. Active opposition members are in a minority today, but are increasingly widening their influence. In many industries there is a broad state of balance between former Social Democrats and Communists. Many reports indicate that the old differences are no longer of such importance and that the aim

is a unified movement which is radical, democratic and socialist in outlook.

5. Most important, the discussions about what is to happen after the war among the more progressive industrial workers are among the most positive to be heard anywhere in Germany. Much thought is being given to the construction of a new state, the trade unions, etc., and to a realistic relationship with the occupation forces. Most of those under this heading are aware that special efforts will be required of Germany in the reconstruction of the devastated areas. Nationalist attitudes are not strong, although it is frequently stressed that there is no desire to be faced with demands that would render them the drudges of foreign powers in the eyes of their own population. The most decisive attitude towards dealing with the Nazis and their allied groups is expected to come from the workers. For this reason the German work force can be relied on more than any other section of the community to collaborate with others anxious to see a democratic and peaceful system of relationships in Germany and Europe.

(16)   AIMS OF DEMOCRACY IN GERMANY

We do not yet know today whether Germany will be occupied by the victorious powers together or whether it will come to a division into zones in the east and west—with different conditions for development on the basis of the differing approaches of the occupation forces. But independently of this we do know that the coming big changes in Germany will be largely dependent on forces outside the country. The possibilities of a German revolution will be predominantly dependent on the international balance of power.

There is naturally also the possibility that defeat will bring such utter exhaustion that there will be hardly any scope for the positive reconstruction of society. All that is certain is that a Nazi collapse will involve both administration and industry.

None the less the main weight of evidence points to the fact that military defeat will induce an uprising among large areas of the population. Then all manner of different interest groups will be in evidence, and the widest variety of statements of intent will be made. There will be a wild outburst against the Nazis and many will take the opportunity of destroying Nazi organisations and institutions with the utmost despatch. Regardless of other social aims, many Germans will feel able to associate themselves with the demand for restoration of basic democratic rights : freedom of opinion, freedom of organisation, freedom of the press. Thus the uprising after Nazism will take on a democratic character in Germany, although there are grounds to suppose that neither the German anti-Nazis nor the occupation forces will go so far as to accord such democratic rights to the Nazis.

Thus we can take the view that a revolution inside Germany will grow partly on the basis of anti-Nazi sentiments and partly on democratic foundations. Some of the German people will certainly ask not only what is to be done with the Nazi leaders but also with those bodies which aided and abetted the Nazis in their seizure of power and which supported their policies in principle ...

But the democratic revolution will also bring social consequences in its train. If these consequences are not faced squarely the achievements of democracy will be put at risk. There is no doubt about the co-responsibility of heavy industry and high finance in the rise of Nazism. If the power of Germany's monopoly capitalism is to be broken, cartels and financial institutions must be nationalised. In factories with Nazi owners or directors it is most likely that the workers themselves will take over the plant, probably in the name of a state authority which will still be in the process of constituting itself. Social control of industry will be a natural consequence of a determined anti-Nazi movement ...

A new German government will be immediately confronted with the following tasks, if it is to hold its position before its own population on the one hand and to be able to offer the guarantees of peace demanded by the victorious powers on the other :

First, the Nazi criminals must be sternly and ruthlessly crushed. They must be imprisoned and punished and, as and when as demands to this effect are made, handed over to the Allies. All public institutions must be denazified. Members of the SS and Gestapo together with other hard-core Nazis must be interned and if they are not punished in any other way at least detailed to compulsory labour. It is highly dubious whether this task can be carried out if—as has been hinted by certain of the Allies—the German police is taken over in its present form and allowed to retain its weapons. For regardless of whether many of them are honourable members of the force, they still remain Himmler's police.

Secondly, basic democratic rights must be restored to those who recognise democracy as a basis for work and discussion. Apart from freedom of opinion and confession, freedom of organisation and of the press will be reintroduced. On the other hand no early elections will be held. The foundations for a new democracy must be laid in such a way that free unions and parallel organisations on the one hand and political parties on the other can be brought into existence.

The third objective is to ensure that the population is fed, to initiate the reorganisation of industry and to avoid mass unemployment and the social chaos which it would bring in its train. These tasks can only be carried out if a large part of the Nazi machinery for the control of industry is 'taken over as it stands'. If this is not done, then there will be breakdowns all along the line. The decisive issue here is not a conflict of dogma between socialisation and free enterprise but the avoidance of starvation and a return of members of the armed services to normal employment as far as is possible. But care must be taken to ensure that the administration of the machinery for economic planning is taken over by reliable individuals and that provision is made for a satisfactory form of democratic control. Co-operative agencies for production and distribution must be allowed an important position in any such regrouping.

The fourth task will be to democratise the administration, the legal and education systems, etc. Local self-government must be strengthened. Social and administrational decentralisation must be co-ordinated with pressure towards strong centralisation in the industrial sphere.

The solution of these tasks as a basis for further advance towards democracy does however depend upon the foreign policy of the German revolution and on the attitudes of foreign powers to the German revolution.

Even after defeat nationalist forces will continue to operate. We can only hope that sincere German democrats will hold fast to European and international objectives and make a concerted effort to win over the majority of the people on to their side. On the other hand democrats can hardly be expected to put their signatures to each and every document placed before them from abroad without demur.

After all that has happened, any peace will be 'just' by comparison with the crimes of the Nazis against other nations. On the other hand it will be difficult to establish conditions for peace which the Germans will regard as 'just'. The sole solution is to tackle the German problem in its wider European context.

Finally, as far as dealing with Nazism and the re-establishment of democratic organisations and institutions is concerned, such tasks are clearly in the common interest of the Allies and the German democrats—regardless of their relative numerical strength. The appraisal of economic problems and their solution should also be conducted in terms of what makes sense in the context of European and international interests.

... At the end of the day we shall not be contemplating a picture (17) of one single co-ordinated countrywide resistance movement. The true picture is rather one of a whole variety of frantic efforts to resist those who had power and were able to reinforce it because of the cowardice of great masses of the people. Those who undertake such efforts need not be ashamed. ...

THE JULY PLOT

... In 1942–43 I myself received the first reports on the work of co-ordinating various groups, the reason being that they might take up the reins after a coup against Hitler. In the winter of 1943–44 I met up with one of the outstanding men of the religious wing of the opposition, who took part in these efforts towards co-ordination but who was no supporter of a coup. He was the then controller of the transport system in Oslo, Theodor Steltzer, who is now State President of Schleswig-Holstein. I was also in contact with my old friend Julius Leber, the previous Social Democrat Reichstag deputy and editor-in-chief, who informed me about internal political conditions. A month before the last attempted coup I was with Adam von Trott, the embassy official from the Wilhelmstrasse[2] who was hanged in September 1944. He was—like the negotiators of 1942— particularly concerned with an exploration of the effect of political conditions abroad on any uprising against Hitler.

But the events leading to 20 July could lay claim to interests above and beyond the context of foreign politics. As long as the war lasted it was impossible to give a clear picture of the situation. The Gestapo could not be allowed to find out any details which they had not already discovered.[3] It was indeed expedient to represent certain things in such a way as to mislead the Gestapo. But today such considerations are no longer important.

In Germany a great deal has already been written about these happenings. Much of it seeks to demonstrate the magnificent and dignified conduct of the conspirators after they had got into the clutches of the Gestapo. And this is indeed true. The *Neue Zeitung* was correct when it wrote that they were real men, even if all of them were not really great men.

Notes

1. Brandt's opponents took statements like this to mean that he was making 'a confession of political faith as a Communist' and that he was demanding 'the establishment of a Soviet Communist Germany'.

2. Seat of the German Foreign Office in Berlin.

3. Suspicion was directed against Willy Brandt when a book entitled *Misslyckad Revolt* (*The Plot that Failed*—Stockholm, 1944) appeared anonymously. Events in Germany leading up to and following the July plot were explored in the form of ten 'Letters from Berlin'. It was claimed that Brandt was the author of this book, and had been guilty of breach of confidence by making use of the writings of a member of the opposition who had fled to Stockholm. Brandt has energetically denied the charge. The man concerned who was involved in the July plot has also strongly denied the possibility of a breach of confidence. Over and above this, a journalist living in Stockholm has stated that he was responsible for the book in question. He has explained that the material on which the 'Letters from Berlin' were based was drawn from various individuals, among them Fritz Tarnow and Willy Brandt, who was involved in the writing of a few sections only.

III

For and Against 'The Other Germany'

III

For and Against 'The Other Germany'

INTRODUCTION

The occupation of southern Norway was virtually completed by 1 May 1940. With my colleagues from the People's Aid I had been continuing the work of alleviating human suffering. In the confusion of those weeks our efforts were well-intentioned, but met with little success. Immediately before the Norwegians capitulated in Mittetdalen on the west coast where I was staying, I had followed the advice of good friends of mine and put on a Norwegian uniform. As a civilian I would have run a greater risk of falling into the hands of the Gestapo. My calculations were correct. After a few weeks in Dovre POW camp—in buildings belonging to a country school—I was released by Hauptmann Nippus with a free pass to 'my home city of Oslo'.

However oppressing the situation was at that time, in general and for me personally, the experience of talking to the German guards remains important for me even now when I look back on it. They were nearly all young men from the Rhineland, and they were nearly all 'apolitical'. And there was no lack of lighter moments. When the announcement came at the beginning of June that King Haakon and his government had fled from northern Norway to England, one young lieutenant made the remark which was as rude as it was wrong, namely that the king was a coward. I replied in my gently broken German and deliberately ignoring the laws of logic that if he did not take that back I should feel able to assert that Hitler was a coward. That caused a bit of a stir but it was cleared up by someone telling the lieutenant: 'Leave that silly student alone.' And perhaps that was not so far from the truth.

Then there came a lonely summer holiday on an island in the Oslo fjord. But it was doubtless more sensible for me to regularise my status by escaping to Sweden. And then again I returned secretly to Oslo from Sweden in December 1940, partly for personal reasons, partly to hold discussions with leaders of the civilian Norwegian resistance. Then it was that I met Einar Gerhardsen whom

I knew well from prewar days and who was to be Prime Minister for many years after the war.

My disappearance into the POW camp and my illegal residence in occupied Norway were naturally not without danger. But the risk was far less than in Germany at that time. In spite of the Gestapo and the informant system it was possible to hide among a broadly based mass opposition movement which was both national and democratic in character. At any rate the years in neutral Sweden were not so secure as people today may be inclined to think. On more than one occasion there was a real danger that this part of Scandinavia would also be invaded. Among my papers from the year 1941 there is an application for entry into the USA just in case. It says: 'Swedish officials have advised me to leave Sweden. If Sweden's position were to become more exposed there is no guarantee for my personal safety. I have already been deprived of German citizenship and I have definite news that the Gestapo have tried to trace me in Norway.'

In later years I have been exposed to a certain amount of ill-will because my disguise, that is to say my being taken prisoner in Norwegian uniform, has been misrepresented. The assertion has been made that I fired on my own countrymen.[1] This is demonstrably untrue, and I have ensured that the truth was stated openly in the German courts. Having said that, I have never accepted the idea that it would have been dishonourable for a German opponent of Hitler, especially for one deprived of citizenship, to contribute to the defeat of the Hitler régime by all means at his disposal. I am grateful to providence that it has never placed my conscience in the dilemma of having to take up arms against my German countrymen. Such a dilemma, however it might have presented itself, would always be tragic, but would never bring shame.

In France it has never occurred to anyone to call General de Gaulle's patriotism into question because he became involved in armed conflict against his compatriots.—No, my sole purpose is to refute false accusations and to oppose those who sought to stimulate feeling against me by their false accusations—which they have indeed had some success in doing.

I have not had nor do I have any need to justify or excuse my political and journalistic resistance to Nazism. In the metaphorical sense of the word I naturally regarded myself as a 'combatant'. I have equally never concealed my strong ties with Norway which owe their origin to more than a debt of gratitude. But, at that same stage of the war which led many people into emotional outbursts to the detriment of their reason, I never renounced what I regarded as my duty towards the other Germany, the real Germany. And that has occasionally brought me into conflict with good friends abroad. For myself and others like me, Nazism represented the enemy within. Hitler had to be defeated so that Germany might live. But this does not mean that I identified myself with other powers and their governments. My friends and myself maintained our independence and a critical outlook towards the governments of the western powers, since the latter had repeatedly shied away from confrontation as long as the risk of a large-scale war was comparatively remote. After the German-Russian treaty and the attack on Finland the attitude we adopted towards Russian policy was that it had compromised socialism and the peaceful policies of socialists. In my book which came out in 1940 I proceeded on the basis of this assessment:

'Whilst the war machines on the European continent have still not yet been set rolling in deadly earnest, it is apparent to everyone that there is a second front cutting across those other front lines which in the early stages have been unclear and fluid—and that is the front where the socialist movement, freedom, democracy and historical progress are making their stand against the power of big finance, dictatorship, reaction and imperialism. It is the battle on this front which will decide at the end of the day whether this war will terminate in a genuine peace or whether it will be just another phase in the continuing state of war which has prevailed since 1914.'

During the war the debate about Germany culminated in a clash of views over 'Vansittartism'. This term derives from the school of thought named after Lord Vansittart, for many years Secretary of State at the British Foreign Ministry, which sought to explain Nazism in terms of the history and national character of the Germans, and drew the conclusion that Germany should receive stern treatment after the war. From the very first I have always considered this attitude as unhistorical, unjust and above all irrational, although seen against the background of Nazi crimes it is not completely incomprehensible.

There had already been forerunners of the Vansittartist debate in 1939–40, and in France a particularly lively discussion took place in the period between the Munich agreement in the autumn of 1938 and the outbreak of war just a year later. The rightwing journalist Henri de Kérillis supported the theory dubbed 'realistic nationalism', which states that Hitlerism is an expression of the destiny of the German nation, and that Germany has always been a predator state and must be crushed once and for all time. Others set out to prove in their own way why no distinction should be drawn between the régime and the people. They demanded that Germany must prepare to become a second Carthage.

The main spokesman of the opposite line was the leader of the socialists and former Prime Minister Léon Blum, who like so many others was shortly to suffer a cruel fate in German imprisonment. He did not deny that Nazism had its roots in German history. But, he wrote, Hitler would hardly have come to power if other countries had demonstrated more foresight towards the Weimar Republic. Blum laid the greatest emphasis on the necessity for the establishment of new forms of international justice after the war. A future democratic Germany must take her place on equal terms within a United States of Europe. In England too public debate in the winter of 1939–40 swung between these two poles, but with a clear majority in favour of a just peace. It is a moving experience to call to mind today what the Labour leader and later Prime Minister Clement Attlee announced as the first point in his programme after the oubreak of war: 'The first principle is that there should be no dictated peace. We have no desire to humiliate, to crush or to divide the German nation. There must be restitution made to the victims of aggression, but all ideas of revenge and punishment must be excluded.'[2]

Looking back over what I wrote at that time, I am astonished to see just how clearly the necessity for the unification of Europe was recognised in England at the time and how clearly the Labour party was saying that all those involved in the conflict including England would be well advised to yield up a little of their national sovereignty to the authority of common European institutions.

I was well aware that at later stages of the war it would no longer be so easy to conduct a carefully considered argument based on the facts:

'The intensity of interest in what is to happen after the war and what forms the new peace will take became evident whilst men's spirits were still not yet thrown into a state of total confusion by war propaganda and the effects of mass slaughter. But we must be prepared for the fact that the spread and intensification of the war will alter this picture. Instead of sober-minded and factual evaluations, emotional and irrational factors will come strongly to the fore. The further the horrors of modern world war spread, the less thought will be given to plans for the future of a new Europe. There is a real danger that the din of artillery and the rivers of blood will once again deaden the longings of the nations towards a real and lasting peace.'

At the same time I held firm to my view: 'The new peace will depend on the new balance of power situation. But the battle for the terms of the new peace will itself contribute to the formation of new power structures. This is one of the most important tasks in the work of preparation for the coming peace. Work for the new peace is one and the same with the battle for justice and freedom in every single country, and this work takes on a more substantial form once the transition from matters of principle to the solution of specific concrete tasks has been made.'

RESPONSIBILITY OR GUILT? (1)

The Germans must bear the responsibility. But responsibility is not the same thing as *guilt*. Those who do not regard themselves as guilty and who are not guilty of Nazi crimes, still cannot—if they seek to continue working among this nation and improving its standards—dissociate themselves from the consequences of a policy which all too many of the people were prepared to support. They cannot place themselves outside the community of responsibility and suffering. If they are sincere in their work of reform and education, they will be well advised not to seek to make light of the injustices that have been committed against other nations. They must refrain from holding forth about other countries' share of the responsibility for as long as they do not speak the complete and whole truth to their own countrymen. They must avoid playing for sympathy at a time when the bodies of the murdered are still fresh in their graves.

The actual responsibility must not be dealt out indiscriminately, it must be laid at the door of the right people. And the question of guilt must be applied to individual criminals and their criminal groups and organisations.

Only once it has been established beyond doubt that there is no intention of absolving the Germans from implication in what has happened do we have the right to point out that the responsibility cannot be restricted to Germany and the German people alone.

German democracy—which really only had five quiet years of existence, from 1924–25 to 1929–30—went bankrupt because of internal dissension, weakness and incompetence. But was not precisely the same process repeated on an international scale from 1933 to 1939? The Germans must bear their share of the responsibility. But it serves no useful purpose to make them into 'whipping boys' for circumstances over which they had no control.

It is the Nazis—in Germany as in other countries—who are *guilty*. Nuremberg has revealed a complex of guilt which exceeds the bounds of the wildest fantasy. Not only are the party leaders and Gestapo terrorists guilty but also Junkers, big industrialists, bureaucrats and professors : all were implicated in the unleashing of terror and war. These groups must be stamped out and their influence in society stripped from them if there is to be any hope of establishing a just German state and an enduring anti-Nazi democracy.

The opponents of Nazism—the real, democratic opponents, not the desperadoes of anti-Nazism and belated opportunists—are not guilty. But they too cannot escape co-responsibility for Hitler's rise to power. Nor can they evade the consequences of the Nazi policy of mass murder. They must realise that for a long time to come suspicious eyes will observe their endeavours. They cannot hope to be offered *carte blanche* to power. Confidence cannot be forced. It must be earned, not by words, but by actions, by a coincidence of word and deed. On the other hand, German democrats should not expect *every* chance to be denied them.

Between the Nazis and their opponents lies the great mass of the more or less indifferent. Their responsibility is great. But there is no sense in burdening them with an excessive liability. Such a sense of liability which people seek to impose upon them from outside is not the happiest start for reconstruction. But this is no reason for not hammering the message home that they have incurred responsibility through their very indifference and submissiveness. I am not convinced that the best way of doing this is by punitive measures which provoke action in self-defence and possibly renewed hatred. But I can find no good reason why anyone should be spared seeing the films of Buchenwald and Belsen. Not in order to make them confess that they were personally involved, but so as not to spare them the sight of what they made possible. They must not be allowed to regard everything that has happened as a kind of natural disaster. They must be shown their responsibility before history and then be challenged to acquire a greater sense of responsibility in the future... Germany has learned that war does not pay. The people have seen the extremes to which racial hatred can be taken. Now the immediate task is to prevent their newly-acquired realisation from being wasted because the population falls into a state of national and social despair. Productive work is the best doctor and teacher. And proven anti-Nazi Germans are those best suited to look after 'holding the reins'. The most important consequence of a sophisticated democratic attitude must be to give the friends of democracy support against its enemies.

The partition of Germany would be a poor gift to the opponents of Nazism. It would fly in the face of economic common sense and there would be a strong risk that positive forces would once more be absorbed into a more or less underground struggle for a national assembly.

The securities demanded by other nations can be achieved in a completely satisfactory manner by exercising controls in Germany. Disarmament and the most resolute suppression of any Nazi and militaristic attempts to restore the former *status quo* are in the interest not only of the Allies but also of German democracy.

CHURCHILL, ROOSEVELT AND STALIN : AGAINST NAZISM, NOT (2)
GERMANY

When the war broke out Churchill declared in the Commons that Great Britain had no quarrel with the German people. But so long as the Hitler régime was in power and resorted to the methods which it had been practising over the last two years, there would be no peace in Europe. In his reply to Hitler's offer of peace in October 1939 Chamberlain declared that British policy did not aim to prevent a Germany which was ready to live in trust and friendship with other nations from gaining her rightful place in Europe. We did not go to war with thoughts of revenge but quite simply in defence of freedom.

By and large, leading British and Allied statesmen have retained this attitude to the conflict with Germany. They drew a distinction between Nazism and the German people as such. At the beginning of 1941 Churchill stated that his sole aim was to stamp out Nazism in Europe.

But it was made clear all the same that the concept of Hitlerism should not be defined too narrowly. Chamberlain's formula would have rendered it possible to make peace with Göring as well as with Brauchitsch. Churchill, Roosevelt and Stalin on the other hand had declared that defeat should involve not just the Nazi system but also German militarism.

When in August 1941 Churchill returned from the Atlantic pact meeting, he stressed that Britain and America were firmly resolved to act differently from the last time in two areas. First they wanted to disarm their opponents, whilst they themselves saw to it that they had the appropriate protection. The other difference should be that 'instead of trying to ruin German trade by all kinds of additional trade barriers and hindrances, as was the mood of 1917, we have definitely adopted the view that it is not in the interests of the world and of our two countries that any large nation should be unprosperous or shut out from the means of making a decent living for itself and its people by its industry and enterprise.[3]

These views were more closely defined in a speech by Lord Cranborne in the Lords in May 1942. He said that policies after the last war had inflicted, even if unintentionally, economic and military punishment upon Germany. The Atlantic declaration was based on quite different premises. It expressed the firm resolve to prevent Germany or any other aggressor state from ever again getting into a position which would enable it to spark off a world-wide catastrophe. But in the economic sphere there was no intention of treating Germany any differently from any other nation.

On 21 September 1943 Churchill declared : 'We do not war with races as such. We wage war against tyranny.'[4]

On the American side Vice President Wallace explained among other things that the outline of the future economic policy in the Atlantic declaration was interpreted in the same way there as in Britain. In May 1942 he said : 'The peace must mean a better standard of living for the common man, not merely in the US and England but also in India, Russia, China and Latin America—not merely in the United Nations, but also in Germany and Italy and Japan.'[5]

In August 1943 Roosevelt commented on the capitulation demands of the Casablanca conference as follows : with the exception of the responsible Fascist leaders no one in the Axis countries needed fear unconditional surrender. The population of the countries under Axis rule could be certain of this : an unconditional surrender did not mean that tyranny would be exchanged for misery. It was the goal of the Allies to grant the liberated peoples the possibility of a political life under the banner of freedom, which they were able to shape themselves, and to economic security.

In a message to the Congress in September 1943 Roosevelt also stressed that, if Hitler and the Nazis were forced out of existence, the 'Prussian military clique' must go with them. Churchill followed this up with a declaration in the same vein.

In a radio speech which he gave on Christmas Eve 1943 Roosevelt again emphasised the difference between the planned treatment of the Nazis and militarists on the one hand and the German people on the other : 'The United Nations have no intention to enslave the German people. We wish them to have a normal chance to develop, in peace, as useful and respectable members of the European family. But we most certainly emphasise that word "respectable"—for we intend to rid them once and for all of Nazism and

Prussian militarism and the fantastic and disastrous notion that they constitute the "Master Race".'

On the Russian side particular weight can be placed on two speeches by Stalin. In an order of the day in February 1942 he made reference to the fact that the foreign press had maintained that it was the aim of the Red Army to stamp out the German people and destroy Germany. 'The Red Army does not nor can it have such foolish objectives,' said Stalin. 'The goal of the Red Army is to drive out the Germans who are occupying our country and to liberate Soviet soil from the German-Fascist intruder. It is more than probable that the battle for the liberation of Soviet soil will lead to the rout or destruction of the Hitler clique. We should be overjoyed at such an outcome, but it would be ridiculous to equate the Hitler clique with the German people and the German state. The lessons of history tell us that people like Hitler may come and go but the German people and the German state live on.'

In his speech on the anniversary of the Revolution in November 1942 Stalin returned to the same question and declared : 'It is not our task to destroy Germany, for it is impossible to destroy Germany, in the same way that it is impossible to destroy Russia. But to wipe out Hitler's state—that is both possible and imperative.' His speech continued to the effect that it was not the task of the Russians to destroy all forms of organised armed units in Germany. 'But to wipe out Hitler's army—that is both possible and imperative.'

VANSITTARTISM

Stockholm, 14 August 1943

Dear H.,[6]

... On the other hand the British and Americans should be in no doubt that, failing the achievement of a clear and positive attitude towards the German problem, the German people might well feel more and more strongly that the surest guarantee for their continued national survival would be accorded them by the Soviet Union. This must be said particularly to the Vansittartists inside the British Labour party. They should also be left in no doubt that the position is clearly recognised even by many comrades in the occupied countries and they have indeed suffered a great deal more than the British. In the latest issue of *Fri Fagbevegelse* for example —which, as you know, is the main publication of the underground trade union movement in Norway—there is an excellent article demonstrating that the war is directed against Nazism and not against the German people. It goes on to say that the establishment of a democratic Germany is not just in the interest of the Germans, but also in the true interest of other nations...

...I have been exposed to a shabby attack in the main publication of the Norwegian Communists. Their principal argument is that I am a German, and they insinuate that I am to all intents and purposes an agent of the Gestapo. This criminal accusation has already been denied by the rest of the underground press. I have myself written an open letter to the Norwegian Communists in which I stress the vital importance of unity, and state that they should desist from such underhand methods once and for all if they want to play an effective part in the opposition. As far as my position as a 'German' goes, I wrote these words:

The 'revelation' that I am German in origin is no revelation at all. I have never concealed my German origins and have no reason to be ashamed of them. It is quite correct to state that I came to Norway from Germany in 1933 as a refugee. At that time I was less than twenty years, old but for a number of years I had already been actively working against Nazism. The Nazis took away my homeland, and Hitler took away my citizenship into the bargain...

Friheten [the underground CP paper in Norway] is seeking to mobilise against me the anti-German mood which has greatly intensified as an understandable reaction to Nazi methods. The argument was supposedly strengthened by the question of who the Norwegians operating in league with the German Willy Brandt really were, and also by the assertion that in my capacity as a 'German' I had renounced the concept of a guerilla war in Norway. For me—and I have good grounds to suppose that this holds good for the majority of the Norwegian camp—the war against Nazi Germany is no racial war. I am thoroughly aware of the responsibilities which should be laid at the door of a great many Germans, but the question of responsibility concerns not only the German people, and in the course of recent years many of them have carried on the fight against Nazism under the most unfavourable conditions. It will be these men—who are my friends—who on the morrow will be comrades in arms in the task of constructing a world safe to live in. I feel bound to Norway by a thousand ties, but I have never given up Germany—the other Germany. I am working towards the destruction of Nazism and its confederates in every country, so that the Norwegian and German people and people of all nations might live. In recent years I have twice lost a homeland. I am working to regain two homelands—a free Norway and a democratic Germany.

It will certainly not be easy to take up the reins after the Nazis, but the day will surely dawn on which the inevitable hatred of the war years is finally overcome. One day a Europe in which Europeans can live together will become a reality . . .

Stockholm, 15 March 1944[7]
I have a very bad conscience about not yet having answered your letter of 15 December. But I have two excuses to offer. First I fell ill in the middle of December (so I even had to celebrate my thirtieth birthday in bed with a temperature). It was jaundice, a most unpleasant affliction (clearly a result of having got myself too angry . . .), which also leaves you feeling flat out for weeks after. At the same time I had promised to have the manuscript of my new Swedish book (on post-war problems) ready for 1 February. When 1 February came, I hardly had anything prepared, and I had to put everything else to one side and apart from my normal work just concentrate on writing. Now at last I have a little more breathing space.

. . . The news that has come out of Germany recently is among the saddest I have ever heard. It is becoming evident that even people who had until recently resisted the pressures and propaganda of Nazism are now under the influence of the mood of national solidarity. I have to hand statements by radical workers to the effect that this war must be regarded as a war of national defence, because—as they see it—the enemy seeks the complete destruction of Germany. The air raids naturally also work both ways. It is even becoming evident in Berlin, where critical attitudes have been much more marked than in many other areas, that people are influenced by the general feeling that they are all in the same boat anyway and must make the best of a bad situation. Fear of the Russians is also an important factor . . .

Once and for all we must be in no doubt that nationalism will be the most serious threat to the growth of a new German democracy . . .

Crimes without number have been committed in the name of the German people and continue to be committed unceasingly. Hatred against everything German has become ever more intense. Among the Allies and especially in occupied countries many people have taken the view that the official objectives of the war are inadequate and that the demands of the Atlantic declaration must be made harsher.

So, the assertion goes, any distinction between Germans and Nazis is a fiction. To all intents and purposes, every German is a Nazi. Nazi ideology and Nazi policy are, it is argued, the logical outcome of the historical development of Germany and an accurate reflection of the German mentality. The war comes exclusively from the megalomania which forms part of the German character, according to Vansittart...

At the time of Hitler's seizure of power, the English naval treaty with Germany, the occupation of the Rhineland, the wars in Abyssinia and Spain and the annexation of Austria, Vansittart was Secretary of State in the British Foreign Office and worked on until 1941 as chief diplomatic adviser to the British government. People of many political persuasions in England and America, spokesmen of governments in exile, individual Russian writers and a number of German emigrés have together given Vansittartism the character of an international movement. Their aim is to fight the war 'to the bitter end' and to resolve the German problem 'once and for all time'.

Even before the war there were a few groups in France that sought consolation for the feelings of helplessness and shame after Munich under the slogan 'realistic nationalism'. Henri de Kérillis maintained that Hitlerism was an expression of the German nation and the way fate had determined her historical development. Germany would always be a predator nation if she were not crushed once and for all, just like the Spain of Charles V was crushed in his time. He saw no distinction between Germans and Nazis. Germany's power had to be utterly broken. The outbreak of war gave 'realistic nationalism' a strong shot in the arm. However there was considerable inconsistency between his vociferous demands and the inadequate state of readiness of the French defence forces.

In England as well after the outbreak of war it was possible to read opinions in the newspapers in which the readers expressed the view that the best thing would be to stamp out all Germans or to raze Germany to the ground and turn the country into a desert waste. More responsible discussion, however, was far less immoderate in tone than in France. Certain circles did indeed betray their extreme disappointment when the Germans did not rise up in a revolution after they read the leaflets dropped from British aircraft in the first winter of the war. The demand that there must be a second Carthage and not just another edition of Versailles was to be made with ever increasing frequency. But the overwhelming majority of British public opinion was still determined by quite different attitudes. Not even during the worst bombing raids did a genuine national hatred become widespread among the British population. And many people from other countries have described to their astonishment how the British felt sorry for the Germans when they were repaid more than in full for the bombing of British cities.

It can well be imagined that a change in mood came after the establishment of the second front and reports of heavy losses started coming in. In America a marked shift in public opinion has already taken place. In the summer of 1942 a Gallup survey showed that 79 per cent of the population thought that the war was directed against Nazism. Only 6 per cent regarded the German people as a whole as enemies. At the beginning of 1944 a majority of Americans were apparently holding the German people responsible for the war and for what was happening inside Germany. In the First World War feeling did not become intense either in Britain or in France and America until just after the armistice.

In the Soviet Union propaganda diverged sharply from official pronouncements. It has been asserted in their press that we 'cannot vanquish the enemy without learning to hate him body and soul' (*Isvestya*).

In all the occupied countries there is a massive hatred of the Germans. People find it difficult to believe in a better Germany when they see daily evidence of the worst side of a bad Germany. People who are fighting a war have no time for subtle distinctions.

And this is the emotional basis of the mass support for Vansittartism. Millions upon millions in tormented Europe would be prepared to subscribe to the theory of this English Lord that the great mass of Germans had in the course of between three and four generations developed into a nation of brutal, organised and savage aggressors.

In the *Black Record* Vansittart goes back to Hermann the Cheruscan in the year 9 BC—'It is worth noting that the first German national hero to make himself a name for treachery was Hermann in the year nine'[8]—and then traces a clear line of development in Germany via Charles the Great (the French Charlemagne), Frederick Barbarossa, Frederick the Great and Bismarck up to the new Hermann. This is supposed to prove that throughout their history the Germans have inclined towards aggression, law-breaking and terror. This is part and parcel of their national character. They are rotten by nature. He even goes as far back as 55 BC in order to prove with the aid of quotations from Caesar that the Teutons were a

predator nation then and that those who became Germans
have not changed in the course of two thousand years. So we are
now involved with something not so far removed from Hitler's
racial doctrines.

Vansittart has asked not to be held responsible for everything
which trades under the name of Vansittartism. He has also retreated from his racialist doctrine and goes so far as to put the
number of 'good' Germans as high as 25 per cent. But at the same
time he is still thinking in terms of 'national character', 'national
spirit' and 'political mentality' as quite inflexible categories.

Vansittart's arguments are worthy of more serious attention when
he restricts himself to a more limited time span. He states that since
1860 Germany has initiated five wars and that the people made
each of these wars their own. The master race ideology and the
mentality of aggression are deeply rooted and continue to flourish
today. Democracy has never really gained a foothold in Germany.
The so-called democrats were no better than the rest of them. The
Social Democrats, he says, were the Nazis of the First World War.
In the Weimar Republic everything possible was done to prepare
the way for a new war. The representatives of German cultural life
saw their real mission as one of preaching nationalism and spurring
on aggression . . .

The Vansittartists also claim that Hitler came to power through
democratic elections. The overwhelming majority of Germans support Hitler's platform, want war, and have declared their solidarity
with his policies of aggression and occupation—at least as long as
all goes well . . .

The way the Germans behaved under the Weimar Republic
supposedly demonstrates their incapacity to govern themselves. That
they followed Hitler and the policy of war confirms that they are
militarists. The terror in occupied countries has unmasked them as
sadists.

Vansittartists deny the existence of the other Germany. They
may concede that 'good' Germans do exist, but these are so tiny in
number, so ineffective and impotent that nothing much is to be
expected from their quarter. The passivity of potentially anti-Nazi
Germans is compared with the resistance put up in the occupied
countries. And the question is asked : 'Where is the engagement of
the German opposition, where are their sacrifices, where is their
underground press?'

Some but not all Vansittartists direct the main weight of their
attack against the German left wing. Schwarzschild concludes his
analysis of the inter-war period to the effect that all democratic

experiments in Germany have been doomed to failure. Others accuse the German socialist movement of being just as militaristic as the rest of Germany and of having lent support to Hitler. We are warned against sentimentality and faith in a democratic or socialist Germany. This tendency can partly be explained by the fact that certain circles exploited the anti-Nazi attitude as a front for a consciously reactionary policy. Many earlier admirers of German Fascism have suddenly changed horses in midstream—a lot of them at a very late point in time—and have gone to the other extreme.

Some people even count the refugees from Germany among those who are at least potentially war criminals. They are accused of being implicated in a pan-Germanic conspiracy which sought to prepare for the coming war. In France some people got it into their heads that the refugees were responsible for the fall of France. They had supposedly given false reports about internal difficulties in Germany—as if the Deuxième Bureau and the Secret Service were dependent on information from refugees! No one made any effort to recall that the refugees had been striving to convince the peoples of other countries that Hitler meant war.

The most radical solution of the German problem would be to wipe out all Germans, that is to say, to subject the Germans to roughly the same kind of treatment as their representatives had applied against the Jews in recent years. Many have declared themselves in favour of such a prescription. Some sought to be more moderate and content themselves with sterilisation. But that at least was no part of the programme of Vansittartism. At the end of the day it will perhaps even prove the case that some of those who were the most implacable in debate found themselves in two minds when the sentence was to be carried out not just against the Nazi leaders but also against their industrial friends and their generals.

Lord Vansittart wants a Germany under the slogan : 'Full warehouses, empty arsenals', and this indeed does not offend against the Atlantic Charter and the declaration of the Allied leaders regarding the disarmament and economic equality of rights for the Axis powers. Further, Vansittart wants the Germans to be declared minors in law and their country to be occupied for at least seventy-five years, as he said earlier, or twenty to thirty years as he suggested later. The Germans should be educated under the watchful eye of an international police force to become peace-loving and democratic.

Many place the main emphasis on weakening the power of Germany by partitioning it into a series of smaller states. There is no clear dividing line between the more extreme demands for frontier adjustments to the detriment of Germany and the establishment of independent little German states.

In England Duff Cooper came forward shortly after the outbreak of war as a spokesman for the policy of partition. He took the view that Bavaria and Austria should be brought together, perhaps even with Otto von Habsburg as Regent. For the remaining part of northern Germany it would be possible to find some kind of solution once the demands of Poland were accepted. Others were more pre-occupied with detaching the Rhineland and the Ruhr from German control. Those who thought on traditional lines and wanted to avoid social upheavals were also eager to see the re-establishment of the old German individual states and the reinstatement of the former princely houses. The English political economist Paul Einzig who—along with others—put forward such suggestions has said that Prussia should be placed into a special category and kept under occupation for a longer period than the rest of Germany—perhaps indefinitely.

The notion that German particularism with its kings and grand dukes should be brought back into being is not unfamiliar to certain elements among the reactionaries. Some of the Rhineland indus-trialists have no objection to plans for setting up an independent republic of the Rhineland. They are even discussing plans for link-ing a west and northwest German state to the British Common-wealth, and this would in their view offer guarantees for the main-tenance of the present pattern of private ownership. In Bavaria some of those who assisted in preparing the way for Nazism are in sympathy with union with Austria, not only out of dislike for the Prussians and Nazi control but because they fear a possible develop-ment of 'Prussian Bolshevism'.

Another section of the Vansittartist programme centres on the question of how Germany's economic potential can be weakened. That can easily lead to anxiety for peace being mixed up with matters of economic competition.

Representatives of the governments of occupied countries have repeatedly put forward the view that the industrial capacity of Germany should be no greater than is necessary for supplying home demand. Neighbouring countries should take over superfluous German industrial capacity. Sir Rowland Evans maintains (in *Prelude to Peace*)[9] that Germany is overindustrialised and that her huge industrial capacity represents a threat to peace. The whole of heavy industry must be placed under the control of an international commission and all industrial concerns in important centres—above all in the Ruhr—must be managed under international control.

Paul Einzig has made out a case (for example in *Can we Win the Peace?*)[10] for a Germany which—as he put it—is disindustrialised. He proposes an 'inverted New Order' in Europe with the following principal points in his programme : German workers are to be employed in reconstruction and then in the building of fortifications in those countries which were invaded. Over and above this the democratic countries should claim German workers as unskilled labour for all time . . . Food supplies will be made up exclusively of imports from overseas. Similar measures are to be taken against Japan, Italy and the smaller tributary states.

Further Einzig suggests that 51 per cent of the shares of all German industrial undertakings with more than twenty workers should be transferred into Allied possession. The victorious powers should not only destroy and put a ban on armament factories but also the engineering industry as well as the production of synthetic rubbers and oils. The engineering and electrical industries may only be retained to the extent necessary for the maintenance of direct production of consumer goods in Germany. The object of the whole exercise is to deprive German industry of its leading position in Europe and effectively depress the German standard of living so that Germany will never again be in a position to subordinate other peoples with the aid of her industrial potential.

It is true that Vansittart himself also proposes 'the elimination of the industrial potential of Germany' but he does not intend this to lead to the ruin of the people. He does not defend proposals for the partition of Germany, but he is a supporter of decentralisation to break the strong position of Prussia. He places the main emphasis on 're-education'. The idea that the German people could be educated to live peacefully and democratically under the surveillance of an international police force has also formed the basis of a large number of statements from Poland, Holland and others on the Allied side.

'Germany has got to go into a reformatory; the discipline will be severe and salutary, but there are compensations and encouragements', states Vansittart.[11] He also wants the Germans to learn 'how to be happy'. What he has in mind in the first instance is international control of education, the press, radio and literature. The legal system and the administration are to be reorganised on democratic lines and where necessary placed under external control for as long as supervision is maintained. Even the church is to be filled with a new spirit. For this reason certain circles are thinking in terms of the necessity for sending shock troops of foreign teachers to Germany. On the other hand there are also proposals for the introduction of an Allied 'Gauleiter' system.

Vansittartism is opposed by the view that there is a real difference between the Nazis and large areas of the German people and that this difference must be one of the keys to the solution of the German problem. (But just as many Vansittartists let emotion conquer reason, various anti-Vansittartists demonstrate an evident ignorance of the facts. This relates partly to Germans, who out of misguided patriotism do not want to look squarely at the real misfortunes of their people, partly to more or less well-meaning 'friends of Germany' with no awareness of realities.)

In the discussions which took place in France before and after the outbreak of war, Léon Blum was one of the most outstanding personalities opposed to 'realistic nationalism'. He held fast to the working hypothesis of the 'other Germany'. Blum and men of the same mind did not surrender the belief that there were other and better forces alive among the German people than those which found expression in the Nazi régime. They hoped that these forces would come to power and sought to help wherever possible to bring this about. Blum accused the aggressive supporters of the political right of conducting a racialist policy from a different starting point but on the whole on the same principles as Nazism.

He did not deny that Hitlerism has its roots deep in German history, but added that Nazism would scarcely have become possible if Europe had not treated the Weimar Republic in such a short-sighted fashion. The peace of Versailles, stated Blum, was by and large founded on just principles but was put into practice in an irresponsible manner. As a glaring example of this he points to the occupation of the Ruhr. A logical conclusion of this attitude was that a future democratic Germany must have an equal place among the European nations.

Professor Carr and Professor Laski are two of the sharpest critics of Vansittartism in England. Carr states that the theory of the wickedness of the Germans resulted from an emotional reaction to an enemy known from all the wars of history . . . Nevertheless it must be assumed that hatred generated after the end of the war would be an important factor. Laski (in *Reflections on the Revolution of our Time*)[12] warns against regarding Germany's conduct of the war as a product of one aspect of the German national character. All those who have maintained views of this kind and who continue to do so are saying nothing different from the Nazis when they speak of the 'master race'. The men of Lidice were not described as barbarians by the British when they bombed Guernica. Many who wished for friendship with Nazi Germany would have pointed with disgust to the terror in the Soviet Union and called it a product of the Russian national character—up until 22 June 1941. Human nature is however conditioned by its environment, to which it adapts itself. If we want to change human nature, says Laski, we must alter the historical environment.

The history of every nation has its blacker aspects. There are many in the history of Germany but not every aspect of her past is black. In Douglas Smith's *Guilty Germans?*[13] and Julius Braunthal's *Need Germany Survive?*[14] a whole series of arguments are brought to bear against the Vansittartist exposition of history. As far as the recent past is concerned, it is a fact that in 75 years Germany has waged five expansionist wars. But imperialist policy in other countries was decisive in this. France experienced four wars in the eighteen years of the reign of Napoleon III. In the 75 years of her existence Italy has been involved in eight wars. And England holds the record for involvement in wars in the period from 1850 to the turn of the century. But this does not get round the fact that there is a 'Prussian' tradition in modern German politics. In this regard there is a continuous line from Bismarck to Hitler. Prussia owes her greatness primarily to her military power and has been a stronghold of reaction and militarism. And Prussia came into union with Germany. The Junkers and the Prussian military class were the final arbiters of German policy. And that states in a nutshell that the Prussian problem like the problem of Germany is in the first instance a social issue.

It may be established that Germany owes the blacker aspects of her history to Prussia, but we must be careful not to oversimplify the picture. During the time of Napoleon in 1848 the forces of freedom in Berlin received stronger support than in many other parts of Germany. In the Weimar Republic the Prussian state government conducted a considerably more progressive policy than that of Bavaria. Most of the leading Nazis do not hail from Prussia.

One of the principal arguments against Vansittartism is that the crisis of democracy is universal and that Fascism is not a peculiarly German phenomenon. It is a product of the cross-currents of capitalist society. Quite different notions are generally held about the Italian character, but there Fascism came to power ten years earlier than in Germany. Fascist movements which gained a large following made an appearance in Hungary and Portugal, Finland,

Spain and in many other countries. Even before the fall of France, Fascism had already become a force to be reckoned with there. In Vichy their policies were even able to secure a fairly broadly-based consensus.

But Fascism acquired its strongest and most dangerous exponents in Germany. However, the opponents of Vansittartism stress that this does not imply that Nazism is an expression of an unalterable aspect of the German national character, although it did acquire a particular national flavour in Germany. It is not necessary to support the doctrine of racialism in order to be able to recognise that common historical experiences, common language, religion, economic and social backgrounds, common climatic and geographical conditions are all contributory factors in the creation of specific national characteristics. The military tradition doubtless worked to the advantage of Nazism. A number of German writers have bred an extreme form of nationalism, reverence of authority and racial mysticism which have exercised some influence on teaching in the schools. But the importance of the stolen ideological property of Nazism is usually overestimated. And it is frequently overlooked that what goes by the name of the ideological roots of Fascism can be found in most other countries in the world.

The victory of Nazism can be explained principally in terms of social conditions. It is all too easy to forget that Germany was a backward country when it suddenly became caught up in imperialist policies ... The state of tension became more acute in Germany than in many other countries because of the more rapid polarisation of the socialist movement and the reactionaries. In spite of Bismarck's legislation against socialism, the socialists fought their way through to a position of power which earned respect in the Second Internationale before the last world war. But the socialist movement did not stand alone; Germany's liberal, humanitarian and cosmopolitan cultural life gave her a good standing in the world. Democracy was not firmly established in Germany, but in the fight against the 'bad' Germany, German democrats were not entirely unsuccessful.

The struggle between 'the two Germanies' continued into the Weimar Republic. The revolution of the year 1918 did not really bring things to a head. The old social forces were still holding their own ...

The main stream of the socialist movement lacked resolution just as it had when faced with nationalism at the outbreak of war. Weimar was nevertheless not just 'the spirit of Prussia' in disguise and a policy of revenge. Large areas of the population were filled with the desire for peace and supported the advance of democracy. Policies of reform made considerable strides. Time and again strong movements in the direction of Fascism were repelled. But then came the depression. It hit Germany with particular severity. And unlike the long-established democracies it struck at a country with little internal stability . . . Capital, the Junkers, the military and the reactionary bureaucracy threw in their lot with Nazism. The Nazis absorbed the discontent of the middle class and the farmworkers and exploited their antipathy towards both the reformist movement and the revolutionary socialists. But the socialist movement which should have risen to the challenge of Nazism was preoccupied with internal squabbles.

In spite of the burning of the Reichstag and the terror, Hitler did not get a majority in the Reichstag elections in March 1933. Resistance against him continued to be very strong. Perhaps a nation of individuals would have reacted with greater vigour. But here there was no drive towards a national resistance movement. The anti-Nazis were weighed down by the demoralising after-effects of defeat. They were crippled not only by a terror machine which had no equal in all history but also by the unbroken chain of successes of their opponents. The compliance of other nations swept most of the ground from under the feet of the German opposition. Passivity was encouraged by the feeling that they were faced with a natural force which it was hopeless to resist.

The fact is that in 1933 about half the German people voted for Hitler and that many of them did not become caught up in National Socialism until a later date. In this process the elimination of unemployment was of great significance. But the assertion that all Germans turned into Nazis simply does not hold water. No socialist leader of any importance and only a handful of Liberals went over to the Nazis. An underground anti-Nazi movement continued to survive although not very much was heard of it. Many more sentences of death were passed against German anti-Nazis than is generally believed. At the outbreak of war around 300,000 people were in concentration camps or prison for 'political offences'. One-and-a-half million Germans passed through the concentration camps.

The Vansittartists are of the opinion that the overwhelming majority of the German people wanted war. William Shirer and many other foreign correspondents maintain that this is not so. But there is evidence to the effect that a very large proportion of the people fell for the Nazi war propaganda.

Hitler and his cronies bear the responsibility for unleashing war.

If one accepts the tenet that every nation is responsible for its government then it follows naturally that the Germans were responsible for the war. But if we are talking about responsibility, then the lion's share of the blame must fall upon those who assisted the Nazis in their seizure of power in 1933.

In any case certain sections of the German population can plead 'extenuating circumstances'. There is moreover the question as to whether it is appropriate or if there is any point in making a whole nation collectively responsible for the actions of its government. If this is the case then the English nation would for example be held responsible for Chamberlain's support of Hitler's preparations for war. We will not get very far by asserting that the Hungarians are collectively responsible for the policies of Horthy, the Italians for the policies of Mussolini and the Rumanians for the policies of Antonescu. The Austrians have been promised independence after the war, and rightly so, even if their mountain troops have been fighting alongside soldiers from Hamburg and Lübeck.

This kind of questioning leads nowhere, because it is simply impossible to punish a nation in the same way as an individual. Laski wants Hitler and his henchmen to be given the same sort of punishment as men like Al Capone. It is not impossible to take the view that it will be necessary to put a substantial number of Nazis out of harm's way—a process of purging from which many Vansittartists draw back—while at the same time rejecting punitive measures against the nation as a whole.

The opponents of Vansittartism do not make light of the German Fascist terror which is unequalled in modern times. All too many Germans have allowed themselves to be used as the tools of the real terrorists; all too large a number of the German people have adopted a passive attitude towards the vile acts committed against the Jews, Poles, Russians and the populations of other occupied countries. Still the assertion must be rejected that the Germans are a nation of sadists. Terror has been highly developed in Germany but does not originate from there. The most primitive forms of maltreatment were applied by Mussolini and Franco, in Jugoslavia, Rumania, and Greece. Arthur Koestler writes in his book about France that the French concentration camps set up in the autumn of 1939 for anti-Fascist refugees could in many ways bear comparison with their German models. The British and French were not innocent of aggression in the colonies. The Americans have their pogroms against the Negroes. There has been the bloodiest persecution of the Jews in many countries. In Germany it went further than anywhere else.

But people ask why did German soldiers not mutiny when they realised what they were being used for? Why was there no uprising by the anti-Nazis of whom there has been so much talk?

It is rare to find victorious troops mutinying . . .

Because of the 'Prussian spirit', discipline is more strongly rooted among Germans than many other peoples, but also the Nazis took modern terrorist techniques to their highest point of development. German Fascism became so strong because Germany is a large, highly industrialised and thoroughly well administered country. But even the Austrian 'sloppy Fascism' was powerful enough to crush a strong socialist movement. Italian Fascism was considerably weaker than its German counterpart—none the less there was no popular uprising against it, at least not until serious rifts appeared in top government circles as a result of military defeat. In the case of Germany it has long been clear that a decisive military defeat is essential before the forces for good can be liberated.

As far as the war goes, one objection to Vansittartism is that it is helping to prolong the war. It unites the forces of the enemy instead of tearing them apart. As early as the autumn of 1939 Goebbels had posters put up throughout Germany listing the most extreme demands which had been raised on the Allied side, in order to make the Germans realise that they were waging a war of national defence against the western powers' schemes for their destruction. The *New Statesman* wrote on this subject that it would be unfair not to grant Lord Vansittart the credit due to him. He had succeeded in developing German resistance to its highest pitch. His assertion that the Germans had almost always been Nazis welded them together into a solid block around Hitler.

The anti-Vansittartists base their views on the need for waging the war against Nazism and the conditions which brought it into being. A régime and its representatives can be hated without that hatred being directed against the whole of the nation concerned.

The consequence of the anti-Vansittartist view would be to place the main emphasis on a revolution which there was good cause to expect would take place after the defeat of Germany and to grant support to the friends of democracy. Plans to partition Germany were rejected since they would fly in the face of vital economic considerations . . .

However, those who support the line that collaboration with the other Germany is crucial broadly base their view on the fact that Germany will be kept under Allied military control for a transitional period. The Allies, it is said, have a claim to control the course of events inside Germany in order to obtain guarantees against a repetition of what happened after the last war. On the other hand they must ensure that in so doing they do not sow the seeds of a new Hitlerism and a new war. Above all they must not prevent the German revolution from settling the account with those forces which bear the chief responsibility for Nazism and its militarist programme.

Official spokesmen and others have underlined time and again that a new Germany—by which it is assumed that the country will achieve a democratic form of government, even if only by degrees— must play an active part in future European and international collaboration. The British Labour party took a very firm stand on this point. Attlee declared in November 1939 that Germany must neither be humiliated nor mutilated. All thoughts of revenge must be cast aside. This view was underlined in the party programme of February 1940, which stated : 'History teaches that any attempt to keep Germany an outcast after the war, or to deprive her of such security as her neighbours rightly claim for themselves, will fail.'[15] The most farsighted and safest policy is one which sets out from the view that co-operation must be sought with a related political leadership in Germany. At the Labour party congress in June 1943 other views made themselves felt. There a resolution was passed which went some way in the Vansittartist direction. But at the TUC congress in September 1943 there was a majority holding fast to the view that responsibility must be sought among the Nazis, not among the German people.

Carr moves away from the idea of dealing out punishment to an entire nation. Without denying the necessity for punishing war criminals he says that it would be far better to turn an enemy into a friend than to create undying mutual hatred. German nationalism must be overcome by an atmosphere of internationalism which would also be in the German interest. The top men in the occupation authorities must be given the task of supporting a new German administration whether or not it is national or just local in the first instance. No predetermined form of government should be forced upon the country under occupation. Every care should be taken to respect freedom of opinion, to reintroduce equality before the law and respect of the legal system, and also to prevent racial discrimination. Germany, continues Carr, may be defeated by an overwhelming force, but at the same time the country must be convinced that the victorious powers have something other than military superiority to show for themselves when it comes to the reorganisation of Europe.

Occupation must not be allowed to mean that everything without exception should be dictated from above and that the occupier should exercise control over the entire administrative machine. We would not get far with Gauleiters who have taken part in month-long courses in the 'law, morality, economic life and psychology of the German people'. One way or another, we are confronted with the necessity of supporting one group of Germans against another. There is no point in selecting a group which does not form part of the popular movement. The new government must not be allowed to take on the character of a Quisling régime. The consequence would be resistance in German society on a national scale.

The occupation of Germany can mean not only that no one is left in any doubt about who lost the war but also that the armistice terms are properly implemented and support given in the initial stages of the reintroduction of democracy into Germany. It is on the cards that SS troops and other fanatical Nazis will continue the fight on their own soil for some time after the Wehrmacht have surrendered. With the occupation, the victorious powers will take over the responsibility for such disruptive elements. Perhaps troops will also be needed to keep the peace on the frontiers between a disarmed Germany and its maltreated and at the same time armed neighbours.

The Vansittartists are now in full cry against the projected compassionate treatment of Germany. But it is to be hoped that it will not come to the point where compassion is shown towards the privileged groups who bear the responsibility and that at the same time those who come out of the concentration camps will be refused an opportunity for political expression. Hitler gained a great deal from what had been denied to the Weimar Republic. Those who were more or less irreconcilable towards democracy in Germany behaved in a compliant or even sympathetic manner towards Nazism. After the last war the Allies placed great difficulties in the way of a provisional government based on the socialist movement.

The poisoning of German youth has created a European problem, and the re-education to democracy is therefore an important task in the interest of Europe as a whole. The plan of sending in shock troops of foreign teachers is too impractical for words. Under normal conditions in Germany there are around 300,000 teachers. In the Murray report it is regarded as self-evident that democratic forces should be supported in the German re-education programme. But the view is taken that not everything can be left to their unaided efforts. The teaching profession in Germany must be denazified. There is also the belief that teachers for specific subjects can be

brought in from abroad, for example, from Switzerland, the Nether-
lands and Scandinavia. The whole educational system in Germany
should be placed under a senior member of the Allied
commission.

Foreign experts can doubtless render valuable assistance in a
reconstruction of the German educational system on democratic
lines. But the Germans will have to resolve the main task for themselves. Labour party member Aneurin Bevan wrote in an attack on
Lord Vanisittart that there was only one man capable of educating
a bad German, and that man was a good German.

Benes said in a speech in America in May 1943 that the German people must be re-educated and led on to the path of democracy, but he stressed that no one should believe that any one other
than the new Germany herself would be able to realise this re-
education programme. Carr placed the main emphasis on the
achievement of reconciliation through collaboration. There is, he
said, only one way to turn the Germans into good Europeans. They
must be given a part to play in the new Europe so that they can
regain their self-respect.

The war and the defeat form one part of this re-education programme. The German people have learned most emphatically where
Nazism and expansionist wars lead. Thomas Mann's optimism rests
on these factors : 'Our hope for a moral recovery in Germany...
reposes on the fact that National Socialism... was as extreme as it
was physically and morally extravagant, an experiment in the utter-
most forms of immorality and brutality, which can never be ex-
ceeded nor repeated... If this experiment fails... then [Germany]
will feel able to go off in an entirely different direction. The world
needs Germany, but Germany also needs the world, and since she
cannot make it "German", she will have to assimilate the world, in
the way that she has always been accustomed to do with all great
and noble things, affectionately and sympathetically.'[16]

Marshal Smuts was pursuing a similar train of thought when he
spoke about the revolution of the German spirit in the autumn of
1943 :

'What has happened inside Germany, what has been done to
innocent neighbouring peoples in recent years has sunk deeply,
scorchingly, into millions of German minds. There is another and
better Germany who must have passed through hell in witnessing
this brutal and lawless inhumanity of their people.'[17]

The democratisation of German society can only be achieved in
collaboration with German democrats. In southern Germany democracy in the community has a comparatively long tradition. Social

legislation even in the period before the First World War was democratic in form. Democracy can draw on large reserves from within the German socialist movement. If democracy is to be rebuilt, no obstacles should be placed in the path of the formation of political parties. It naturally will not work if the British conservatives form a German party of the right and British Labour party members establish a new German Social Democrat movement, even though it may be a good thing to end up with fewer parties than there were in the Weimar Republic. International trade union circles have been extremely active with plans for the reconstruction of a new German trade union movement using leaders from abroad. But however important the intervention and encouragement of foreign advisers may be, the real work must be carried out by forces inside the country.

From an economic point of view the Atlantic Declaration and official utterances from the Allied side seek to prevent the extreme proposals brought forward by the Vansittartists from being carried through. Carr points out that the economic punishment of Germany would lead to the collapse of the economic unity of central Europe. The European standard of living cannot be maintained without the productive capacity of Germany. *The Economist* has expressed the same view : poverty in Germany means poverty for Europe. The ruin of Germany means that her neighbours will lose their markets.

I do not believe—unlike Lord Vansittart—that an outside power (1) can teach a nation 'how to be happy'. I believe—in spite of all that has happened—in the moral, constructive forces among a minority of Germans which could gradually develop into a stable majority and make its mark on the life of the entire community. The occupation authorities can do a great deal. The new and—as I hope—democratic and peaceful life of Germany must none the less be built up from forces from within . . .

I am firmly convinced that the propaganda of Vansittartism and the influence it exercised on Allied policy during the war have not helped to shorten the war by a single day. The opposite is more likely the case. The Germans were brought closer together. No encouragement was given to the opposition. The psychosis which arose limited the freedom of action of Allied statesmen. They did not dare to venture upon bold policies when it came to the *political* conduct of the war. No real contact has been established between the Allies and the German anti-Nazi opposition which, however weak it may be when Hitler achieved his greatest victory, has had a certain significance. No one can claim that any such collaboration would be able to produce big results. But the attempt would have been worthwhile.

THE FALL OF GERMANY AND A NEW BEGINNING

After unconditional surrender came total occupation.

The Wehrmacht was crushed, and what was left disarmed. The Nazi organisations ceased to exist. Hitler had ejected Göring and Himmler before he took his own life. After the tragi-comic epilogue in Flensburg had been played out, the German state itself ceased to exist. Administration, transport networks and social welfare services were crippled. The Nazi leaders left behind heaps of rubble, a bankrupt economy, an uprooted and apathetic people. The collapse really was unique, without parallel in modern history. The victorious Allied powers had to take over the bankrupt estate. It would have been worst of all for Germany if they had left the country to fend for itself. Then every man would have turned against his neighbour. The collapse would have gone to its ultimate conclusion.

The occupation first dealt with the task of isolating a centre of contagion. But that did not solve the problem. In the territories occupied by the Allies in the middle of Europe over 60 million people were living. Yesterday's 'master race' became today's beggar race.

Hitler—and others before him—had attempted to persuade the Germans that it was their calling to become the masters of Europe and of the world. He managed to recruit the largest and most dangerous band of criminals in history. When he vanished, the novitiates of the master race were prisoners, beggars or—at the very least—inmates of a vast poorhouse.

The assertions of Nazism were taken *ad absurdum*. Their crazy aspirations ended with a mighty fall. Those who sallied forth to conquer the world led their own land and people into a crisis which imperilled the very existence of the nation. The name of Germany was stained with blood. The stench of corpses sticks to it and it summons up associations of plunder, cruelty and treachery. The unique challenge of defeat has brought forth strong reactions. The Germans will feel the effects for long after the last Nazi leader has met his just punishment. The dream of the master race will never be dreamed again. Germany is neither the 'navel of the world' nor the 'heart of Europe'. For the time being, the Germans will have no voice in international policies . . . It was madness to spur the

Germans on to play the part of masters of the world. They marched on—until they had lost their own country. But that does not necessarily mean that they are all—and always have been—criminals.

The reality is considerably more complex and subtle than Nazis and other racialist politicians would have it. The Nazis built on the basest instincts and most criminal attributes ruthlessly and systematically. Hitlerism was a well-organised gangster tyranny on a world-wide scale. His gangsters acquired a hitherto unknown faculty for exploiting the power of organisation, propaganda and terror. They organised the dregs of society and manufactured human carnage on the production line. And they did everything in their power to implicate as many others as possible. But that does not mean that the Germans were predestined to become a race of criminals. In many respects they are an immature nation. But they are not born wearing SS badges. Their children are like the children of other countries when they come into the world. When they grow up they model themselves according to their social and educational background. They slot into a community which is itself determined by social and historical factors. The inheritance of history can be a serious impediment. But social factors can be overcome. Even given a specific set of social conditions it is not a matter of course that there is only one direction which can be taken. It is possible to redirect into new channels the lives, conduct and ideals not only of individuals but also of an entire people.

It would be simpler but terrible if the Germans were criminals by birth. But it is not so simple as that nor so terrible. Circumstances have turned them into the tools—and victims—of Nazism. Like all people they still have another 'background' in good and evil. They are recognised as industrious and loyal, really loyal. Keenness to work and a sense of duty are not bad qualities in themselves. It is all a matter of whom the work is being done for and to whom the sense of duty is felt. The capabilities which have established a good name for German skills and German technology—and earlier the German talent for organisation—may be led into the wrong channels but they have not disappeared altogether. The Germans are not so exhausted that they cannot work their way up again if they are given the opportunity, if social guarantees are created against nationalist relapses, and if they succeed in establishing a democratic leadership which has some degree of stability.

The Germans are not in a happy state after the Second World War. Many of them are bewailing a fate which they consider undeserved. Few of them are yet aware of the great opportunity that has been offered them. They must not be allowed to continue to live in the past. They cannot make any progress by living from hand to mouth. What they must do is to build an entirely new national and social existence from the ground upwards. That is their great opportunity. The path which they have to take is not yet clear. The occupation will surely not continue for all eternity. The rubble of the bombed-out houses and factories will gradually be cleared away. It will be a far more difficult task to clear the ideological rubble from men's minds. But the difficulties should not be allowed to mask the most important fact : Germany has gained her new opportunities because she has suffered total defeat. A struggle for power on the old scale is now out of the question. However things may stand with the Germans, they have not been chosen by destiny to rule other nations. They will have their work cut out governing themselves . . . Now that there is no necessity for their nation to be in arms it is possible for them to grow together into a truly unified society. There could be a worse breeding ground for a new patriotism than common need. Perhaps even German culture has a task to fulfil. I am fully aware that this is a bold aspiration so soon after Maidanek, Belsen and Auschwitz.

I have become convinced that in spite of all that has happened Germany has forces at her command which can ensure her a peaceful and democratic future. It does not depend on internal factors alone whether these forces will gain the upper hand . . . The final outcome is perhaps in the stars, at any event it is not to be found in these pages.

Not all Germans belong to the band of Nazi criminals, and the German as such is no criminal. But at the same time I take the view that the reconstruction of Germany will never be a 'new construction' if one step is taken from the path of responsibility and strict probity. The new construction cannot be founded on lies and wishful thinking. It would fly in the face of truth for anyone to try and claim that a Nazi propaganda monopoly lasting twelve years had not left strong traces in the German consciousness. It would be wishful thinking to maintain that any specific group or class has retained its immunity from the Nazi poison . . .

In a crisis of existence like the one the Germans are going through we need love of truth and a sense of responsibility above all else.

The period after lost wars has in the past been a time of growth for German society. The years following the First World War were no exception. Defeat brought out progressive as well as reactionary forces. The mistake was that the latter came off all too lightly from the defeat. The imposing work of 'red Vienna' was accomplished in a country that was almost dead on its feet and had been wrenched out of its economic context. After the defeat of 1917 and despite civil war, foreign intervention and famine, the Russians built an entirely new state. Norway was never greater than at the time when its militant democrats were maintaining their demands for justice and freedom against the German occupier. Immediately after Dunkirk invigorating breezes blew through the fabric of the British state. Those whose national existence seems threatened with extinction are not *merely* to be pitied.

...Many of the young are silent for ever. Many others have precious little to say for themselves. They have gone through a great deal. Not all of them had a good time at the expense of the subject nations. Many were in the front line. They saw their comrades die. Children became men. Lads of seventeen talked about their terrible experiences in the war as if they were quite everyday occurrences. Those who are now twenty-five have been in uniform for eight years. Some have been called up even longer if labour service is included.

The troops come back home. Many of the houses they grew up in are no longer standing. If they are lucky they still have arms and legs. That apart, they do not really have much left. Their clothes are a mixture of army rags and civilian bits and pieces which they have scrounged together. There are no jobs waiting for them.

These young people have lost most of their illusions. And what was it the seventeen-year-old said to an American woman reporter? 'I envy those who can still believe in something, even if they believe in Hitler. In spite of it all they've still got something to hold on to. I've got nothing, absolutely nothing.'

And then these people are told that it is they who are branded as the very worst Nazis. The generation which led them into all this misery have set themselves up as judge and jury of the young and pronounced them guilty.

...Work is perhaps the most important need of the young. But it is not everything. A great deal hangs on the task of re-education which is to be carried out among the younger generation. Those who note where the shoe pinches know that the new political parties and the Allied controlled press have found it difficult to speak a language which German youth understands. All those catch-phrases like 'we must win over the young' get them nowhere. Anyway, it is hardly appropriate to talk to the young as if they were all bandits and incorrigible Nazi terrorists. On the contrary, a clear distinction must be drawn between a criminal régime and a spontaneous youthful idealism abused by the propagandists and sirens of the Nazis.

I am not trying to make the youth of Germany out to be any better than they are. But one factor that must be taken into account is that the young have had more than their fill of propaganda. And they are also suspicious of 'party politics'. They do not find it easy to understand the slogans of the years before 1933. But they are receptive to the language of realism. They will tolerate—as indeed they must—being put into the picture about the true state of affairs with no attempts at cheap idealisation. That does not mean that the young must be steeped in black pessimism. They need an objective, a goal they can look to with enthusiasm, a 'new faith', if you like. The task of rebuilding a country is surely a great one calling on true heroism. Especially if this reconstruction is carried out within a European context so that the young people of Germany can set their sights on a supranational objective. They must be told that the Germans are to be given a place in a new world not on military but on economic and cultural grounds.

I feel strongly that there should be less talk of abstract democracy and more about basic human values, rights and duties, moral uprightness, clean living, truth and integrity. The Nuremberg tribunal provides a whole mass of material for such a reorientation, if only it were used to good advantage. I know of more than one young German who has said that what he despises more than anything are the Nazi leaders now they stand revealed in their true colours and the way they have shown themselves as they really are.

In the end new leaders of the younger generation will rise up. Until that happens they must be helped to acquire clarity of mind. We must appeal to their sense of responsibility—it has not entirely disappeared...

(3)   GUERILLA WARFARE[18]

The Second World War has been marked by embittered guerilla campaigns on several fronts. For years hundreds of thousands of guerillas have held their own against the Japanese in China. The Russian partisans play an important military role. In the Balkans the 'small war' is at its height. In other parts of Europe the devastation of guerilla war threatens.

History has not kept to its prophecy of the inter-war years that machines alone would determine the outcome of the new world conflagration. The war is indeed a battle of machines but also one between men. Nations have reverted to the 'primitive' fighting methods of past ages in order to hold their own against modern military and political techniques. International conflict has been far more closely linked with upheavals within individual social groups than in previous wars. Very much against the expectations not only of 'the man in the street' but also of the experts, the words 'guerilla' and 'partisan' will figure prominently when the history of our war-scarred times comes to be written.

The present work seeks to offer a few sidelights on the history of guerilla warfare from the Napoleonic wars to the present day. The material must of necessity be limited, and the main emphasis is deliberately placed on European conditions. This restriction is achieved at the expense of factual and military matters. The present author is no military expert, and has no intention of offering an exposition of the tactics and techniques of guerilla warfare, but a topical historical study. Perhaps it will contribute in some degree to an increased understanding of what is actually happening at the present time. Stockholm, April 1942

The Hague Convention of 1907 put irregular warfare outside the law. The question which confronted those who were drafting the Convention was whether the defence of the homeland should be in the hands of regular armed forces or whether individual citizens should be permitted to fight for home and nation in the hour of danger. The answer came in the form of a compromise. Spontaneous national uprisings were not to be forbidden in themselves but they should be conducted in an organised manner. But under certain conditions a national uprising against an enemy invasion could be recognised, even if it was not immediately organised in every respect.

The Hague Convention is of course still valid but—in this as in other areas—its provisions have not been observed in practice. Total war has stifled such modest initiatives in the direction of an international legal order. Totalitarian systems only recognise 'international law' in practice when it coincides with their own power interests. It would not be reasonable to expect nations fighting for their very existence to stop and ask first whether the methods they are employing in the struggle to regain their freedom are in accordance with an international law which is valid only on paper. Contemporary warfare has decisively swept aside the distinction between combatant and civilian ... The thirty-five-year-old provisions of international law no longer offer a viable basis for judging present-day guerilla warfare. And a 'moral' evalution which equates guerilla units with marauding bands and partisans with cut-throats is not much help either. Any nation with a genuine desire for freedom will not be slow to exploit each and every expedient type of warfare against an enemy which has either removed or is in the act of removing their freedom, even when such types of warfare are designated irregular or immoral by their opponents. Something is amiss with a nation which takes the view that it cannot conduct a war of liberation because its regular army has been wiped out. History would laugh it to scorn.

Is that any defence against 'inhuman' methods of warfare, which expose countless innocent non-combatants to the acts of retaliation by the enemy? I am not trying to defend or condemn anyone. But all the same no one should overlook the fact that the methods of warfare which are branded as inhuman are never the first step. They form part of a wider military context, and the question is whether it would not be far more just to describe the reprisals as inhuman. What is more inhuman : when bombs are dropped on defenceless individuals or when vast numbers of men willing to sacrifice themselves set out, often under skilful leadership, to attack enemy *troops*?

An historical outlook offers more reliable points of reference for an answer to this question than 'legalistic' or 'moralising' judgements influenced by the propaganda requirements of the moment. The classical example of guerilla warfare, the fight against Napoleon by the Spanish, turned out to be a widely-based popular uprising which took place independently of or alongside the regular army. This army had proved incapable of preventing the occupation of the country. The volunteer corps, irregular bands of guerillas, drove the occupiers out of Spain after a year-long bitterly fought battle. They could not engage in fights to the last man, for that would simply have meant their own destruction. But they were able to conduct a 'small war' and in every way possible deal destructive blows against the supply lines of the enemy and smaller enemy divisions. The Spaniards have shown that the same can happen in war as did to the king of beasts in Lessing's fable, in which the lion succumbed to the bite of a flea ...

On the whole it can hardly be said that military terminology is particularly precise. The German word 'Kleinkrieg' can refer to either of the two extremes we have mentioned. In French they use the terms 'petite guerre', 'guerre de guérilla' and 'guerre de partisans' as synonyms, and in English 'small war' and 'guerilla warfare'.

Talking about current events, it is evident that the partisan struggle in the Soviet Union is organised and publicised by officialdom. But it is equally evident that in many cases partisan divisions have grown up spontaneously and operate without reference to the regular army. Conditions in China are broadly the same, although with the difference that there are stronger contacts between the free and occupied zones so that a greater part of the guerilla strike force is linked to general defence measures. In Serbia in 1941 the new Balkan war was begun partly with what remained of the regular army, partly with newly organised volunteers. In other occupied countries partisans and saboteurs—potential guerilla fighters—are operating without any connection with companies of regular troops. But large numbers of them are doubtless in contact with the authorities in exile.

In order to arrive at a definition of the term, we must set out from the point that guerilla war is carried on by the native population of a country or region. The population itself organises or participates in the organisation of military forces for defence against the enemy or in order to liberate itself. In its purest form guerilla war is the military expression for a popular uprising that employs every means which genuine patriotism or some equally powerful motivation is capable of exploiting . . .

. . . There has been a strong tendency to take the experiences of Belgium and the brutal and relatively swift destruction of the guerillas as proof positive that guerilla wars against modern armies and occupation troops are completely pointless. Most recent experiences have however shown that such conclusions are over-hasty. In any case other lessons can be drawn from the tragic events in Belgium. Ehrhardt underlines two of them : 'In a densely populated free country with a highly developed social pattern and a sophisticated road network it is impossible to bring about a mass uprising in the event of war quickly enough and then to hold on if the enemy strikes resolutely and swiftly. The fighting techniques of guerilla warfare are ineffective at the centre of operations.' But it is in any event evident that it demands much greater sacrifices from the population in a country like Belgium than for example in the Balkans . . . A popular uprising under west European conditions demands significantly more thoroughgoing preparation, more resolute execution and a great national willingness to sacrifice than in less advanced countries, which have both a guerilla tradition and also the terrain on their side.

The guerilla war in Belgium was the first practical test in the 'civilised' world of the Hague Rules of War on Land laid down in 1907. These regulations were already on the table at the Brussels conference of 1874 and the Hague conference of 1899 but were not ratified until October 1907. These rules distinguish between organised and non-organised popular war and for both cases lay down the legal limits...

It is less to do with international law than with the character of the war itself that irregular military operations played such a small part in the First World War. And in the Second World War just about all that was left of the provisions of international law was the paper they were written on.

The conditions of occupation created the ideological climate under which even people with a basically positive attitude to law and peace can react differently and—if other factors come into play—can be readily swept along in an uprising which in the past would have been inconceivable. Occupation brings out nationalist passions and a brutalisation of the spirit which can cause large masses to go over from unarmed opposition to rebellion. Inhibitions are swept aside and fear of inevitable sacrifices is overcome in the face of the desired goal, freedom.

A serious state of emergency is a mitigating circumstance when a man oversteps the bounds of the law. Necessity knows no law. A desperate situation involving a whole people can lead to actions which may contradict certain rules of international law. What can be said against such people when they maintain they are not capable of observing the small print because their right to live and the very existence of their nation are at stake? And if at the same time the majority go on to maintain that it is they who are fighting for just conditions against the domination of injustice? And once again we are faced with the age-old problem of whether a nation has a moral right to incur guilt in law in a just cause. History has repeatedly supplied the answer to this question. A state which offers its citizens security and human dignity need fear no revolution. An international order which secures all individuals the same rights to exist and live their own lives will not be plagued by civil war on an international scale.

Throughout the occupied countries a state of unrest has arisen which can with considerable justification be regarded as constituting a 'third front'. It becomes all the more apparent the closer we approach the final phases of the war. There are many signs that the last period of the current war will be marked by extended guerilla campaigns and national uprisings.

Notes

1. Much has been said to refute such assertions. The Norwegian ambassador in Reykiavik, Johan Zeier Cappelen, made a statement on 12 February 1963 to the effect that it was he who suggested to Brandt that he should put on military uniform. Cappelen met Brandt the day before he was due to go into a POW camp, and Brandt followed his advice that it was less dangerous to spend a little time in a POW camp than to be arrested as a civilian. Brandt's perfect Norwegian allowed him to pass himself off successfully as a Norwegian soldier for the couple of months he spent in the camp. Cappelen adds: 'When Brandt put on Norwegian uniform, we were already without weapons . . . I have never witnessed nor heard reports of Brandt firing on German troops during the war.'

2. Attlee speech 8 September 1939.

3. Churchill speech on 24 August 1941.

4. Churchill, House of Commons speech 21 September 1943.

5. New York, 8 May 1942.

6. This letter is to Herbert George in London. George had engaged in political activities with Brandt in exile, and in 1940 had escaped to England from Norway. Only a small part of the 'open letter to the Communists' which Brandt mentions in the course of the letter is quoted. Brandt was defending himself against accusations such as these: being a German 'with a dubious past'; betraying Communists into the hands of the Gestapo; and being one of the 'bitterest enemies of the Soviet Union in the socialist movement'.

7. Letter to Herbert George.

8. *Black Record—Germans Past and Present*, London, 1941.

9. London, 1942.

10. London, 1942.

11. *The Leopard and the Spots* (Win the Peace Pamphlet No. 1) London, n.d.

12. London, 1943.

13. London, 1942.

14. London, 1943.

15. *Labour, the War, and the Peace. A Declaration of Policy by the National Executive of the British Labour Party*, Transport House, London, 9 February 1940.

16. *Reden und Aufsätze*, Vol. 2, Frankfurt a. M., 1965.

17. Broadcast, September 5 1943.

18. The book from which these extracts are taken (*Guerillakriget*—see List of sources) has also played a role in the smear campaign against Willy Brandt. What he says in it has been twisted round to mean that Brandt was really giving hints on how to fight a partisan war against German soldiers. It was taken as a 'handbook for Norwegian resistance fighters' and even as advice on 'how to murder hundreds of thousands of German soldiers'. In fact the work is an historical study which does nothing of the sort.

IV

Spain

IV

Spain

INTRODUCTION

Writing history at short range can easily get no further than the journalistic or polemical level. But we know that even at a greater distance it is by no means easy to overcome the effects of prejudice and legend. The 'traditional emnity' taught in French and German schools for all too long now is just one example among many.

There is scarcely one event of our age which has given rise to such contradictory assessments as the war in Spain 1936–39. When I write the words 'war in Spain', I am already on the verge of bringing out a contradiction. Many people will ask: Why didn't he put 'civil war'? I write plain 'war' because the events in Spain went far beyond the bounds of an embittered internal dispute.

We in Germany more than most are still largely ignorant of those dramatic and confusing events. That is not so remarkable, since our country was at that time cut off from free reporting of news and it was not possible for us to form an objective opinion. And in contrast to the events at home and to what has happened in the Second World War, people were not particularly concerned to correct their image of Spain at a later stage. So we continue to live on with the distorted picture of a Communist revolt which was crushed by the forces of civilisation and perhaps also of freedom. I take a quite different view. Even thirty years after, it all still seems fundamentally different. It was indeed different. Both the reactionary and the Communist Spanish legends call for critical examination.

The first thing that should be made clear is that there was no Communist uprising in Spain in July 1936. What did take place was a putsch by generals with the support of lawyers against a government which had come to power after free elections and which moreover did not have one single Communist member.

Next it should be made clear that Spain became the setting for an international conflict. Mussolini's Italy and shortly after Hitler's Germany both intervened massively on the side of the rebellious '*nationalists*'. *The western powers kept strictly to a policy of non-intervention to which other states were content to pay lip-service. Thus the Soviet Union was able to exercise a strong influence on republican Spain by her arms deliveries.*

In the third place it was the case that, throughout Europe and far beyond, Spain was the focal point of the hopes and fears of all who saw in the onward march of Nazism and Fascism a deadly threat to progress. This held true not only for the 'left', in the current sense of the term. It was equally valid for the liberals, for conservative moderates who stood a good way right of centre, and for many who were deeply committed to their sense of Christian responsibility. Much was oversimplified at the time. Light and shade could not be so clearly distinguished as was claimed. But that is no wonder. For me the Spain of today has not become an idée fixe. I know that there too things have progressed and I can but hope with all my heart that the forces of freedom and a European vision will come out on top. The Spanish people certainly do not want another civil war. Democracy which is still being suppressed in Spain can only gradually emerge victorious. It needs European solidarity. In any event, I do not understand that part of the 'left' which is confident that the Communist dictatorships are capable of bringing about great changes but exclude the possibility of an evolutionary process taking place in Spain.

At that time—February 1937—I was glad to go to Spain. Since my time in Berlin, which had anyway been put out as a stay in Spain, a good month had passed. I wanted to experience for myself what I regarded as the most decisive event since the Nazis seized power. Apart from journalistic work I took on the task of keeping up political contacts in Barcelona for my SAP friends, which was a quarrelsome and thankless enough chore.

The southward journey itself was an adventurous undertaking, although hardly fraught with danger. I made the crossing from Kristiansand on the Norwegian south coast to Jutland together with my friend Per Monsen, who is now Director of the International Press Institute in Zurich. He started off with the false supposition that he would find in me a companion already thoroughly familiar with Spain, and I had to tell him on the way down that I knew as little as he did. We travelled from Esjberg to Le Havre and had to wait days in Paris for the necessary official stamp ...

If I think back now on that spring and summer nearly thirty years ago, those unedifying squabbles and sordid intrigues which then dominated the scene have now entirely faded into the background. What remains alive in the memory is the beauty of the countryside, and it was unfortunate that I only got to know Catalonia at close quarters; I have never been to Madrid, for example. The image which remains most clearly of all in my mind is that of the proverbial pride of the Spanish people, their vitality, love for freedom and faith in the future, and the creative power which time and again would fight its way to the surface in the midst of the painful conflicts of wartime.

I remember also the fellow feeling of bitter misery. For this reason I felt particular satisfaction in being able—when back in Oslo again—to work on the Spanish Aid programme which provided food and medical supplies right to the bitter end, that is until the aid given to the republicans, who in 1939 fled to France, exhausted and humbled, and were accommodated in camps under the most wretched conditions.

The party with which my group was linked by membership of the bureau of independent socialist parties bore the name POUM (Partido Obrero Unificada Marxista, that is, the United Marxist Labour Party). The centre of their influence was in Catalonia, but as early as December 1936 they were forced out of the Catalonian government ...

My first contact with POUM took place when I was participating in an international conference in Paris in May 1936 with its president Joaquin Maurin. Maurin was a persuasive and militant phenomenon. But his formula—'We are for the popular front because we are against it'—left me cold. It was generally believed that Maurin had fallen in the very first days of the civil war, whilst in reality he had survived into Franco's Spain in prison under a false name. I learned this secret through his wife, but not until after I had left Spain. Everyone treated Jeanne Maurin as a widow.

The POUM, in partial agreement with the Anarcho-syndicalists and a section of the Social Democrats, supported the view that revolution was the overriding concern. The Communists, in partial agreement with the 'bourgeois' Democrats, took the opposing view that the demands of war took precedence. In trying to arrive at a view of my own I fell out with the revolutionaries, who seemed to me to have overshot the target by a wide margin, but I disagreed even more violently with those who sought to exploit the discipline which the military situation demanded by establishing a system of one-party rule.

I came to the conclusion that the POUM had 'taken up a false position on virtually every practical issue' and accused them of 'sectarian conduct' and 'ultra-left subjectivism'. This applied particularly to their youth league which summoned its followers to join battle against Fascism and 'against bourgeois democracy' and with whom I was in fundamental disagreement. I tried, at least up till 1 May 1937, to bring all the youth leagues under one heading, in which I had some success to begin with, but which later brought friction with every single group. My participation in such discussions, which was not restricted to the role of passive observer, was rendered easier for me by the fact that I had acquired some Spanish as a fourth foreign language at the Lübeck Johanneum.

Principal among the leftwing socialist leaders in Barcelona whom I learned to respect for their balanced attitudes was Julian Gorkin. But I naturally regarded it as my duty to intervene on behalf of the POUM leaders when they and others were persecuted, dragged before the courts, or even murdered by the Communists. This sort of thing was at its height after the bloody and tragic May week in Barcelona, which was a civil war within a civil war. I know it is not easy to explain these confusing events. In any case I learned a great deal from them.

As so often happens in life, the ridiculous was always rubbing shoulders with the sublime. Right in the thick of those days in May the Swedish poet Ture Nerman was in Barcelona on a visit. He was one of the founders of the Swedish Communist party and represented the leftwing socialists in the lower chamber. My friend Paul Gauguin, the grandson of the famous painter, who had also made a name for himself as an artist, and myself could hardly stifle our amusement when Nerman came into the hotel one afternoon in a state of considerable disarray. The 'revolutionary socialists' had taken him for a class enemy because he was wearing a hat and he had only been allowed to go free after much deliberation.

These experiences at the age of 23 have exposed me to reproaches from two opposing sides right up until recent years. On the one hand I was taken to task as a 'social Fascist', 'agent of Franco' and 'Gestapo spy' in Communist writings. On the other hand 'rightwing' opponents have tried to brand me as a 'Communist fighter' for the 'Red front'.[1] But it is not always so that opposites cancel one another out. Sometimes one complements the other, or their respective exponents even pass the ball among themselves.

(1)   DEMOCRACY AGAINST FASCISM

On 19 July the uprising of militaristic and Fascist forces took place as a preventive measure against the revolution that was steadily advancing towards power. For years rumour had been rife in Spain. The victory of Gil Robles in October 1934 remained a bloody episode. In 1935 a powerful democratic popular movement rose up under the banner of a popular front. In February 1936 the popular front experienced its great election victory. The democratic popular movement formed the basis for the development of the forces surging towards the socialist revolution. Conditions for the struggle had become more favourable. Bad though the policy of the popular front government was, the masses in the country and the factories were doing well politically. And on the whole the popular front movement made it possible for such a broadly-based resistance against the Franco party to rise up in July.

The working class was bound to become the mainstay of this movement. It was the working class which in association with the broad mass of the anti-Fascist population broke the Fascist insurrection in the key areas of Spain on 19 July and the days following.

Since July 1936 war has been raging in Spain. The fronts are (2) clearly marked. The Franco camp represents the medieval forces of Spain, the nobility, the big estate owners, the reactionary ecclesiastical hierarchy, and a decadent officer cadre. The dark powers of the Middle Ages have fused with those of big finance. This camp also numbers foreign imperialists among its supporters.

Spanish youth knew what the battle was about. They recognised the necessity for driving out the forces of medievalism and for fighting for national freedom. They stood their ground under far from favourable conditions. More than that—they took the initiative. During those days of glory in July they stood at the barricades and helped to bring the Fascist rebels to their knees in the key Spanish centres. The young workers took the lead in the towns. And the young people in the villages also played an important part. They were freer than the older generation. It was the young more than any others who filled the ranks of the first people's and workers' militia. Young men and women took up arms. And in the many places where there were no weapons, they made ready to use their fists. The first period of the war has been called the 'children's war'. And on the Guadalajara front Ludwig Renn said : 'I love the young because they seek to do great things. Here in Spain most of the combatants are young and that is why there is so much verve in their fight against Fascism, both in the front line and to the rear.'

It would of course be wrongheaded to fall into the temptation of idolising the young. But today the young of anti-Fascist Spain are in the people's army. Over half the troops of the people's army are made up of members of the anti-Fascist youth organisations. The youth leagues also fill over half of the posts of the political commissariat in the army. Young officers stand at their head. There are generals of twenty-eight and thirty.

The young people of Spain also play a vital part in the rear, in the shock brigades in factories, in the process of transformation in the country, and in the cultural revolution. Republican Spain is gaining youthful vigour in the midst of war although thousands of the younger generation have had to sacrifice their lives. In the autumn of 1936 Catalonia gave young people full political and civil rights from the age of eighteen. We come across young Spain not just in the army, but also in the inner councils of economic and political life, in the people's courts, in fact everywhere. The leader of the giant young socialist organisation is just twenty-four. An eighteen-year-old girl is one of the functionaries in the Catalan youth movement. One of the people working on the youth newspaper *La hora*, Azcárate, is a secretary in the Foreign Ministry at twenty.

The heroic epic of the Spanish milizianos is the battle of fists against machine guns, of shotguns against aircraft, of tins of explosives and petrol bombs against tanks. The young drew their strength from the knowledge that they were battling for a better future.

A simple fighting man at the Estremadura front put it in these words : 'The most educated of us know a bit about Karl Marx' teachings, know the odd thing about the French revolution, and perhaps know who Lenin was as well, and that's about it. The others fight without political ideals, just for the right to eat and live. They're fighting so their kids can go to school and get a better education than their parents, so they can live free and happy.'

At the end of August 1936 the republican government recognised the militia as the Spanish government army. At the beginning of October they published their decree on the militarisation of the people's militia. The romantic period came to a close. The internal hold was strengthened. At this time Madrid fell after an heroic defence in which peace-loving young people from all corners of the earth had played a crucial part.

Then the build-up of the new people's army took place. After a few months the first great victory was achieved in Guadalajara. Up until Teruel the new force consistently consolidated its position. Those of the young who showed qualities of leadership became the new officers and commissars. In the autumn of 1937 200,000 of the

300,000 members of the socialist youth movement were in the front line. All together the anti-Fascist youth organisations made up the overwhelming majority of the people's army. The best of them were commissioned or entered specialist brigades. These latter made up the anti-tank units, the dynamiteros and guerilleros who led the battle behind enemy lines.

They went through war training and took with them their pre-military education. With Madrid as starting-point, the Alerta schools were set up. Theirs was the task of implementing the cultural, athletic and pre-military education of the fourteen to twenty-one age group. In Madrid the Alerta movement was organised by the youth front. Antonio Lopez, secretary of the youth front and member of the Youth of the Republican Union, was at the same time chairman of the Alerta movement. As early as the first part of summer 1937 there were 60 schools in Madrid with 10,000 pupils and 500 teachers. By the end of 1937 the number of pupils had risen to 40,000. During the terrible bombing raids on the Spanish capital children are to be seen going round in stretcher parties. They are members of the medical battalion of the Alerta. For the girls special nursing courses are being laid on as part of the Alerta movement.

On all sectors of the front there also grew up the 'soldiers' hostels' of the young people's army. Some of them are right in the front lines, even in the trenches. There the soldiers can learn to read and write. There they study books about the war and other subjects.

Troupes of actors come to the front with all their artistic paraphernalia. In the rear the soldier' hostels are used as resting places. Wall newspapers bear witness to the fighting spirit of the young. The young women come along and repair the soldiers' clothing. Peasants in the neighbourhood frequently come too and take part in the discussions and activities of the soldiers . . .

THE REPUBLICAN ACHIEVEMENT

Apart from an underdeveloped agrarian economy, Spanish reactionaries left another sad inheritance behind them : a backward culture. Over half the population could neither read nor write.

Young anti-Fascist Spain has made a start on the revolution of the spirit. As schools, hospitals, children's homes, museums and invaluable monuments to their cultural heritage are being bombed the anti-Fascist Spanish people protect the old and are creating new cultural values. It is not just a matter of right against wrong, truth against falsehood, but also culture against barbarism.

It was FETE, the teachers' union, which took up the initiative for the formation of the cultural militia ... The tasks which these cultural militia have taken upon themselves are legion. They not only teach reading and writing, but they also deal with the equipping of libraries, establish wall newspapers, give talks and organise the presentation of cultural and social films.

On top of this they have collaborated in and helped to run newspapers at the front, organised lectures for enemy troops, created cultural and soldiers' hostels, worked on educational films, radio transmissions and theatrical performances.

And these labours are even now beginning to bear fruit. There are already formations of the people's army in which a short while ago 80 per cent of the soldiers were illiterate but whose entire complement can now read and write.

In the country as a whole the work goes on of establishing libraries on all sectors of the front and in every village ...

The cultural struggle in republican Spain has not been dictated from above, but has been borne along by the enterprise of the broad mass of the population ...

In his speech at the Nuremberg party rally in 1937 Propaganda Minister Goebbels expressed his eagerness to destroy the cultural values of 'Red Spain'. He maintained that the school system in republican Spain was in a deplorable state. He prudently refrained from referring to the destruction of Guernica by German bombers and also the terrible bombings of children's homes, schools and hospitals.

The opposite to Goebbels' assertions is the truth. At the outbreak of the civil war there were, according to the figures of the Barcelona civic authorities, 70,000 children receiving no formal education, in other words, 39 per cent of those of school age. For Madrid the number given was 50,000. But even the schools that did exist were in a wretched condition. The buildings were falling apart. At the beginning of 1936 a Spanish primary teacher's salary was only two-thirds that of a policeman at the bottom of the scale.

The Catalan trade unions had been working since 1880 for the establishment of modern school buildings. Francisco Ferrer, the leader of the free school movement, was executed in 1909 on the Montjuio near Barcelona. He had wanted to guide children out of ignorance into knowledge. For this he was regarded as a revolutionary and had to forfeit his life.

The seeds he sowed were only later to germinate. Just over a week after the rebels in Barcelona had been defeated, on 27 July, the CENE was set up, the Council for the New Standard Primary

Schools of Catalonia. Its foundation was the result of collaboration between the teachers' union and the two large union central offices. In the autumn of 1937 they had got as far as reducing the number of children in Barcelona with no schooling from 70,000 to a mere 16,000.

Throughout the whole of republican Spain there are 60,137 schools in existence. From July 1936 up to July 1937, that is to say in the course of one year of bloody war, 7,578 new schools were established. In the second half of 1937 a further 10,000 schools were at the planning stage. These figures bear comparison with those of the old order. The monarchy established 945 schools in 1930, the reactionary government set up a total of 1,399 in 1935 . . .

The Spanish republic's entire budget for state education totalled nearly 497 million pesetas in 1937. That means an increase of 143 million since 1936. In the middle of a war a sum of 40 millions was set aside for the opening of new schools.

Ten million pesetas were used in the fight against illiteracy, 7 millions for teaching materials, 50 millions for building new sports centres, swimming pools, etc. The income of the worst paid teachers, the young and country members of the profession, was raised by a quarter, and a sum of over 42 million pesetas was allocated for this purpose.

At the same time republican Spain has turned its attention to the social welfare of the youngest members of the community. As early as the beginning of August 1936 a 'Committee for the protection of orphans of the defenders of the republic' was brought into being. State aid is guaranteed to those unfortunate children whose fathers have fallen in the fight for freedom.

A decree of the republican government in November 1936 proposed the establishment of secondary schools for those who wanted to matriculate at secondary level in order to be able to continue their studies. These schools have now come into existence.

Special schools for country children and specialised farming schools were set up.

Young Spain has a profound respect for its cultural inheritance. In every province a Junta (council) was established for the protection and state ownership of the cultural heritage. Artists, scholars and technologists offer their services to these preservation councils.

In Madrid alone more than 70 large libraries, which originated from religious foundations and individual palaces, were saved. The archives of the church were also brought into safety. The cultural preservation council in Madrid rescued over 10,000 works of famous painters, among them 32 Goyas, 30 Cranachs, 11 El Grecos as well as numerous works by Velasquez, Murillo, Titian, Breughel, Reynolds and Gainsborough. They were able to save around 100,000 other *objets d'art*. Most of them were despatched to Valencia where they were put into bomb-proof store. And in Madrid itself steps were taken to protect artistic treasures from bombing . . .

In the country thousands of farms are without a man in the family. Women and girls have taken over the work on the land. There as in industry they have frequently formed community groups and carry out training courses in order to increase production.

The more men that are called to the front, the more jobs the women have to take over.

Moral support supplements practical collaboration. There is the proud statement of La Pasionara :[2] 'We would rather be the widows of heroes than the wives of cowards !'

The Spanish reactionaries and their backers set themselves up as the protectors of the church, of religion, of Christianity, of faith. But what is the true position?

In Spain about 30 evangelical priests have been murdered. Without exception they fell victim to the terror in Franco's Spain. Guernica, the holy city of the Basques, was razed to the ground by German bombers. After the victory of 'national' troops in the Basque many priests were executed, others sentenced to up to 30 years' hard labour, because they had held services for government troops. These sentences were published in the *Gaceta del Norte* in Bilbao. That is the real truth : the Fascists are only friends of the church when the church is a friend of the Fascists.

It is also true that a number of monasteries and churches were sent up in flames during the first days of the civil war. Many were turned into fortresses from which shots were fired in anger.

The Spanish people nourished an intense hatred against the old reactionary forces which had held them enslaved for centuries and which at this turning point in history had again thrown in their lot with the enemy. The church was furthermore regarded as an instrument of exploitation. In the February elections of 1936 the Bishop of Barcelona could still be heard preaching that a right-wing vote was a vote for Christ. Numerous church leaders were actively engaged in preparations for the insurgence and entered the provisional Fascist government.

None of this has anything to do with religious faith. This is why not only the Protestants, not only the Basque Catholics, but also a very large number of practising Catholics of high standing and reputation throughout Spain have come out on the side of the people and against the reactionary forces of the church. The republican government, with the support of the fighting youth, has from the outset pledged itself to freedom of religious belief. Over and above this, forces have come into being among the youth of Spain which are working towards the defeat of dogma and prejudice.

Republican Spain is opening thousands of new schools and leading a crusade against illiteracy. In Franco's Spain the schools are closed. We learn of this not only from the reports of foreign correspondents. The official Burgos newspaper has announced the closure of a whole series of grammar, secondary and elementary schools.

Republican Spain does not have enough teachers. Union and youth officials must be drawn in to make up a full complement of teachers.

In Franco's Spain teachers and academics are shot. In the province of Galicia 80 per cent of all primary teachers were put before the firing squad. In the villages of other provinces the Fascists shot down 60 per cent of teachers, and 20 per cent ended up in prison. The rest have their liberty, but no work, as the schools are closed. Many university professors, teachers in grammar schools, medical men and lawyers were shot. In the province of Granada there was a large contingent of intellectuals among the 23,000 people executed. The number of women shot there was so great that a rightwing professor set up a kind of orphanage specifically for the care of their children.

Republican Spain established generous social provisions for mothers and children.

In Franco's Spain children are given military training from five years upwards. The Falange takes children between five and ten into the 'Flechas' (Arrows) and makes five-year-olds bear wooden weapons and uniforms. The ten to seventeen-year-old 'Infantas' are armed. The 'Requetas' (Monarchists) dress up the members of their children's organisation 'Pelayos' in khaki uniforms with red Basque caps. That is playing at soldiers. But in Franco's Spain even twelve-year-old children are driven to the front as soldiers. In Carabanchel twelve to fourteen-year-old children were made to work in the trenches. At Oviedo fourteen-year-olds were forced on ahead in attacks by Fascist troops. At Oviedo one of the most terrible acts of this war took place : during the storming of a civil guard barricade the dynamiteros suddenly stopped in their tracks. They were unable to take a step further, and so they withdrew, because the barricade was alive. The Fascists had roped six to ten-year-old children of anti-Fascists to the barricade.

Republican Spain sets up schools for the workers and establishes libraries in every village.

In Franco's Spain, following Hitler's example, the burning of books is organised. This is what happened in August 1937 at the feast of Saint Ignatius in Bilbao and in the province of Biscaya. A pyre was constructed in front of the monument to Ignatius Loyola, into which books were flung for hour after hour, works by Galdes, Zola, Blanco Ibanez, Anatole France, Pi y Margall, Thomas Mann, Valera, Palacio Valdes, Dickens and many others, and of course the works of Marx and Bakunin.

Bombardments of the Fascist air force and artillery against Madrid caused in one single month—February 1937—the destruction of 980 buildings. Among them were 14 schools, 8 churches, 9 old people's homes, 4 hospitals, 2 museums, the Academy of History and the Academy of Languages.

In republican Spain a new youth movement is in the making.

In Franco's Spain by contrast even the Fascist youth have no freedom. Hundreds of rank and file members and leaders of the 'Falange Espanola' are executed. These nationalist young people dreamed of a national socialist movement, of a national syndicalism.

The Franco régime is simply incapable of operating with the language of socialism, it knows no other means than terrorism. The formation of the Fascist unity party, which made Franco the ultimate authority, responsible only to 'God and history', shifted the balance on to the side of the monarchists, those reactionaries who fear even the radicalism of Fascist youth like the plague.

The anti-Fascist youth organisations of Spain have strong traditions. The Socialist Youth fought in October 1934 against the coloured and foreign legion troops in Astruria. They became the motive force behind the mobilisation and unification of the socialist workers . . .

WHO IS THE REAL ENEMY?   (1)

In Barcelona far too many wrongheaded discussions are taking place. But that in itself is no proof against the necessity for accounting for the developments of the past eight months of war, and the character of the armed conflict raging all round us.

There are two contrary theories. The first is most actively supported by the Communist party and by the PSUC, the Socialist party of Catalonia affiliated to the Comintern, and the United Socialist Youth. Large sections of the socialists and of the socialist UGT unions follow this view, which runs like this: 'We are not faced with a war among Spaniards ... but a war which foreign powers are waging against Spain ... We are not faced with a class war, but a war of national independence.' This proposition, which is also supported by the popular front parties of the middle-class left, leads to a call for the whole nation to unite against the foreign powers.

On the other hand the Anarcho-syndicalists (CNT and FAI) and especially the POUM (Workers' Party for Marxist Unity) defend the proposition which Andres Nin has recently expressed in these words: 'What is happening in our country is not the defence of the independence of the homeland ... What is developing is a fight of the Spanish proletariat against the Spanish bourgeoisie.'

The fact is that the revolution stood still, but so too did the war. International circumstances were inhibiting, in particular the weakly and largely treacherous attitude of the democrats towards Spain and the efforts of the Soviet Union to prevent the struggle within Spain from turning into the lighted fuse of the powder keg of Europe.

But in the meantime a tricky situation had developed. The character of the war was shifting more and more into the direction of a war of independence. Every organisation is faced with the necessity for taking due account of the situation, of the fact that public opinion was insufficiently mobilised, that the revolution got bogged down and that nowadays normalisation of life is the order of the day.

Salvation lies in victorious offensives on the front! Only then can the right mood be established for a resurgence of the revolutionary spirit. What must be done is to reinforce the achievements of the revolution to date and to do everything possible to win the war.

AN EPISODE IN THE BATTLE

Barcelona, 15 March 1937   (3)

A few observations on my *Impressions from the Front*: In this work I was not entirely led by what I have seen with my own eyes, I have also made use of reports from various well-informed colleagues.

During the attack on 17 February which we watched from very close quarters, I observed among other things the following: (*a*) Everyone had known hours beforehand (and, I was told, even days in advance) what kind of action was in the offing, and it was the object of much discussion. (b) The transportation of the battalion into the line of trenches took place between 1½ and 2 hours too late, and for this reason the start of the attack was considerably delayed. (c) There was no officer in command during the operation, as he had gone off up the hill with the grenaderos, while the riflemen remained behind without orders. (d) There was no co-ordination with the artillery; in contrast to the enemy, they were firing all over the place, and some of their shells actually landed among us. (e) There was no air support. (f) Our boys were simply far too badly equipped, quite apart from the fact that they completely lacked the effective weapons of the other side, for example, the mortars. (g) There was no fatigue party standing at the ready with sandbags and spades for throwing up trenches. (h) The battalion in the first line of trenches gave up the ghost altogether when it turned tail on seeing the boys driven back from the hill by the Fascists, instead of giving them cover by firing on their pursuers. They had to be stopped at pistol point (and, we were told, by even stronger measures). (i) Afterwards no disciplined analysis of the action took place, instead something of an orgy of mutual recrimination . . .

VALENCIA

Valencia, April 1937

It is our duty to see things clearly as they are.

The first impression of Valencia is that it is hopelessly over-crowded. And there is no wonder. There used to be a mere 300,000 people living here in the town, and now there are over 900,000. Two things in Valencia immediately leap to the eye after Barcelona : (a) *the atmosphere is far, far more serious* (by way of comparison, a friend described to me the mood in Barcelona as one of light operetta), the town is filled with the military, grim-faced workers and anti-Fascists, there are throngs of heavily armed patrols, and large posters remind the inhabitants that the enemy is a mere 100 miles away (in Teruel). There are many wounded to be seen all over the town. There is war in the air and also the feeling that the forces of war are concentrated here. (b) *The revolution was halted at a much earlier stage here in Valencia*, or had gone to the limit of its possible progress. And that brings out the differences in the suitation between Catalonia and the rest of the country. Valencia offers a much more middle-class and 'respectacle' impression than Barcelona.

To take just one example : the more or less universal greeting in Barcelona even today is 'Salud', but this is far from common in Valencia. On the shops there is no sign 'collectivised', but rather 'controlled'. (All undertakings of over five workers are controlled, but my information has it that the extent of the control is highly variable.) But in this context I must add at once that the syndicate signs are already evidence in themselves that close co-operation between the CNT and the UGT has been achieved.

The food supply system in Valencia seems to be better than in Barcelona. The accommodation of vast numbers of refugees has evidently been organised in a masterly fashion by the unity committee. There are fewer posters on the streets than in Barcelona. The Communist party is well to the fore, and in contrast to Barcelona there is scarcely any sign of the POUM. The SP posters relate exclusively to the challenges of war : 'Unity command !' 'Socialist : your duty—to the front !' and the like.

In chasing round for members of the SP and youth movements I did after all meet a few people who gave me some useful pointers. *A young lady in the Social Democrats,* a lawyer, first asked me the question : *What are they doing abroad?* She voiced her disappointment over the attitude of French socialists and spoke with a tremor in her voice of *the Soviet Union which alone comes to our aid.* 'The Soviet Union will help us'—this is surely not just the isolated voice of one comrade.

Anyone seeking to arrive at a picture of the situation in Valencia must realise that the Fascists were once very strong here. Even today they are not to be underestimated. Valencia is a significant stronghold of the fifth column.

Only a few days ago *a complete broadcasting station was captured* which had been sending daily reports to Franco and which even had access to *information in very high quarters indeed.* The police and military authorities comb the town and surrounding district day by day. The resulting atmosphere bears no comparison to that in Barcelona.—A well-informed individual also told me that in the population at large there is no small number of people who try to get Franco or Llano on their radio sets in the evening, or whose prayers end up with a hope for a Franco victory.

WAR, REVOLUTION AND THE FUTURE OF FASCISM   (4)

The CP, which has now become the central political force in anti-Fascist Spain, has a period of rapid growth behind it. In the February elections of 1936 it gained fourteen seats thanks to the popular front, whilst previously it only had one. Today it numbers

250,000 members, whilst its membership a few short years ago could have been accommodated in a medium-sized hall. It is true that this growth largely owes itself to lower middle class elements which see the CP as the strongest defender of their interests. But that is just *one* part of the story. What is far more important is that the CP has been more successful than any other party in attracting the proletarian and activist young.

The leftwing Socialist Youth has hitherto formed the main body of the left wing of the Socialist party. The United Socialist Youth which the CP entered with only a few thousand members is now with its 300,000 members—even if that figure is too high—predominantly under the leadership of the CP. And in addition the PSUC in Catalonia which represents the Comintern section there has 50,000 CP members. How is this quite extraordinary growth to be explained?

The first factor is the stream of Unity and Popular Front slogans, as whose supporters after the seventh Comintern congress in Spain the CP members gained the ear of the masses. They were the representatives of a policy of strength through unity which led to the February election victory. And then it is impossible to overestimate the increased weight the CP has gained as the Spanish representative of the USSR, the land of military aid. But we should be blind if we did not see further that in the eyes of large masses of the population the CP has become the staunchest supporter of the exigencies of the military situation. Day in and day out the CP have driven home the message : unified command, unified army, shock brigades at the front and to the rear, pre-military training of the young, etc., etc. And that is not just for the sake of appearances. We should arrive at an entirely false conclusion if we did not recognise the rewards the Communists have reaped for themselves on military questions, if we did not recognise the way in which progressive and reactionary elements in CP policy were intermixed.

The Comintern and its Spanish sections claim to be striving towards a radical democracy with a strong social content. In the early months they were saying quite simply : First win the war and then we will talk about what happens next. And that had some attractions. But it also happened that the selfsame CP in its principal publication was fighting for the democratic republic and in front-line newspapers for socialism. Recently José Diaz has made an attempt to throw out a catchphrase which expresses the double nature of the conflict more clearly when he says : Win the war and save the people's revolution.

What are the realities of the situation? They are that the leaders of the USSR, to which the Comintern is subject, desire the defeat of Germany and Italy in Spain. The leaders of the USSR regard the danger of world war as extremely serious. They no longer place any hope on international working class solidarity. They seek to achieve the defeat of Hitler and Mussolini and the prevention of a Franco victory by coming to terms with France and England especially. This is why the Comintern is making such an effort to force the Spanish revolution into a middle-class and democratic context.

The Russians really want Franco beaten. And without Russian military aid it would already have long been over. That must be made absolutely clear. But it is at this point once more that the interaction of progressive and reactionary forces makes itself sharply apparent. The active involvement of the Russians last October has clearly resulted in a break in the external policies they had been pursuing for many years. They have started to pursue an active and independent foreign policy line once more. And this is the point at which their interests coincide with those of the Spanish and international working class. The Russian intervention aimed at the destruction of Franco was an extraordinarily progressive move. But this very new activity on the foreign policy front is evolving within the framework of their changed outlook. They have never delivered nor are they delivering now with no strings attached. Now no one in his right mind has requested them to deliver weapons accompanied by the declaration that they are intended for the victory of the proletarian revolution. They were needed for and aimed at nothing more than the support of the Spanish government. But they went further. They tied up political conditions with their deliveries, conditions which grew out of their attitude that on international considerations Spain cannot and must not go beyond a democratic republican system.

But every beginning has its end. Forcing events into the democratic framework has led to the destruction even of those revolutionary achievements which had already been made in the July revolution. This leads to conflicts with the militant sections of the working class. And this turn of events brings about the result that the initiative in the anti-Fascist camp has shifted towards the *petit bourgeois* and the anti-Fascist elements among the middle class and that the influence of the British and French middle class on the leadership of anti-Fascist Spain has been strengthened. The Russians are well aware of this. And what conclusions do they draw from it? Everything points to the fact that they give the battle cry of the new brand of democratic republic—and mean a Spain under its monopoly leadership . . . It is plain for all to see that they have not achieved the success in international policies which they have striven for. Despite the fact that the middle class now sets the tone, the British and French governments have not surrendered their non-interventionist policies. On the contrary, they have started to come more boldly out into the open with their compromise plans which operate to the disadvantage of the Spanish working class.

The Communists use every means at their disposal to achieve the creation of the one-party government towards which they are striving. But in a situation where everything hangs on bringing forces together against Franco, the CP methods of defamation of their proletarian opponents, witchhunts and indiscriminate acts of terror against them, taking all others into the fold or destroying them—normalisation after the pattern of the PSUC and the United Youth—all undermine the fighting spirit and have a fatal impact on the conduct of the anti-Fascist war. Such tactics threaten to embitter and set back the whole international socialist movement once again and to reduce the initiatives towards unity to a heap of rubble.

In Spain these tactics have already halted the development of the anarchist mass movement and have to some extent set in train a dangerous retrograde motion.

Today the CP is the decisive political force in anti-Fascist Spain. Although it does not have its hands on the reins of government, it still dominates the greater part of the apparatus of the state at the present time. The officers are largely in the CP organisation, and the overwhelming majority of the police are in their hands. Spain is moving towards a Communist party dictatorship.

The international socialist movement can do a great deal to influence the ultimate outcome of the Spanish conflict. For the international working-class movement, for freedom and socialism throughout the world, the outcome of the war in Spain means a very great deal indeed.

But the international socialist movement must also put its whole weight behind the prevention of a continuation of the fight between political allies and a cessation of the persecution of the POUM and other revolutionaries.

Thus two crucial questions for the further progress of the Spanish   (5)
civil war arise : will Spain lead to a world war? Or will the Spanish conflict be de-escalated by an accommodation between the great powers?

The socialist movement has a vital interest in the prevention of a worldwide conflagration. But it must also recognise that there is no point in helping those who provoke war to become more daring and powerful just for the sake of peace. Spain is a test case for the great events that are to come. Already international Fascism has suffered great moral defeats. Now of all times the socialist movement must not lose heart. It must go beyond simple expressions of solidarity toward a positive attitude to external policies. In this period of transition the socialist movement must have answers to offer to all the questions the nation will pose. Looking at the position as a whole, the situation in Spain is now favourable to the cause of freedom and socialism.

There is no doubt any more that the conflicts between the various   (6) political factions in Franco's Spain are of a pretty serious nature. In many places it has come to the point of hostilities between the Falangists and the monarchists . . . As long as the war continued and foreign weapons and troops were needed for victory, internal tensions were set aside. After victory the question arose as to which paths should be taken towards the reconstruction of Spain after three years of devastation. Now the forces of Fascism and reaction are clashing. But in contrast to Germany and Italy, Spanish Fascism continues to draw its strongest support from abroad; in Spain itself there is no broadly-based Fascist movement . . .

The Falangists have taken over the Nazi vocabulary and have turned themselves into 'Spanish socialists' and 'national syndicalists'. Their threats against the capitalists are not taken very seriously, but they clearly want to take over the big estates. They are also challenging the might of the Catholic church. But above all else they are eager supporters of close collaboration with the Rome-Berlin Axis; in the event of war Spain is to go on the side of the Axis powers. The Falangists have therefore worked out a programme—with regard to land reform, for example—which signifies a break with the conditions which led Spain into civil war. They may have gained some support for these points of their programme. None the less the opposition view has a stronger position among the population.

What the Spanish people want more than anything else is peace, and also they want to rid themselves of foreigners. The monarchists say that they seek to secure the independence of Spain. They want to achieve this by not binding themselves too strongly to the Axis, but instead of this by working out a form of collaboration with

Britain. But at the same time they defend the old rotten social conditions... These struggles behind the scenes will continue and we can count on more surprises coming out of 'liberated' Spain.

Notes

1. These accusations may be the result of mistaken identity. A certain Wilhelm Philipp Liborius Brandt (born in 1907, now living near Frankfort) went in 1936 to Barcelona as a journalist. While he was on a trip to Madrid the civil war broke out, and he placed himself at the disposal of the republican government, taking part in front line fighting. In December 1940 he was abducted off to Germany by the Gestapo. In the course of his imprisonment (which included Dachau) the Gestapo frequently asked him what he had been up to in Sweden and Norway.

2. La Pasionara = Dolores Ibarruri, the most notable Spanish Communist.

V

Norway

V

Norway

INTRODUCTION

As I have said before, I went to Norway to take on a political task. But at the same time it was my chosen place of exile.

During the summer holidays of 1931 I had travelled across Scandinavia and seen with my own eyes the incomparable beauty of the Norwegian landscape. Even before then, in 1928, I had gone on a school exchange visit to Vejle in Denmark. I was attracted by the unforced friendliness, reserve and natural sense of justice of the fjord and mountain people. I read the Scandinavian writers and in the brief year after my matriculation, when I was trying my hand at shipbroking, I was in day to day contact with Scandinavian sailors. And I was no stranger to their language.

But it was not entirely due to my personal inclinations that my flight ended in Oslo, an attractive city in its austere way, rather than among the beauties of Copenhagen.

The real reason was that the SAP, which was small by German standards, and the NAP (Norwegian Labour Party), which was large by Norwegian standards, had in common the fact that they both stood somewhere between the Social Democrats and the Communists. They did not belong either to the Second or the Third Internationale, but came together in a study group which had been dubbed the 'Second-and-a-Half Internationale'.

After the First World War the NAP had decided by a large majority to join the Comintern. In 1923 they broke off from Moscow. In 1928 the NAP had become the majority party and Haakon VII called upon the leader of their parliamentary party to form a government. When some of the conservatives at court objected that he had no business handing over power to such Communist-inspired radicals, the king replied: 'Gentlemen, I am also King of the Communists.' But this experiment in political power only lasted a few weeks.

This could be taken as if I was trying to belittle the political situation in Norway at the time. That is far from being the case.

There was a strong democratic tradition, even in the rural areas, from which many of the industrial workers came. But when I went to Norway, it was a country suffering from an economic crisis yet at the same time overflowing with political passions. The Labour party came into power in 1935 after an election on the platform of 'Jobs for all'. I witnessed the evolution of a great leftwing socialist party into a Social Democrat party which none the less retained its own peculiar characteristics.

In the sectarian discussions of the emigré groups the 'NAP question' played an enormously important role at the time. I found them accusing me of lacking firmness of principle. When in 1935 I had delivered myself of the profundity that you cannot climb mountains simply by charging straight at the summit, I was countered by the remark: 'But Brandt has the NAP in his rucksack.'

In 1939 I explained to my emigré friends the real significance of the formulation of a new programme by the Norwegian Labour Party. I pointed to the difficult task that lay before the Scandinavians in 'surviving the period of reaction'. This had created problems which were 'hard for members of underground revolutionary parties to understand', especially as understanding was rendered difficult by differences in terminology. In contrast to their previous programme the present line was not 'founded on a total commitment to Marxism'. Instead of 'classes' they were talking about 'the working people': 'The prevailing social circumstances have brought to the surface the common interests of workers, smallholders and fishermen. The policy of the party in accordance with socialist theory towards the management of society and the planning of economic life is characterised as a policy of national well-being for the security of country and people.' And also: 'In its new programme the NAP declares itself opposed to dictatorship in any shape or form. In the discussions now taking place within the party, this statement is explained as a withdrawal from the classical concept of dictatorship against which is to be set an effective democratic structure as a means by which the common people can seize power.'

This was a moderate forerunner indeed of the Godesberg programme, but the path of the Norwegian Labour party from a class platform to a broader radical-democratic platform was, if I may say so, parallel to my own. In my first years in Norway I was still swimming against the current. Thus in 1934–35 I had rather overhastily joined forces with a strong leftwing opposition on the Youth League of the Labour party as a result of misunderstanding the lessons to be learnt from political defeat in Germany.

My contacts with the intellectual organisation 'Mot Dag' ('To-

wards the Day') were instructive, if problematical; this group was influential in the academic world, but in political circles did not come into prominence until their for the most part very able members joined the Labour party and rose to high office ... The Mot Dagists encouraged me to go and study at the University of Oslo. However it was by no means an easy task to reconcile this idea with the supposed obligations of a politically engaged young German in exile. None the less I obtained a good pass in the qualifying arts examination in 1934, a year after I matriculated; then I turned to the study of modern history, without however sitting any final examinations.

Foremost among my close acquaintances and friends in Norway were members of the youth movement, among them the present party chairman Trygve Bratteli. In spite of his oddities, I had a great respect for Martin Tranmäl, the 'grand old man' of the Norwegian socialist movement. I was made to feel at home among the personalities surrounding Einar Gerhardsen, who was Prime Minister for many years after the war. And I was soon on very friendly terms with Halvard Lange, later to become Foreign Minister —he did not belong to the leftwing socialist majority of the Labour party but rather to the Social Democrat minority group.

But I did not draw on the party membership lists for all my friends. They were not even restricted to leftwing writers of the time like Arnulf Överland and Sigurd Hoel: I moved in 'bourgeois' circles as well.

There is the story—actually from Denmark, not Norway—of the young man who was sent to Berlin by Prime Minister Stauning in 1932 to find out if there was still a chance that the Weimar Republic might survive. A few days later the young man returned to Copenhagen. He had seen enough. When he had visited the restaurant in the Reichstag he was struck by the fact that certain tables were reserved for members of this or that party. His conclusion was: 'In a country where the members of parliament are not capable of eating and drinking together democracy is on the way out.' And there is certainly more than a grain of truth in that.

It was of great importance for the years I spent in Scandinavia that I had become thoroughly at home with the Norwegian language, and it also saved me from more than one tricky situation, and not only in the prison camp in 1940. In Berlin in 1936 for example, when I met up in the state bank with a Norwegian student who had matriculated in Oslo the same year as I was supposed to have done under my pseudonym of the student Gunnar Gaasland, he invited me into a club in the city for Norwegian National Social-

ists. Or the occasion shortly before the outbreak of the war in an Oslo restaurant, when an agent became suspicious of my accent and I explained to him that I had been born in the north of Norway and that my father who was a postmaster was moved around a great deal, as a result of which my accent was very much a mixture of dialects.

I have already related what happened to me at the beginning of the war. Even the time in Stockholm was spent in predominantly Norwegian surroundings. The Norwegian cause was a most worthy one. And in their darkest hour they showed convincing greatness. By and large civilian resistance was a moral, even more than a political, force.

My contacts with the Norwegian resistance movement was on a personal rather than organisational level, even to the extremely personal extent that close and intimate friends were shot as hostages or found death in other ways. I supported the Norwegians in words and writing. The main purposes of my contributions to Swedish newspapers and the Swedish and Norwegian press bureau was to tell the truth about the resistance movement against the Nazi authorities and their Quislings.

My Norwegian citizenship was not confirmed until 1940 by the government which in the meantime had been established in London. My application dating from 1939—after my loss of German citizenship—had been shelved. When I regained my own citizenship once more in Schleswig-Holstein in 1948—for which, a year later, according to the constitution, there would have been no need to make an application—I did not surrender my Norwegian citizenship, it lapsed automatically. But that has not altered my personal attitude to the country in which I grew into manhood.

Of recent years I have been presented with many honours. I was especially delighted to receive the Olav order. It was presented to me on 15 June 1960 by the then Ambassador to west Germany. He said: 'You have many friends in Norway, and the Norwegian people have followed your progress with pleasure and admiration. In all your activities, from early youth to the present time, a clear and consistent line can be observed: you have fought for the right of the people to rule themselves in freedom. This is a struggle crucial to the future survival of our western culture and civilisation. In recognition of your services and with regard to the special place you hold in the hearts of the Norwegian people, His Majesty King Olav V has accorded you the Grand Cross of the Order of Saint Olav, the greatest honour that Norway can bestow.'

In my speech of acceptance I replied: 'There is naturally some difference between the nineteen-year-old refugee of the year 1933 whom the Oslo immigration authorities expected to behave with political circumspection, and the mayor of 1960, able to accept the Grand Cross of the Order of Saint Olav. Reference to this gap renders it easier for me to say a few words about my relationships with Norway and state openly my debt to my years there as apprentice and journeyman in life.

'From many points of view, my Scandinavian years were the most important of my life. The experience I gained there and the lessons I learned have in my view been invaluable to me. There I was fashioned for my subsequent activities.

'Norway gave me citizenship when others had made me stateless.[1] Despite this my Norwegian friends did not think ill of me when I remained in Berlin in 1947 to give of my best in the work of reconstructing my own country and to serve this sorely tested city in the cause of freedom ... Even in the hour of its deepest distress I could not cut myself off from the true Germany. But I have worked to the limit of my ability to make my own modest contribution to the struggle against the forces of enslavement ... I ask my Norwegian friends to regard me as irrevocably bound to them for all time. I ask them to have faith in the vigour of a German people purified by their bitter experiences. We must not forget the past, but we must learn its lessons. But we must also turn our eyes to the future and, working together in mutual trust, seek to accomplish the tasks that lie before us.'

NORWAY AND THE DEMOCRATIC TRADITION (1)

Norway, where I had been living since 1933, was not just a place of refuge for me. It became a second home. On that morning when Hitler's planes flew across the rooftops of Oslo, I felt it my natural duty to serve the just Norwegian cause with all my might. I was not making a stand against Germany, but against a régime which was devastating both Germany and Europe. Thus it was that my war years in Stockholm were spent working as a journalist and writer for the Norwegian cause.

I have never regarded the Norwegians' fight for freedom in isolation. What I was working towards was a free Norway and also a democratic Germany. When the hour of freedom struck for Norway, a new period of great hardship began for Germany. My decision to devote all my energies to the German homeland did not mean I had turned against Norway. Nothing had changed in my relationship to its people, my love for its landscape, or my affection for its mode of living.

What I have written draws upon these profound ties. Perhaps it will contribute to the removal of obstacles. Bound up with it is the awareness of all the things which have burdened the name of Germany with shame. Only when we are prepared to recognise the truth will we be able to interpret correctly the lessons which another people fighting for their own freedom in different circumstances offer us.

The means of overcoming the postwar crisis is not a retreat into nationalism but a consistent drive towards realistic forms of European and international co-operation. One of the most important prerequisites in this respect is that different peoples should come to learn more about one another.

That is why I hope this book will have brought the reader a little closer towards an understanding of the destiny of Norway. He should also know that democratic Scandinavia will be happy to co-operate with a democratic Germany to their mutual advantage.

The Norway which was invaded on 9 April 1940 was one of the oldest constitutional states. For centuries the principle had been firmly rooted there that the country should be built up on the rule of law and not destroyed by despotism. The constitution of 1814 was influenced by the American Declaration of Independence and the French Revolution, but had nonetheless grown up naturally on Norwegian soil. In it the law provided that no man should be sentenced outside the law nor be punished without due sentence having been passed. No retrospective legislation would be countenanced. The citizen was guaranteed freedom of expression. The civil code of 1857 was highly advanced. When the death sentence was abolished in 1905, no one had been executed for thirty years previously.

The sanctity of the law was one of the cornerstones of the state. Nothing angered the people more than the way justice and the law came to be flouted soon after the occupation began. Any serious attempt to discover the sources of energy behind the resistance cannot help but come to the conclusion that perhaps the most important single cause was the Norwegians' highly developed sense of justice.

But this factor cannot be isolated from that thread of freedom which runs throughout the country's entire history.

It is true that the Viking kingdom of medieval times was followed by impotence, national defeat, and four centuries of subservience to the throne of Denmark. But the urge towards freedom never faded. In the last century townspeople and peasants alike struggled for complete independence. It was secured in 1905 with the dissolution of the union with Sweden which had been entered into in 1814. The national character gained its unmistakable identity on the basis of geographical conditions and a firm stand aginst foreign influences. Nothing was able to deter them in their drive towards freedom and independence. Even the Gestapo could not break them.

They gained autonomy by peaceful means and their independence of Denmark and Sweden was one of the necessary conditions for renewed union with their Scandinavian neighbours on equal terms. When the Germans invaded, 125 years of peace came to an abrupt end. Modern Norway had no military tradition. Peace was the foundation of her material and cultural development.

Norwegian man had been fashioned in the struggle against the forces of nature. The country is somewhat larger than Great Britain, but three quarters of its land mass is rocky and infertile. After Iceland Norway has the world's most thinly distributed population with only twenty-three inhabitants per square mile. The distances are vast. It is as far from the most southerly to the northernmost point as it is from the southern tip of Norway to Rome. Including all its bays and fjords Norway has a coastline of 12,500 miles, which corresponds to about half the circumference of the earth. The winters are long, even though the climate is considerably less severe than in other countries on the same latitude.

The people had to work hard to wrest the necessities of life from land and sea. They did not have easily accessible and abundant natural resources at their disposal. The conditions of life in the extensive mountain areas criss-crossed by fjords demand an individualistic turn of mind. By 1940 a great deal had already been achieved in economic, social and cultural spheres.

At a round figure 800,000 people were dependent on agriculture and forestry for a living and the same number were in industry. Fishery was the means of livelihood of a further 200,000 inhabitants. The agricultural system, based as it was on low-acreage farms and smallholdings, was not in a position to provide for the needs of the whole population. With a catch of over a million tons a year—the highest in the world—the fishing industry had developed a valuable export outlet. Whaling, which the Norwegians had pioneered, was also of great importance. It was the merchant fleet that played the really decisive economic role—in the prewar years it was the fourth biggest and most modern in the world. The majority of the tonnage was engaged in international freight transport. This brought about a considerable balance of payments surplus.

Alongside agriculture, fishery and shipping, modern industries had grown up. These were in the main dependent on the exploitation of water power. In the last seven years before the war alone the exploitation of 'white coal' had risen by 50 per cent. But there were still many sources of untapped energy, as at the time only 14 per cent of the available energy was being exploited . . .

These industries afforded the population a comparatively high standard of living. It is true that even in Norway the work force had to fight hard to gain recognition, and also that some of the population were still living under far from satisfactory conditions. But there were fortunately no particularly acute contrasts between the classes. The standard of living rose through peaceful expansion and not on the basis of economic and socio-political measures. In many respects, social legislation was a model to other countries. Infant mortality was lower than in any other country. In the immediate prewar years—under the leadership of the Labour party which had come into office in 1935—much had been done to advance social equality.

Norwegian poets, musicians and painters were known throughout the world. Intellectual and artistic activity was evocatively indigenous in tone but never descended into complacency. There was a ready interchange of ideas with no need to fear international competition. Education had reached a relatively high standard. Mass education was broadly democratised and offered the majority of young people the opportunity of qualified vocational training.

It would be no exaggeration to maintain that in Norway democracy had very deep roots. In contrast to nearly all other European countries the peasant never lost his individual freedom in Norway. It was the agricultural workers themselves who had been the main creators of its modern democracy. Feudalism had played virtually no role at all in the history of this nation. The constitution which came into effect at the onset of the previous century was one of the most advanced of any country. Since 1837 local authorities had been autonomous. Women got the vote in 1913. The rule of the people was virtually free from class privilege.

The national character was an important factor, but it did not inhibit a wider international vision. Partly responsible for this was a long nautical tradition and also an early involvement in European trade. After the First World War the Norwegians placed great hopes in the League of Nations. Fridtjof Nansen was one of the great spokesmen of humanitarianism and conciliation. Norwegian families took in children of the starving Viennese. They gave spontaneous support to rescue operations for the suffering and oppressed—for example, to the Spanish republicans. The men of industry, the intellectuals and not least the modern socialist movement strove for international union and international collaboration . . . Those qualities to which I have referred to left their mark on the events of the years 1940–45. Norway had a great deal to defend.

INVASION AND THE QUISLINGS

The attack on Denmark and Norway was one of those 'crimes against peace' for which many leading Nazis were brought to justice in the Nuremberg trials of 1945–46. Keitel regarded the question of whether it was a matter of illegal aggression as a political issue which was none of his concern. Dönitz equally referred to the fact that it was the business of the political authorities and not the military command to draw the dividing line between wars of aggression and wars of defence. Jodl and Raeder held firmly to the view that the events of 9 April occurred because the British had forced Germany into protecting herself against their plans. Raeder maintained that he had received reports of British intentions in this area as early as the first month of the war.

The defence submitted French documents and also made reference to papers which in April 1940 had been taken from captured British officers in Lillehammer in Norway. There was also the matter of material which had been published even during the war in the form of a white paper and among other things contained references to 'Operation Stratforce', the British code word for the occupation of Norwegian bases. But unequivocal proof of Allied intentions had not been secured. In any event it was clear that the documents captured at the end of April and in June 1940 were hardly able to justify the measures taken by the Germans in the winter of 1939–40. It is quite another matter that we cannot arrive at the final historical explanation of the events leading up to 9 April as long as Allied secret archives remain closed.

The German official record of the war at sea has an entry under 13 January 1940 giving details of the 'Studie Nord'. It is based on the consideration that it would be intolerable to the Germans to allow Britain to gain a foothold in Norway, and that such a development could only be prevented by anticipating the British. Raeder projected—drawing on the same source—that Britain would take steps to cut off German imports from Norway and Sweden and to harass German operations in the North Sea and the Atlantic. He was also of the belief that the British government

would put pressure on Sweden not only to check her exports to
Germany but also to force her to come into the war against Germany. On 8 April, the official record states that the minefields should
be regarded as the first stage in the Allies' strategic plans.

On 26 April reference was made to the papers captured in Lillehammer and the conclusion drawn that the German action came
in the nick of time, just a few hours before England had planned
to put her operation into effect. But he was simply trying to justify
himself in retrospect.

It is worth noting a memorandum in the official record for 22
March to the effect that a massive British drive into Norwegian
waters was not an imminent possibility. Raeder's reaction in
Nuremberg was that this entry did not accord with his own views.
He was equally at odds with Admiral Assmann, the historian of the
German navy, who noted in his diary on 26 March that Raeder
had given a negative reply to Hitler's question as to whether the
danger of an British landing in Norway was acute. In this context
it is also worth noting the assessment Jodl made when he reported
on 7 November 1943 to the Reichsleiter and Gauleiter in Munich.
There he advanced the view that Denmark and Norway were in
no immediate danger in the early part of 1940. None the less there
was still cause to fear that Britain intended to establish herself in
Scandinavia in order to effect a strategic encirclement of Germany
from the north and to cut off the importation of the deliveries of
iron and nickel which were essential to German war industry.
Moreover the success of Germany's maritime interests was at
stake.

Jodl made reference both to Swedish iron ore and nickel imports
from Scandinavia. But it is not likely that the interests of the arma-
ments industry were decisive in the decision to invade. On the other
hand the German experts were naturally well aware that Norway
was the sole European producer of molybdenum and that her copper
production almost equalled Germany's. Her enormous fish harvest
was not to be taken lightly in view of the fat shortage in Germany.
As early as April 1940 war industry commanders were given the task
of exploiting to the full the vital industries of Norway and Denmark
and harnessing them to the German war potential. Exploitation of
current possibilities was not really put into effect until the German
dream of a short war came to an end. This clarifies the fact that in
the events leading up to 9 April strategic considerations were decisive.

The Nuremberg court then addressed itself to that part of the
verdict relating to the question of the German attitude, and firstly

to the treaties which had been concluded between Germany and
Norway and with Denmark. In addition to specific agreements,
the member states were bound by the Briand-Kellogg pact of 1928
which specifically outlawed wars of aggression. All these treaties and
promises were broken after Hitler came to power. The claim that
Germany was compelled to forestall an Allied invasion was not
acknowledged by the tribunal, which considered a preventative
offensive to be admissible under international law only when no
other possible course of action presented itself in the interests of
self-defence and negotiation was impossible at the time.

In the judgement of Nuremberg it was not denied that an Allied
invasion was considered likely in leading German circles. But the
court came to the conclusion that the German attack did not take
place in order to anticipate impending Allied operations but in the
first instance to render impossible any subsequent Allied occupation.
The German plans, which aimed at the exploitation of Scandinavian
bases for a more effective combating of the western powers, had
been worked out long before the Allied plans which had been used
in retrospective justification of the German action. The undertaking
given on 9 April 1940 that Danish and Norwegian territory would not
be used for aggressive operations was equally broken. Taking all
the evidence into account—which, although not exhaustive, was
none the less comprehensive—the conclusion was reached that the
invasion of Denmark and Norway could not be considered a defensive
measure. It was an act of aggression in defiance of international
law.

After 9 April 1940 articles appeared in the international press
representing the German invasion as a victory of the 'fifth column'.
Such reports were exaggerated out of all proportion. Norway gained
the dubious honour of enriching the international vocabulary with the
'Quisling' concept. But it was unjustly stigmatised as a country
riddled with Nazism.

What can be said is that the Nazis thoroughly prepared the ground
in all those countries selected as targets of attack. It was true to the
character of the Second World War that it was not a matter of
purely 'national' front lines, but that Hitler was at the head of an
international Fascist movement. In Norway as elsewhere there were
groups sympathetic to Nazism which were baited with a mixture of
pan-Germanic fanaticism and anti-Bolshevist slogans and harnessed
to the German cart. And these apart, all manner of dubious personalities came along after the invasion making friendly noises to the
new authorities. But the idea that Norway was riddled with traitors
who handed the country over on a plate is far from the truth.

There were some traitors among the Norwegian officers, but by comparison far fewer than there were in France around 1940. Many of them lost their nerve, others proved to be of no use. Many people distinguished themselves by creditable conduct in a situation which on the face of it was hopeless. The condition of the defence as a whole naturally could not help but leave its mark on the officer corps. And an officer corps which had been neglected, undervalued and untried was no basis for a force of international standing.

Major Quisling played a decisive part in the preparations leading up to Hitler's operation. It has been proved that at least from the beginning of 1940 his party was receiving considerable financial support from Berlin. The Norwegian Nazi leader had transmitted precise proposals to the German authorities and had laid the chief emphasis in his advice on a swift occupation of Oslo in order to put the palace and government out of action. He warned against an assault on the inner Oslo fjord and recommended that the main emphasis be placed on airborne and seaborne landings on both banks of the outer fjord. Later he pointed out that the German action would have been far more successful if his advice had been followed more closely. He claimed that the evacuation of the government would probably have been rendered impossible if the airborne landing on the Gardermoen drill-ground—on the Oslo to Hamar road—had taken place in accordance with his recommendations.

German-trained Quislings were to be transported to Norway in colliers to make an attack which had been agreed with Rosenberg in the first instance, but this did not materialise either. Nor did Quisling receive an exact date for the commencement of the German operation. Still, he was not so obtuse that the announcements of 8 April did not enable him to put two and two together. On the evening of that day he took up quarters in one of the big Oslo hotels from which he directed operations with his crony Hagelin and chief administrator Scheidt. When the invasion troops had marched into Oslo, Quisling took himself off to the Ministry of Defence in a German military vehicle and ordered the chief of police in Elverum to arrest the King and the government.

At half past seven in the evening he appeared with Scheidt in the radio station building to deliver the proclamation in which he announced he was 'forming a government' and revoking the order of general mobilisation.

Quisling maintained that Germany had come to the aid of Norway. The government of Nygaardsvold had resigned and he had now taken power. This Putsch-type self-appointment came as a surprise

both to the German Ambassador and to Falkenhorst. But Quisling
was able to count on Hitler's support. Dr. Bräuer held long telephone
conversations, first with Ribbentrop, then with Hitler. The Ambassador, now the chief executive officer of the Reich, requested the
dismissal of the Norwegian Nazi chief. But it was made clear to him
that Quisling enjoyed Hitler's unqualified support. Thus the sub-
stance of the next day's conference with the king was established.
But thereby the German leaders committed one of their crudest
political blunders. The Quisling affair even more than the surprise
invasion itself was responsible for sparking off resistance by the
Norwegian population.

Quisling had once been an officer on active service. He collaborated with Fridtjof Nansen in the rescue operations in Russia after
the First World War and even before then had shown evidence of
considerable ability. But he soon revealed his true identity as a
political power-grabber and daydreamer. He started by making
overtures to the extreme left and when they rejected him he later
took command of a Fascist organisation. In 1931 the Agrarian party
appointed him as Miniser of Defence to their government which fell
at the beginning of 1933. During this period he became implicated
in various provocative actions. When Hitler came to power in 1933
he decided the time was ripe for establishing his 'Nasjonal Samling'
(National Assembly).

In the Storting elections in the autumn of 1933 the Quisling party
had to content itself with a mere 28,000 votes, that is, something
over 2 per cent of the total. None of its candidates entered parliament. In the Storting elections held in 1936—the last before the
occupation—they did not fare any better; 26,000 votes, under 2
per cent of the total, and again no mandate. The National Socialist
candidates slumped even more disastrously in the local elections of
1937. The membership in 1935 totalled 15,000. In 1940 it must
certainly have been far smaller. Many of Quisling's original supporters had turned their backs on him. Only a few country people, some
desperate members of the middle class and a number of sixth
formers remained with him.

9 April brought a new defeat. Quisling was then unmasked before
the whole nation as an agent of Hitler and a traitor to his country.
The emergency committee set up by the Oslo city council informed
the German High Command that they had no intention of co-
operating with the régime that had seized power.

Administrative chaos threatened in the occupied zone. This
worried German officials in Oslo. The High Command did not

welcome such a development either. They were delighted a few days later when the opportunity arose for getting rid of the Quisling régime.

RESISTANCE AND THE 'HOME FRONT'

The occupation had taken the Norwegians by surprise. Their democratic heritage and parliamentary tradition, their directness and trusting nature were scarcely a good grounding for the conditions of underground national resistance. In the conflict with a blindly ruthless and viciously cowardly enemy they at first suffered one shock after another. Only a few recognised the real aims and intentions of the enemy.

One lesson was learnt all too soon, namely, that internal differences had to be laid aside to allow a united front to serve the common interest. This was less of a problem in Norway than in other occupied countries. Norwegian democracy certainly had its imperfections, but it was a vital force and almost the entire population deemed it a cause worth fighting for. The reality of foreign rule did not of course eliminate social differences and class divisions. But from the outset these were far less important than in most countries. And the occupation lessened rather than heightened them. The workers did not regard themselves as social outsiders. They had gained a considerable voice in public affairs. The government had risen from their ranks. But it is true that in Norway, as in almost all other countries, the people and the popular movement had learnt surprisingly and frighteningly little from the experiences of other nations and their movements. Most lessons have to be learned anew—often at great cost—on home ground. However it was clear to all educated and enlightened workers that Nazism was their arch enemy on two counts : both nationally and socially.

In Norway, the property-owning classes also respected the rules of the political game of democracy. Unlike the privileged classes in many other countries, they did not betray their homeland. For the majority of Norwegian shipowners and directors the national interest outweighed class considerations. Thus the way was paved for others to recognise that self-interest and the national interest were intimately bound up with the victory of the western powers. Norway was also fortunate in having at her disposal an intelligentsia which for the most part was progressive and democratic rather than reactionary. The schoolteachers had for many years formed the backbone of the Liberal party in the country. The influence of socialism was strong among young intellectuals.

The social conditions were favourable for a broadly based anti-Nazi front. Terboven had forbidden the affiliation of the parties which was to have taken place in August 1940 with the support of the trade unions. After the parties were disbanded, a form of collaboration came into being which was soon dubbed the 'home front'. No centralised authority in any one place had called for its formation. The home front grew from the smallest beginnings—spontaneous demonstrations against the provocative behaviour of the Nazis; small groups publishing all manner of underground writings; committees which worked out policies to counter Nazi measures designed to crush the opposition—into a truly national movement. In this popular front previous party allegiances were forgotten. This did not mean that personal convictions were abandoned and swallowed up in an amorphous mass, but rather voluntary submission to the greater common interest. Of course groups of a party political character continued to exist. But the home front as such was not based on a coalition of the parties. It was an alliance on an altogether higher plane. The position of the Communists in the underground movement was exceptional, characterised by their sharper lines of political demarcation, and they developed on their own lines alongside the rest of the home front, as a result of the differences of opinion which came into the open during the first months of the occupation and the persistent atmosphere of mutual distrust.

In the course of the first winter a circle of leading personalities from many parties was already taking shape and gradually became the *de facto* leadership of the home front, but it did not make an open claim to leadership until the beginning of 1944. As has already been mentioned, the President of the High Court was a member of this circle; so too was Einar Gerhardsen, chairman of the Labour party and mayor of Oslo, who had been stripped of both offices by the Nazis. Other members included the bishop of Oslo, trade union leaders, high-ranking civil servants, a young law student and many others. Since the national resistance movement drew largely on the various professions, this was equally reflected in the composition of the leading circle, and above all in the 'co-ordinating committee', which worked with it and directed day-to-day activities. In parallel with the Oslo organisation, committees sprang up all over the country which were given the task of ensuring that the various branches of the resistance movement worked in harmony.

In spite of the illegality of the organisation, mass protests signed in full also played an important part in the national resistance. Such movements however had to be guided along the right lines in order to achieve the desired united front. A further task was the encouragement of the underground press and ironing out differences of opinion. The central group in Oslo published a 'bulletin' in a strictly limited edition, acting as a news source for the underground press which at the time produced around 200 publications. These often left much to be desired technically, but were mostly editorially sound; they achieved high circulation figures, and one copy would pass through many hands. The secret press was extremely influential. This was particularly the case in August 1941 when radio sets were confiscated from all Norwegians with the exception of the Quislings. From then on daily bulletins giving the main stories of the radio news from London were produced in many places, circulated in factories and offices and constituted an invaluable supplement to the 'newspapers' which were for the most part only produced weekly. Throughout the whole duration of the occupation the population kept itself remarkably well informed about events at home and abroad, although of course a large number of misapprehensions and misinterpretations were inevitable.

One of the further tasks of the central organisation was raising capital for underground activities and supporting those families deprived of food and income by the Gestapo. Large sums were collected by voluntary contribution in Norway itself. Gradually substantial sums found their way into the country from the Norwegian government in exile, principally via the Stockholm embassy, which maintained an underground courier service across the frontier. There was constant contact and exchange of views between the leadership of the home front and London. The government operated on the sound principle that the resistance must be allowed to evolve and develop according to its own pattern inside Norway itself. As a rule they contented themselves with an advisory role. In addition, they took the counsel of the leading bodies in Norway in broader policy decisions concerning foreign relations . . .

The comradely collaboration between members of different political organisations and social classes could not help but stimulate romantic illusions about the possibility of a long-term preservation of the unity which had been achieved during the occupation. But it did lead to the breaking down of out-moded barriers and resulted in broadening the outlook of groups in the community which up to now had been isolated. Furthermore, the mobilisation of the energies of the people resulted in social groups which had previously been apolitical taking a lively interest in working with others in shaping public affairs. This applied, for example, to the doctors, engineers and members of other professions who had for the most part refrained from engaging in political discussion and party activity before the war. It can also be demonstrated that a large number of active workers in the underground movement were recruited from the ranks of white-collar workers in both the private and public sectors.

Understandably the new circumstances caused old members of the establishment to fade away, to be replaced by new forces, hitherto unable to gain respectability in public life, which now came into prominence and frequently developed sound qualities of leadership. But it is characteristic of the developments in Norway that this process took place without sharp divisions of opinion and along broadly evolutionary lines.

Nazi occupation

The forms in which the resistance developed in the first years of the occupation were an expression of local conditions. Among these should be numbered a considerably milder German policy than in other Hitler-occupied countries. Norway was not in the limelight of military activity. This fact influenced the conduct of both the population and the occupying power. However, one of the prime considerations for German policy was the insane notion of certain of their leaders that on 'racial' grounds the Norwegians should be expected to demonstrate particular sympathy for Nazi philosophy.

But it was this very attempt to win them over from within that triggered off the resolute and broadly-based resistance of the Norwegians. The conditions were clearly unfavourable to an all-out military attack. It was those measures taken to suppress opposition together with the policy of the Quislings which induced that movement initiated by spontaneous protests and declarations of rights and freedom by groups which at first were quite small but were soon to broaden out into a truly popular movement. The internal readiness to defend, the resolution with which, for example, the fight for the schools began was only possible among a people in whom democratic traditions were firmly established. The militancy of Norwegian democracy, which manifested itself in the most varied ways, formed a contrast to that lack of individual responsibility and moral cowardice which had grown up under Fascism. If you take freedom seriously —this was Norway's message to the world—don't defend it with material might alone, but with spiritual strength above all. It goes without saying that the Nazi war machine could only be destroyed by a powerful and co-ordinated military onslaught. Fascism must have its social foundations swept away by means of a process of social breakdown. However, the blight of amorality can only be cured when justice is set against despotism, freedom against tyranny, faith based on knowledge against the political catchword, personal responsibility against the Führer principle—and then only when you stand firm for the alternatives you have established.

The Norwegian resistance does not however present a picture of a single clear line of heroic decisions. Around 9 April 1940 some confusion became evident. In the summer of 1940 quite a substantial number of the population were prepared to capitulate, and later too a certain lack of resolve made itself felt. Favourable objective conditions assisted the Norwegian people in overcoming their confusion and lack of resolution. But it was their deeply rooted sense of justice and love of freedom which were chiefly responsible for their ability to maintain a tenacious resistance. The resistance was borne along by their passion for justice, which cannot of course win wars unaided, but without which it is all too easy to fall into the danger of being incapable of ending a war on the same terms as it was conducted.

Moral integrity distinguished those men and women who stood at the head of the unarmed struggle. Their strength did not lie in the purely political sphere. It demanded much painful effort to acquire the necessary experience of underground operations. From time to time the decisions they took sorely tested the patience of active fighting groups. They made allowances for this, for they were concerned with the support of the overwhelming majority of the population and the prevention of a split into a small activist advance guard and an indifferent majority. This was indeed avoided. The defence of the constitution and international law was not just the concern of the High Court; the survival or loss of academic freedom was not simply a matter for the professors; attacks on the school system did not affect only the teachers. Questions such as these influenced the destiny of the Norwegian people as a whole.

After attempts at suppressing opposition and setting up a new political order had petered out in a succession of failures, a change of direction became noticeable in 1943. The nazification plans faded into the background. This was partly due to the Norwegian resistance. And for the rest it was due to the fact that the military and war economy aspects of German policy towards Norway came increasingly into the open. An overall evaluation of the state of the war caused the Norwegians too to reassess the direction of their efforts. They continued to defend the basic principles of justice and freedom of opinion, but from 1943–44 military factors began to play an increasingly dominant role. In accordance with the Allied High Command (SHAEF) strategy there was a movement away from the concept of general guerilla warfare, which under the conditions obtaining in Norway seemed unlikely to achieve anything, and instead a concentration on getting all available forces into a state of readiness for the final struggle which now seemed imminent.

The nations under the yoke of Nazi Germany were subjected to a twofold occupation. It was not simply a matter of a military invasion. Characteristically for a totalitarian régime there was also the ever-present police and political government machine.

The number of German troops in Norway rose steeply from the approximately 100,000 men who had been brought in during the 1940 campaign to more than a quarter of a million. But it did not stop at that. By August 1943 the army had 380,000 troops in Norway. This was more than one tenth of the total Norwegian population. And along with them came hordes of police, administrators, technicians, etc. In the Oslo central command more German was spoken than Norwegian. In Kirkenes the local inhabitants shrank to a tiny minority of the total population. The mere presence of so many foreign troops was a severe enough burden on the people. The demands issued by the occupying power, the requisitioning of home and school accommodation, of food and workers, woollen blankets, shoes and many other goods were repeated reminders of the fact of foreign control and created revulsion and a mood of rebellion.

It is a fact repeatedly confirmed from reliable Norwegian sources that German soldiers were well disciplined at the beginning of the occupation and for the most part thereafter. On the other hand it is equally a fact that every occupation involves infringement of liberty and arbitrary actions and puts not only the occupied, but also the occupiers at risk. This latter danger was particularly severe in the case of the Germans, as Nazism was largely Prussian militarism taken to its logical conclusion. Particularly at the time of their apparent great victory most of the soldiers conducted themselves towards the Norwegians with a particularly inappropriate arrogance. But it should be recognised that individual acts of violence on the part of members of the armed forces in Norway were untypical of the situation as a whole. On the Norwegian side, however, the population, regardless of the relatively disciplined behaviour of the occupation troops, took the view that all Germans should be 'cut' and condemned to social isolation. Many Norwegians were

naturally aware that there were Germans unsympathetic towards
the Hitler régime. But there was neither the time nor the inclination
to test the true feelings of the man wearing the uniform. In the
situation as it existed all men in Hitler's uniform were regarded as
enemies of Norway. No one wanted any truck with them. They were
only addressed when official circumstances rendered it unavoidable.
But this hard line was not adhered to everywhere. In the countryside in particular there were all manner of individual contacts.
Some Norwegian women even defied the general boycott to enter
relationships with German soldiers and thereby attracted the hatred
of their fellow countrymen. Of course a distinction should be drawn
between 'regular' relationships and prostitution, which occurs in
every occupied country. This apart, it should be noted that the
boycott cut both ways, because the discipline of the occupation forces was not relaxed, and as a result the men
were frequently obliged to consort with 'undesirable' elements of the
population.

Most German officers in Norway behaved in a correct, and at
times even decent and humane, manner. But there were more than
enough representatives of the arrogance and brutality of Hitler's
Prussian-based Germany. To these men and to the party bosses as
well the Norwegians were merely 'those laughable three million
people'. The life of the civilian was no more a bed of roses in Norway
than anywhere else.

The Norwegians' main feeling towards the Germans can be expressed in the hope that they should speedily disappear whence
they came . . .

When the national resistance intensified, purpose-trained guerilla
groups made attacks on military targets. Even at this point there
were only isolated serious engagements with Nazi army units. Only
an invasion from the west or all-out military conflict would have
wrought a fundamental change in the situation. In the meantime
however it was the police and political machine of the foreign
power which particularly roused the repugnance and hatred of the
population and against which their resistance was principally
directed.

Shortly after the invasion in April 1940 German police divisions
came into Norway. This involved units of the riot police, security
police, SS guards and—dominating all else—the SD. In Norway as
elsewhere they were all grouped together under the general title of
Gestapo. The basic Gestapo unit destined for the Norwegian sector—
200 men originally—mustered on the orders of Heydrich in Pretzsch
an der Elbe and arrived in Oslo on 29 April. They swiftly developed

into an organisation with more employees than all other departments of the Reich commissariat put together. At first they made a considerable effort to behave with some discretion, and were as a result 'softer' than in France and Holland, let alone Poland. Norway was in quite a different category as far as the techniques of Nazi domination were concerned. But in essence the Norwegian experience was the same as everywhere else where the Gestapo reigned supreme. Their concept of 'justice' was summary trial, their normal method terror. Arrest of hostages, collective punishments and torture marked their passing.

The civil administration which had been brought into the Reich commissariat did its work partly under Gestapo protection, partly under internal pressure from them. Among these civil servants numbered several respectable businessmen. But most of the important posts were occupied by SS men who combined incompetence and ignorance with arrogance and fanaticism. Their work complemented the Gestapo reign of terror. The Reich commissar's policy of national castration, the activities of the Quislings controlled by the special 'assault group' of the Nazi party, and finally the industrial harnessing of the occupied country to the ends of Hitler's war were all various manifestations of Gestapo tyranny in Norway. It is hardly the fault of the Norwegians that at that time the words 'Germany' and 'Gestapo' became virtually synonymous.

On the other side of the coin there were Germans in the army and civil administration who risked all to avoid or at least to minimise brutality and injustice. In case after case soldiers, officers and officials felt themselves impelled to offer assistance to the Norwegians in their fight for freedom. Those who acted thus were far from being traitors, for they knew that the Hitler régime had to die so that Germany and Europe might live. But the initiative of individuals, spurred on by their conscience, which had to be kept a close secret during the war and scarcely found mention when peace came, was still incapable of changing the attitude of the Norwegians to 'the Germans' . . .

A few days before the edict of 25 September 1940, General von Falkenhorst summoned his chiefs of staff to Oslo, where Terboven briefed them on the political situation. Falkenhorst took this opportunity to remind them that soldiers must obey orders, and that it was their sacred duty to submit to the will of the Führer. And this situation continued as it began. Relations between the Reich commissar and the Chief of the 21st army were strained. Falkenhorst was no party man. But he was a died-in-the-wool proponent of Prussian militarism and an unquestioning 'yes-man' even when it came to breaches of international law.

This was clearly illustrated by the commando murders. In October 1942 the order was issued from Hitler's headquarters signed by Keitel and drafted by Jodl to the effect that Allied commandos and parachutists should be shot even when in uniform. 'Participants in commando raids are to be killed to the last man', was the wording of the equivalent edict issued by the Reich security office. Falkenhorst passed this order down the line and put it into effect on innumerable occasions. For this he was brought before an English military court in the summer of 1946 and given a sentence of death which was subsequently commuted to a long term of imprisonment because of extenuating circumstances. The 'Führer's command' was also thoroughly examined in the Nuremberg trial against Göring and his henchmen.

Many instances were cited there in which uniformed Norwegian and English sailors were tried and then handed over to the SD by the responsible admiral. Logic demanded that Raeder and Dönitz as well as Keitel and Jodl should be held responsible for this death decree.

Former Admiral of the Fleet Raeder referred to the fact that many leaders had pleaded for decent and humane treatment of the Norwegian population. It was in fact the case that Raeder had indeed made use of Quislings but was a sharply contrasting figure to Terboven. The same applied to the navy chief in Norway, Admiral of the Fleet Böhm who was replaced by Admiral Ciliax in 1943. Terboven won that battle. He made certain that Böhm and the corvette captain Schreiber were sent out of Norway. The navy had tried to convince Hitler that it would be a wise course of action to withdraw Terboven and his crowd. Nothing came of that.

If it is borne in mind how the big men in the forces reacted to the Norwegian situation in 1944, it would be difficult to find any real difference between them and the party or Gestapo chiefs. Because of dock sabotage in Denmark and Norway, Dönitz had recommended a substantial hardening of German policy towards these countries. He also supported the 'concentration' and collective punishment of Scandinavian dockworkers. On the same occasion Keitel expressed the view that the best course of action would be to give Terboven authority to allow 'more executions' to take place.

It should equally not be forgotten that it was Keitel who had signed the notorious Night and Fog decree[2] of December 1941. As a result of this decree hundreds of Norwegian patriots—alongside tens and hundreds of thousands in other countries—were deported to

German extermination camps without their families even receiving information regarding their whereabouts. Regrettably, others followed Keitel's example. In Norway as in other occupied countries the name of Germany was dragged in the mud by senseless excesses and mindless brutality.

Nikolaus von Falkenhorst was regarded in many quarters as a supporter of the German opposition. This was not true. He was a typical representative of the type of officer who would occasionally make an individual stand but never plucked up enough courage to come out openly against Nazi crimes. When German difficulties were on the increase and resistance became more pronounced, Falkenhorst was even prepared to recognise Quisling, which he had up to then refused to do. After the abortive attempt on Hitler's life in July 1944 he was the first army chief to reaffirm his loyalty in true subordinate fashion. A fortnight later he and Terboven were speakers at a propaganda rally where he swore allegiance to Hitler and concluded from an 'analysis' of the military situation that there was no doubt that Germany would win the war.

If the uprising against Hitler had proved successful, Falkenhorst would doubtless have come trotting along at the heels of the new régime. After he had been taken prisoner by the Allies he condemned the Nazis as criminals. In his speech on 6 August 1944 and on other occasions Falkenhorst had given voice to his supposed 'anti-Nazism' by proclaiming that the fortress of Norway must be defended to the last round of ammunition. When things got bad the High Command did not regard Falkenhorst as fit for the task of taking command of the fight for Norway. In December 1944 he was recalled to the 'Führer's reserve' and replaced by Rendulic. Rendulic let himself be known through the Norwegian press as a particularly warm admirer of Norwegian culture. But in the same month he was transferred to the eastern front after Hitler had awarded him the Knight Cross with oak leaves and crossed swords for his 'successful withdrawal' in the north. So the last German commander-in-chief was General Böhme, who had entered Norway with the Lapp army.

When the invasion by the western Allies had resulted in a catastrophic deterioration in the German military situation, the question arose whether the German High Command would come to the conclusion that Norway should be given up. Eisenhower reckoned on this being a possibility. And it was actually the case that Norway was now virtually useless as a base from which surprise attacks could be led. Twenty divisions which were urgently required on the main

battle fronts were stationed in Norway. Still the military economists
took the view that under no circumstances was it practicable to give
up the Norwegian supply lines. The naval command clung on to the
illusion that they could continue to operate using Norway as a base
since the fleet had virtually no ports left on the continent. The transport specialists demonstrated that a complete evacuation from Norway was an impossibility. The men in the Reich commissariat and
Gestapo had a vested interest in proving that they were indispens-
able where they were. For Hitler's prestige strategies the surrender
of Norway was out of the question.

After the 20th mountain force had crossed from Finland and
joined up with the 21st army, several divisions were taken via Denmark back to Germany. Norwegian saboteurs and the Allied air and
sea strike forces made attacks against this transfer operation. But the
21st army was not substantially reduced in numbers. In spite of the
transfers it remained stronger than before the Finnish change of
front . . .

NAZI WITHDRAWAL

At the beginning of 1945 fantastic rumours were flying around
about a 'decisive big offensive' which was to be set in motion not
only against England but the American eastern seaboard as well, with
the help of U-boats and a new kind of flying bomb. It was a fact that
around this time large numbers of U-boats were gathering in Norway
and that an order of the day early in 1945 had stated that a new
weapon was shortly to be brought into service and that bases in
southern Norway would be required for its use.

At the end of January 1945 Terboven was summoned back to
Hitler, who reprimanded him severely for the escalating sabotage. In
autumn 1944—after the sinking of the transport *Westfalen* off the
Swedish coast, in which fifty Norwegian political prisoners who were
on board lost their lives—Falkenhorst and his subordinates had
attempted to put a stop to harsher measures against the activities
of patriots. And indeed an order was sent from Berlin to the Reich
commissariat that no further sentences of death should be carried
out and, secondly, that the deportation of Norwegian prisoners
should cease. But now Hitler was demanding renewed 'drastic
measures'.

Quisling was with Hitler at that time. He learned from him about
the 'favourable' military situation. Hitler let it slip that he had a
terrible secret weapon at his disposal. He said that he prayed God
would spare him the last days of the war. Quisling alluded to the

danger which in his view was threatening from Sweden. Hitler's reply was that if Sweden struck, Stockholm, Gothenburg and Malmö would be in ruins the next day.

Hitler's confidence in his Norwegian favourite was no longer unshakable. In 1944 he had stated after an interview with Quisling, 'You have to keep pumping these rubber pigs up, otherwise they'll collapse'. However, he did not refuse Quisling the 10,000 machine pistols he had requested for the Hird. But Böhme torpedoed their delivery. That apart, Quisling came back from his last visit to Hitler with the pledge that after the war Norway would rise up once more 'in complete freedom and independence'. A few months previously, Quisling Ministers had again broached the peace question in a letter to the 'Führer' and sought his assurance that there had never been any conflict between Germany and Norway.

Terboven was not averse to making such a manoeuvre. But in Hitler's headquarters there was a complete lack of interest in the idea.

A mood of peace was already prevailing in Oslo on 29 April when Himmler's offer to the western powers became known. On the following day the leaders of the home front released a proclamation in which they expressed the view that a complete German capitulation was becoming much more of a probability. For this reason precipitate action should not be allowed to prejudice an orderly cessation of hostilities. There should be no provocation of Germans or Nazi party members. The watchwords were to be : calm, dignity and discipline.

On 3 May a new proclamation was issued by the home front. It warned in the strongest terms against acts of provocation. It had come to their attention that there were forces at work on the German side which were opposed to a disciplined capitulation and sought to stimulate disorders. And such elements were also naturally to be found among the ranks of the Quislings.

But Quisling himself had realised that the game was up. His followers retreated to their earlier 'national' position. On 29 April Quisling made a statement to his Ministers in which he stressed that Norway was neutral and should not be permitted to become a theatre of war. At the same time he reminded them that the Quisling régime was the sole de facto and 'legal' government of the country. But the Ministers all vacated their posts. There was a desperate attempt at forming a caretaker government on a broader basis which was doomed to failure from the outset.

Publication of Quisling's declaration was forbidden. The German leadership had troubles of its own without permitting itself to be publicly disavowed. The Hird organisation was placed under army orders. This was an expression of the shift of power from the Reich commissariat to the High Command. At the beginning of the year Rendulic had already put a physical distance between them by moving his headquarters to Lillehammer.

At the end of April the main organs of the Quisling press took on a conciliatory tone. Articles appeared to the effect that civil war should be avoided at all costs. The 'national government' should admit that it has achieved none of the aims it had set itself. Now we must call upon the united efforts of all Norwegians both inside and outside the country. But the home front did not let itself be deceived by these conciliatory noises. The home army did break off its acts of military sabotage. But in an attack on 3 May they seized the records of the Nazi Ministries of Police and Justice and thus took possession of a comprehensive body of evidence against the Nazis.

Quisling broadcast from Oslo radio on 5 May. By now the capitulation in Denmark had taken place and Terboven had offered him the chance of escape to Spain. There is no evidence of the seriousness of this offer. At any rate Quisling remained in Oslo and in his broadcast enlarged on the ability of the united efforts of all men of good will to preserve Norway from the curse of civil war. The Norwegians were impressed neither by Terboven's supposed offer nor by Quisling's shabby attempt to justify himself. When a Quisling delegation appeared at the Swedish frontier on the following day to hold talks with representatives of the home front and the government, they were turned away. The Quislings were bent on saving their skins and 'nationally' discharging themselves from office. But the Norwegians had no reason to enter into any discussions with them.

The decision lay in the hands of the German military. The home front was prepared to accept the great self-sacrifice which a fight to the end would have cost them. But they naturally found disengagement without military conflict far preferable. For this reason they repeated their appeal for calm, dignity and discipline, a challenge which the population accepted in a most commendable fashion.

The terms for surrender which General Böhme had to sign on 8 May in Lillehammer contained a paragraph to the effect that all members of the Gestapo and SS—in addition to war criminals from the ranks of the army—were to be delivered over to the Allies. At first Böhme protested against this condition by referring to its possibly deleterious effect on the discipline of his troops.

But the Allies were not to be shaken in their demands. Members of the Gestapo were duly arrested as planned. This was no simple matter, as the SD and SS almost to a man disguised themselves as troops of the regular army and made use of false papers which had been prepared for such an eventuality. At first the possibility had to be reckoned with that these elements might still make final desperate attempts at resistance. But it did not come to that. The hard-core Nazis were thoroughly demoralised. As parts of a vast machine of mass murder they were both dangerous and effective. But when the machine broke down each of its components failed as well.

Terboven and Rediess made no appeals for resistance. Even flight seemed pointless to them and so they resolved to commit suicide on the day of the surrender. Rediess lost patience before the appointed date and put a bullet through his head. Terboven had the body carted off to his bunker where he blew himself up on the evening of 8 May.

Other Nazi bosses followed their example. SD chief Fehlis took his own life after the Norwegians had found him in a German camp and demanded that he be handed over . . .

Typical in the behaviour of the Nazis was their cowardice and moral degeneracy. There was nothing left of that heroism which the Nazis had held forth about, whilst thousands who fought them bore silent witness to true heroism under the most terrible conditions. Hardly a man among them was prepared to stand by his actions; they all claimed they were the innocent tools of those set in authority over them. Denunciation was rife. Many of the Gestapo were handed over by their own comrades in arms. This process of collapse had been set in train even before the surrender date and one Nazi had actually gone so far as to let it be known to the Norwegians that he was ready to put the noose round the necks of others as long as his own life was guaranteed.

The process of disarming German forces began with the takeover of air bases, heavy weapons, fortifications and navy vessels. At this time there were around a hundred U-boats in Norwegian harbours. After the troops had been concentrated in the areas designated to them they were ordered to deposit weapons and materials with the exception of reserves so that the Allies could take them over. Apart from a few minor disturbances the 21st army was taken prisoner and disarmed according to plan . . .

Initially conditions among the German reserves were tolerated by Allied officials which should have been impossible after a military victory over Nazism. The reason for this cautious approach was probably mainly attributable to a desire to avoid disturbances in the camps and for this reason the previous disciplinary pattern was widely adhered to. With the exception of military raids carried out with occasional brutality, not one hair of the prisoners' heads was harmed. A proportion of the prisoners were employed in clearing-up operations and other tasks—as for example rendering harmless the $1\frac{1}{2}$ million German landmines.

Naturally the Norwegians were delighted when the German troops were transported away and they lost no sleep over the officials of the occupying power. Still, the attitude of the Norwegians to the German question was comparatively moderate and not inflexible. This was particularly true of the many active members of the resistance movement and those who returned from the concentration camps. They had first hand experience of the worst side of Nazi Germany, but they were equally aware that the recent policy which sought to tar all Germans with the Nazi brush was based on mere fantasy. The Norwegians could hardly be expected to be favourably disposed towards Germany. But the majority were not inclined to prevent a new, free and peace-loving Germany from being given a chance, and they refrained from that narrow chauvinism which itself is allied to Nazism and irreconcilable with the peaceful aims of a democratic society.

In their fight for freedom between the years 1940–45 the Norwegians suffered 10,000 casualties : more than 1,000 who died resisting the invasion, over 4,000 seamen, approaching 1,600 killed in concentration camps, 600 sentenced to death in Norway itself, over 700 sailors, 300 airmen and others who fell on the 'extra-territorial front', and in addition members of the civilian population who died as a result of military operations. Ten thousand human lives are a great deal for a small nation to lose, especially when it has not experienced a war for many generations.

The country had been stripped bare, goods and services totalling many millions had been extorted by the occupying power, and the means of production crippled. Years of effort would be required to make good the damage.

And statistics are incapable of evaluating the destruction of so much human happiness in Norway—and in all the other occupied countries. But it is none the less true to say that next to Denmark, Norway of all the occupied territories came off most lightly. It cannot stand up against those countries who suffered the most severely. But it can hold its head high as far as its achievements are concerned.

Yet it remains untrue—even in the case of Norway—that war ennobles. It was necessary to halt the onrush of the Nazis in order to make possible renewed enlightened progress in a state of freedom. But war has always been and remains a terrible, destructive and brutalising thing. Even those fighting the cause of human advancement and freedom are unable to escape its demoralising effects. Despite the soundest of principles and intentions they are ever in danger of falling to the lower level—in the last war, of being tainted by the Nazi mentality.

This aspect of war must be weighed against the obvious temptation to glorification, although the broad mass of Norwegians were well able to brush aside such dangers. There is another aspect too, namely, that a fight for freedom is actually capable of releasing positive forces. This is evidenced by the Norwegian resistance and their rapid postwar reconstruction. In this sense, despite all the deprivation and misery, the Norwegians came out the richer for the war.

In the Second World War Norway was not fighting for material gain. She fought for the right to exist, for freedom and independence. Naturally, the liberation itself was dependent on the course of events in the main theatres of war.

Hitler's Reich had to be smashed by the eastern and western strike forces before the occupied and subject nations could regain their liberty. But the Norwegians can point out that the assistance they were given was by no means out of all proportion to the contribution they themselves made.

Liberation did not simply mean a return to things as they were before the war. Although there was no question of a violent upheaval in the social order, those forces which after the overpowering of Fascism demanded a consolidation and enlargement of democracy had been considerably strengthened. There was strong pressure to broaden the scope of democratic principles outwards from the political to the economic and social spheres. It was in this spirit and on a basis of national solidarity that the new tasks before them were confronted.

The foreign policy line developed during the war was continued after the liberation. Trygve Lie was called to the United Nations at the beginning of 1946 to become General Secretary. His successor as Norwegian Foreign Minister, Halvard M. Lange, stressed emphatically that there was no question of a choice between east and west for Norway. Peace and the future of the nation depended on success in stabilising international co-operation within the framework of the

United Nations. But it was emphasised from the outset that there was no such thing as neutrality in matters of freedom and democracy. As a necessary result a clear stand was taken against the renewed dangers of totalitarianism.

Norwegian justice and the Norwegian constitutional state remained true to their lights. Production workers in industry and on the land, fishermen and sailors, technologists and intellectuals—all were resolved to build up their country in peace and to live in solidarity with other nations.

NORWAY IN NUREMBERG

Norway was one of the states which associated itself with the convention of August 1945 on the setting up of the Nuremberg tribunal. A Norwegian indictment censured the unprovoked Nazi invasion and its attendant atrocities. Göring and his fellow accused were confronted with the crimes they had committed against Norway. The Norwegian document singled out the attempted nazification of the country as perhaps the worst crime of all. 'For it was a crime against the democratic foundations of a country, and if successful would have spelled the moral annihilation of the population.'

It was established in Nuremberg—and to this the tribunal owes its wider significance—that wars of aggression are criminal acts, and that it is equally criminal to discriminate against minorities, let alone exterminate them. Legal proceedings can and should be brought by individuals against state-organised murder; statesmen are not beyond the reach of the law; a military uniform is no guarantee of immunity—all these became principles of international justice. The prime significance of these basic tenets was not weakened by the fact that the boundless injustices committed by the Nazis were followed not only by reparation measures but in a large number of instances by acts of hatred and revenge. Excesses such as these, in which many innocent Germans had to suffer, did not remain unchallenged but came up against the resistance of those whose humanity and sense of justice had survived the war. The Norwegian government was one of those which unambiguously stressed the necessity for constructive policies in their statements on the German problem.

The end of the Third Reich was a hard lesson and a grave warning. It demonstrated the abyss into which a civilised nation could be flung if it surrenders freedom and the moral foundations of human social existence. But the close of one of the darkest epochs in history also brought the laying of new foundations for European and international co-operation.

THE FIGHT FOR THE UNIVERSITIES (2)

30 November 1943 was the date on which the energetic resistance of Oslo University against the new order came to an end.

... Like other institutions of higher education, the University of Oslo stubbornly and uncompromisingly defended the fundamental issue of academic freedom as an essential element of freedom of thought. This defence had to be initiated at an early stage as it was evident that the German occupation would not restrict itself to military matters and events concerned with the conduct of the war. The policy of the occupying power extended to the establishment of a new order all along the line in accordance with National Socialist ideology.

As the most distinguished educational and research institution in the country, Oslo University had a clear duty towards the Norwegian people. This duty was further underlined by the vital role played by the fight for their own university in the Norwegians' earlier efforts towards freedom, and in the secure position which the university held in Norwegian cultural life. So it was natural that the nation regarded the university as a stronghold of national sovereignty when it faced the challenge of renewed trials.

It was not to be expected that the university would be able to achieve what the national defence forces had failed to do. Its responsibility lay in other areas. The University of Oslo shouldered the task of watchdog of intellectual freedom as one aspect of justice to which the Norwegian population could lay claim under the terms of international law.

On the Norwegian side there was of course no suggestion that the university and its colleges should be closed, as long as the work of instruction and research could continue in intellectual freedom and on honourable terms ... The German programme in Norway however went so far as the gradual erosion of the independence of higher education institutions, at the same time turning them to the services of National Socialist policy.

... During the night of 28 November 1943, a Sunday, fire broke out in the great hall of the university. On the following day the Quisling press announced that 'Communists' had committed arson ... Norwegian state police were stationed in the university, in order to check the students' passes. It did not take much to realise that something was in the air.

What that something was did not become evident until the next day—Tuesday 30 November 1943—when units of the German security police, the SS and the state police surrounded all buildings in which academic teaching took place. Guard posts armed with machine guns were set up to prevent attempts at escape. Staff and students were brought together in the university from all quarters. Motor cycle patrols drove round the city arresting students where they lived.

After a few hours those who had been arrested were taken into the great hall of the university to hear a statement read out by SS-General Rediess under the orders of Reich commissar Terboven . . . The chivalrous and generous conduct which the occupying power had shown towards the students, it said, had been the subject of misrepresentation. For this reason Terboven had resolved that the students of Oslo university were to be transported to 'a special camp' in Germany. Female students would be given leave from the university. They should return to their home towns without delay and report immediately to the local police.

. . . On 30 November there were probably a good 3,000 male students in Oslo. Of these around 1,500 were arrested . . . A first contingent of 300 deportees made up from the students and some 900 of their fellow countrymen drawn from other categories was moved off to Germany on Thursday 9 December.

The university conflict cannot be regarded in isolation from the other battles waged on the Norwegian cultural front. Many Norwegian academics achieved a great deal in the defence of Norwegian interests and ideals against the occupying power. Many of them, students and more senior members of the academic community, had to pay for their involvement with their lives, many others had to make the journey to Germany from one concentration camp to another.

But the cultural front itself is equally not to be considered in isolation. It was just one element, but an important one, in the total resistance movement of the Norwegian people; a part of that whole which the Norwegians themselves called the home front. The exemplary efforts of the High Court during the first winter of the occupation, the fight conducted by the schools and church, the maintenance of the principles of justice and cultural values by doctors and lawyers —all these were borne along by a popular resistance movement in which workers of all kinds, officials and businessmen, farmworkers and fishermen had found a place. Without this lively interaction between the broad mass of the population and the intellectuals, the 'Norwegian front' would not have attained its present nature. At times the intellectuals took the initiative, at others they were carried along with the tide.

The struggle for the university and higher education offers a clear illustration of the typical direction which the Norwegian resistance took. It is true that many students actively assisted in the distribution of information which could not be published in the official press, and that they co-operated in other directions by maintaining contacts within the Norwegian population by underground methods forced upon them by the occupying power. It would equally be surprising if a certain number of intellectuals—like people from other social groups—had not taken an active part in patriotic actions against the power with which Norway had found itself at war since 9 April 1940. But the main thrust came from the civil population. For the universities and higher education the battle was restricted to a resolute defence of national life, justice and intellectual freedom.

The heroic achievement at the University of Oslo and other Norwegian universities in these years lay in their successful pursuit of research, teaching and examination despite insecurity, breakdown in the standards of justice, shattering events at home and abroad, and not least the food shortage. It demands a fair deal of optimism, inner fortitude and faith in the future to maintain university life under such conditions.

THE OCCUPIER FALLS SILENT

Vermerk, Stockholm, 29 April 1945

On Saturday evening (29 April 1945) we booked a call to Reich commissar Terboven in Oslo. The connection was duly made with the Reich commissar but was immediately broken off, all we were able to make out being Terboven's question as to the name of the caller. Then the 'Reich commissar's residence' came on the line. And again the connection was broken off. And then suddenly a voice said : 'Obergruppenführer Rediess speaking.'
Brandt: Half an hour ago we had a conversation with Consul Stören [Consul Stören worked on external affairs for the Quisling régime] and questioned him about reports in the Stockholm press today to the effect that negotiations on a change in the status quo are taking place in Oslo and we should welcome an official statement on this from the German side.
Rediess: What I can say is that the reports are inaccurate.
Brandt: Inaccurate? So no such negotiations are in prospect?
Rediess: You will have to wait for official announcements.
Brandt: There also is speculation here that the release of political prisoners in Norway is imminent.
Rediess: In so far as this was discussed between the leader of the SS and Count Bernadotte [the conversation between Himmler and

Count Bernadotte took place on 24 April in Lübeck], preparations are being made in this direction.

Brandt: But is there then no immediate prospect of this being put into effect?

Rediess: On the contrary. It is in preparation, dependent on the agreement between the SS leader and Count Bernadotte.

Brandt: Can we expect an announcement on the part of occupation officials in view of the latest developments in Germany?

Rediess: No. That's clear enough, isn't it?

That was all Rediess had to say. The Norwegian operator said after a moment : 'I am afraid your caller has replaced the receiver; he doesn't wish to continue the conversation.'

(3)　BERLIN AND OSLO AFTER THE WAR

I have been asked to put down on paper some impressions of a journey I made in the autumn which took me from the city of three million to the country of three million, and from the scene of energetic reconstruction there back to this ruined landscape torn apart by bitter quarrels. This provides me with a welcome opportunity of saying something about the barriers between Germany and her neighbours which are slowly—all too slowly—being broken down.

Berlin and Oslo today are worlds apart. Only when the confines of Berlin have been left behind is it really possible to realise just how much the marks of war are still upon it, and just how artificial and paradoxical much of what happens there seems to be. The traveller arriving in Oslo sees how quickly the consequences of war can be overcome and normal conditions re-established, given reasonably favourable outward circumstances and the strong determination to work hard.

Two years ago no one would have ventured to state that events would develop so rapidly. The physical scene at the end of the war was dark and gloomy. Now it has altered almost beyond recognition. That should offer some hope and encouragement to those who for reasons it would not be appropriate to discuss here have not so far made any effort.

For the rest I shall leave the ruins to one side. Things like this make the strongest impact after a certain absence. I should like to record a few differences in other areas :

1. Oslo is in the middle of a local election campaign which is very much involved with violent differences of opinion over the planning policy of the Labour government. But in spite of this the sense of

community which all men of good will forged in the heat of war still prevails to the present day.

2. In Norway moves are afoot to reduce the daily fat ration from 50 to 40 grammes. The Berliner would be more than happy with ten instead of the five he now receives.

3. The Oslo government is striving to make 'UN lessons' part of the school curriculum. In Berlin people are trembling at the prospect of increasing tensions between as yet no-so-united nations.

Such comparisons—which are perhaps rather too facile—should not however divert attention from the crucial fact that there exists between Norwegian and German a far more fundamental distinction than that the former has what the latter lacks : enough to eat, clothing and footwear, books and furniture. What is of greater significance is that, over and above historical differences, often referred to in terms of 'national character', the background of experience in the recent past is totally different.

It is true that Norway quickly regained her prewar living standards and that in many areas economic, social and cultural advances have been made without violent disruption. But it is equally true that the work of reconstruction, largely carried out in a spirit of unity, is intimately bound up with the specific war experiences of the Norwegians. And for the Norwegians the war represented in the first instance a brutal act of aggression, a period not only of suffering but also of uninterrupted resistance. The attack on their constitutional state and deeply rooted national sense of democracy was countered by unshakable faith in the victory of freedom and justice.

From a distance this is difficult to grasp. And on the other side of the coin, the Norwegians lack the German experience of these years, day-by-day contact with tyranny and destruction, and now the quite unique problems of an occupation which international law could not have foreseen, without a coherent national front, without satisfactory clarity on internal values and without much hope.

The rapid overcoming of the aftermath of war strengthens self-confidence in Norway. On the other hand people there are well aware that the way things are going in the world gives cause for serious anxiety. In Berlin it starts with worry over daily bread and ends with fear of new catastrophes.

Much is going on, but mostly things are stagnant. There is no freedom from fear and want. That is why there has so far been no success in at least exhausting in a fever of reconstruction all those possibilities which do exist, despite the difficulties. And it is not getting any better because of the present tendency, intensified by isolation, to regard local problems as the key issues in world history.

In Norway the men and women who refused to be demoralised but undaunted sought a new path are the object of admiration. It is quite a different matter that there is frequently an appalling ignorance of what is actually happening in Germany. Isolation operates in both directions.

There is one thing the people of Norway want in common with nearly all other Europeans, and that is to have dealings with Germany again, to normalise life on the continent. It is recognised that Europe can no longer afford a Germany sunk in despair, a land which might all too easily become a focus of unrest. Further developments are watched by many with interested goodwill, by others with guarded scepticism.

To put it mildly, it would be an exaggeration to maintain that the average Norwegian is fond of the Germans. But he does not regard him with feelings of hatred. Of course there are voices expressing the opinion that the Germans got what was coming to them. Others take the contrary view that suffering alone has never made for peaceable neighbours. There is almost universal agreement that it would be a tragedy for the German problem to remain unresolved indefinitely.

In the Norwegian Storting there is a Liberal member whom the Nazis first sentenced to death and then left languishing in a German prison until the end of the war. He has made it his particular duty to stress by questions to the government the deprivations in Germany and the means by which the forces of democracy might be sustained. And he is no isolated exception. In the main rightwing paper and in the Labour party likeminded men make their views public. And it is indeed no accident that the greatest compassion is felt among those who have suffered most.

But let us cherish no illusions. European aid, which the son of Fridjof Nansen and other men who have suffered maltreatment in German concentration camps have called for, will certainly also benefit Germany . . . The many letters from Germany begging for food parcels are received with little favour, especially when they originate from people who have not yet understood that implication in the occupation of Norway is not exactly regarded as a service to humanity.

One final word : there are numerous problems standing in the way of genuine understanding. But there are people in many places earnestly fighting for a better future in peace and freedom—people who would come even closer together, if they learned more about one another.

Notes

1. Brandt was deprived of German citizenship on 3 September 1938.
2. This decree was issued by Hitler himself. Its purpose was to seize persons 'endangering German security' who were not to be immediately executed, and make them vanish without a trace into the night and fog ('Nacht und Nebel') of the unknown in Germany. (See William L. Shirer, *The Rise and Fall of the Third Reich*, London, 1960, p. 957.)

VI

International Contacts

VI

International Contacts

I had realised in my Lübeck days that it was far from adequate to consider political problems from a purely national standpoint. But arriving at the right approach was still a long way from a correct evaluation of the practicalities of a given situation. In those early years I had made a great effort to achieve an understanding of political events outside Germany and, most importantly, to gain a picture of socialist parties in other countries. I was particularly anxious to enrich this picture through personal contacts.

As the responsible foreign representative of the SJV (Socialist Youth League), and of the SAP youth league, I took part in the efforts to bring leftwing socialist groups together into an international youth bureau in which Holland was the prime mover. But the conference to found it, which took place in February 1934 in Laaren, was broken up by the Dutch police. Four of my German friends were handcuffed and handed over to the Gestapo. I was able to extricate myself with the help of Norwegian friends and documents. We merely ended up in the Amsterdam police prison and were then deported to Belgium. The conference which had begun so unfortunately was continued, supposedly in Lille, but actually in Brussels.

On the subject of the police prison: there I shared a cell with Finn Moe, who represented the Norwegian youth league and was a tower of strength to refugees in Oslo; later he was not only to become chairman of the foreign policy committee in the Norwegian parliament, but also chairman of the world security council. At that time in Amsterdam, he had to put up with teasing comments like: 'And what does your King have to say about all this?'—The man who was drawing him on came to a sad end. Walter Held (Heinz Epe), who for a while had worked with Leo Trotsky, was one of the refugees who in 1940–41—before the German attack on the Soviet Union— set off on the long journey across Russia, Siberia and Japan to America. Together with his Norwegian wife and child he disappeared somewhere in the Soviet Union.

The work of the 'youth bureau' had no success, and contact with the dogmatic Trotskyists proved far from satisfactory. Apart from the Norwegians who had sensibly held back from the outset, in order not to prejudice possible collaboration with the Social Democrats of neighbouring countries, there were only a few 'independent' youth leagues with any membership worth noting. Still there were groups of a respectable size in Sweden, Spain, England, Poland and Holland. The 'left' in the Social Democrat youth leagues in Belgium, France and the USA kept in contact with us. We were also in touch with loyal lone supporters in Rumania, Switzerland and Israel among other countries.

The so-called London bureau did carry more weight, although not a great deal more. This was a study group of independent socialist parties and organisations, of which the SAP was also a member. The secretarial work was carried out by the ILP (Independent Labour Party) which had a rich tradition but even then did not have much influence outside Scotland. Its leaders were the fiery James Maxton and Fenner Brockway, who had done sterling work on human rights and the liberation of the colonial nations. One of their younger representatives was Walter Padley. As Deputy Foreign Minister he was later to greet me in London; in the meantime he had become chairman of the Labour party.

I took part in four conferences of the London bureau. At the beginning of 1935 we started a peace campaign in Paris. One of the most notable participants was the noble and experienced Swede Karl Kilbom, former chairman of the Swedish CP and later of the fairly substantial group of leftwing socialists. Together with most of his political friends he later found his way back to the great Social Democrat mother party. During the war I had many a good conversation with him. He took a great interest in the community centres and parks which are so important in Sweden, and achieved a great deal towards stimulating an interest in art among the working people. The 1935 meeting was also interesting in that we met Jacques Doriot, who entertained us in St. Denis town hall—I had never eaten so well in my life! He had been expelled from the CP because he had come out too early in favour of the united front. His later career took a shameful turn.

After his break with the Comintern, Doriot was not alone in getting worked up into such a state of hatred that he ended up in the Fascist camp. The Swede Nils Flyg, whom I had got to know as a party rival of Karl Kilbom, went the same way. During the war, together with the few people left around him, he degenerated into the sad role of apologist of Nazi Germany and in his journal denounced many people, including myself. What was intimidating about the pointless party struggles inside the socialist movement were not only failures like these but also the unscrupulous way in which honourable men were abused, defamed and not infrequently ruined by Moscow.

In May 1936 we met again in Paris. It was immediately after the election victory of the popular front, and just before the formation of the Léon Blum government. I can still clearly recall how this spokesman of the leftwing Seine federation of the French socialists behaved. His attitude was bewildering in the extreme, especially to us Germans. He took the view that in spite of the Nazis the Maginot line should be dismantled for the sake of peace. My friend August Enderle was unable to choke back the bitter commentary: 'Anyone who speaks like that could earn himself a great deal of money. Anyone speaking like that without payment shows that he is stupid as well.'

In August 1937 a further international conference took place in England. Now I finally got to know London. At that time we held our sessions in Letchworth, where the ILP summer school met. The country atmosphere was unusually relaxing and peaceful and I found it contrasted sharply with the disputes that flared up in the meetings. There were cavillers who sought to stir up trouble because of my attitude in Barcelona, but after I had expressed my views in detail the conference chairman, the MP Campbell Stephen, declared the matter closed. When an Italian sectarian started up again on the next day there was a painful scene. I had called him a 'mad dog' who really ought to hold his tongue. He insisted on a translation and withdrew in a huff. At that time I was somewhat lacking in parliamentary experience.

In the summer of 1938, this time in Paris again, the main point at issue was whether the SAP could continue to be a member of the London bureau at all. For some we did not hold rigidly enough to our principles. We had begun with socialist unification which we knew could only be realised on the basis of the Social Democrat Internationale. When I visited Kenya at the end of 1963 and met Jomo Kenyatta we recalled the fact that we had already seen each other before—namely at that very Paris conference in the summer of 1938. It was a decided plus for leftwing socialist internationalism that we had been meeting representatives of African and Indian peoples long before many others . . .

On behalf of my own youth league I had made a complete break with the 'Youth bureau' because in Barcelona it had taken an extreme ultraleft course. This happened at a small underground conference

near Gothenburg attended by various delegates from Germany. After-
wards we made contact with Erich Ollenhauer and gained the status
of an allied organisation to the socialist Youth Internationale. Its
chairman at the time, the subsequent Danish Prime Minister Hans
Christian Hansen, called me up in the summer of 1939 to confirm
that I would take part in the last international youth congress
before the war. But as I was tied up with my work in Norway I had
to send a deputy.

Quite a different area of international contacts and experiences
was opened up by the trade unions. In Lübeck I was a member of
the central union of employees, and in Norway I joined an equiv-
alent organisation. In Stockholm I became a member of the Nor-
wegian seamen's union. So I did not become the ship's officer of my
childhood dreams, but I was at least in a sailor's union ...

During my war years in neutral Sweden it was very pleasing for
me—with the encouragement of my Norwegian friends—to be able
to bring together an international study group, in which Social
Democrats from over a dozen countries held regular discussions.
These discussions were not just an end in themselves: they were also
concerned with practical issues which helped us to get our bearings
in a time of confusion. Much was put into practical effect in later
political decisions. We were also kept in touch through friends who
were members of Allied embassies, most of which at that time were
still only legations.

One of the members of the Stockholm party was Bruno Kreisky,
who became the Austrian Foreign Minister after the war, and also
Torsten Nilsson, at that time party secretary and later Swedish
Foreign Minister. Halvard Lange, for many years Norwegian Foreign
Minister, had voluntarily returned with his pregnant wife from
Stockholm to Oslo as late as the autumn of 1940, after an unforget-
table farewell evening together in a Stockholm beer cellar steeped in
tradition. His was an act of sacrifice. He was taken to Sachsenhausen
with both his brothers.

I met my first wife in Oslo but we did not marry until we were in
Stockholm. There the marriage also broke up. My daughter Ninja
became a competent teacher in Norway.

Norwegian and Swedish Social Democrats, many of whom had
years in government, were closely involved in the work together in
Stockholm. On the Swedish side we were able to count on an unusual
married couple: the economist Professor Gunnar Myrdal, who be-
came chief of the ECE (Economic Council for Europe) of the UNO
in Geneva, and his wife Alva, who represented her country as ambas-
sador to India and who is today a delegate at the Geneva disarma-

ment talks. Among the Germans Ernst Paul—who with the Swedish political economist Richard Sterner was one of the two chairmen of the international group—played an active mediating role; he had been secretary of the Sudetan German Social Democrats and later as a Bundestag deputy made a particular reputation for himself in the sphere of European co-operation. The strongest force on the German side was Fritz Tarnow, Reichstag deputy and leader of the Union of Woodworkers. In my youthful years he appeared to me as an extreme representative of a brand of reformism which I was unable to accept, but he did say in his report to the Leipzig party conference in 1931 that Social Democrats must act 'as doctors at the sickbed of capitalism'. And it was with this man that I entered into close friendship in Stockholm. I was delighted at the way he—in contrast to others among my compatriots—understood how to gain the ear of friends from other countries who were of the same political persuasion. And I was impressed by his strivings towards a theory of 'constructive socialism' which was to leave the earlier reformist and revolutionary phases of the movement far behind. It was not so greatly removed from the 'integral socialism' of Otto Bauer, but he found a quite different outlet in Austromarxism. It is more than a pity that Fritz Tarnow is no longer able to take a prominent part in Germany's postwar developments.

The Danish Social Democrats—in contrast to the Norwegians— were only poorly represented in Stockholm, because the Danish parties were not banned by the occupying power. The word was going round that Denmark was the 'songbird of the mass murderers'. But even there things came to a head. My connections in Stockholm to the Danish resistance movement proved strong enough to stand the test even after the war. I first met Hans Hedtoft, the postwar Premier and Social Democrat party chairman, in 1946, but in the years following we met one another a great deal. I am pleased that I was able to be of some service to him and his Foreign Minister H. C. Hansen—his successor as Prime Minister—in removing difficulties on both sides of the German-Danish frontier.

I should not want the reader of this book to go away with the impression that my years in Sweden were entirely taken up in dealings with Norwegians and the international group. I was not just living in Stockholm; I also had many contacts in the Swedish socialist movement and in Swedish life generally. I did not personally have much to do with the then Prime Minister Per Albin Hansson. He was an imposing figure, whether you agreed with him in everything or not . . .

The Swedish Social Democrats had come a long way, even as

regards the theoretical basis of their reformist policies. Gustav Möller drew up a thoroughly co-ordinated modern social policy. Ernst Wigforss as Finance Minister evolved a progressive Social Democratic economic policy and it is only unfortunate that he wrote in the language of a minority nation. To the best of my recollection I had not met Tage Erlander, Minister of Education from 1945, before 1948, at which time he had already become Prime Minister and I put him in the picture about the Berlin blockade. Since then we have had frequent meetings and I am proud to be able to number this man among my friends.

I have already mentioned Gustav Möller. As Minister for Social Affairs he was also responsible for refugees and the police. When early in 1941 I was obliged to spend a few days under not very pleasant conditions on remand in the Stockholm police prison, he was the Minister who ensured that the matter was swiftly cleared up when Martin Tranmäl intervened on my behalf. What they wanted to know was what I had been getting up to around the new year of 1941 in Norway, and I was not inclined to reveal which Swedish authorities had assisted me in what I was doing. In contrast to those who were later to take the view in Germany that you could play on both sides of the law, it was the custom in Sweden to observe the rules of the game. Anyway we did not think badly of Swedish officials or go running off to the press when they took an understandable interest in the protection of Swedish neutrality. It never occurred to us to start shouting the odds against the Swedes when one or the other of us got into difficulties because of national exigencies.

The second part of the material reproduced in this chapter is concerned not with unity among men, but political unity. I have already indicated that I was one of those who took the view that Hitler could have been stopped short by a united opposition from the left. It was all the easier for me to take this view because I regarded the Communist party as part of the German socialist movement, and an important part at that.

The experiences of Spain and elsewhere caused me to modify my opinions. Even before the war broke out I had written down my views on this matter at some length. During the war the pointless propaganda campaigns of Swedish and Norwegian Communists had helped me to gain a greater understanding of the nature of their party machine. In spite of all this I still did not drop the idea of a unified socialist movement. And indeed even after the war serious attempts were made in many countries to achieve unified socialist parties.

As far as the situation in Germany goes, I was also taken up with the idea that it might be possible to win over a large section of the serious-minded pro-Communist workers—even against the will of the Communist leadership. The example of Berlin demonstrates that such an idea was not so wide of the mark. At that time I could not imagine that in my Wedding constituency—in 'red Wedding'—I should gain 72.4 per cent of the votes as against 2 per cent for the Communist SED.

I was able to observe, but not take an active part in, the great upheavals of 1946 over the compulsory amalgamation of the Social Democrats with the Communists in the Russian zone. My admiration went out most of all to those who refused to be beaten down. And if ever there was any proof at that time of democratic forces at work in Germany, then the Berlin Social Democrats' will to survive offered it, before the eyes of European Social Democrats and the world at large.

THE STOCKHOLM GROUP (1)

The intention in Stockholm was to form a group in which socialists from the various countries represented here in Sweden could meet together in fellowship; a group in which socialists on the Allied side, from neutral countries and from the so-called enemy states could exchange views and experiences. It is a fact in our favour that we were able to maintain this co-operation and comradely partnership independently of the events of the war. The majority of us regarded it as our duty to keep alive our contacts with friends from other countries. We need such contacts if we are to preserve our own international outlook and if we are to prepare ourselves to confront the problems which the movement will have to face in the various countries concerned, and if the movement is to present itself not just as the party of constructive policies on a national level, but also as the party with a consistently international outlook.

In Stockholm we have not been trying to play at Internationales, nor are we going to do so for the future in a country in Sweden's position, even if the future can offer us greater opportunities for practical co-operation. What we in all modesty have sought to do, and what we must continue to do more energetically than ever before, is to discuss and where possible elucidate some of the issues which need clarification, in so far as the Internationale is to be not merely a symbol and a tradition, but also a living reality. We are not the mouthpieces of individual parties. None of our conclusions are binding on any one organisation. We represent no one but ourselves. But the fact that socialists from a good dozen countries have found a sense of fellowship and are gradually coming to understand each other's views is no mean achievement. In 1944 the leadership of the international group was the same as before. Richard Sterner and Ernst Paul acted as chairmen, Willy Brandt as secretary. M. Karniol took charge of the very modest finances at the group's disposal. The remaining members of the group comprised: Martin Tranmäl and Lars Evensen (Norway), Henry Grünbaum and—later—Oluf Carlsson (Denmark), Victor Sjaholm (USA), J.G. (France), J.J. (Czechoslovakia), Emil Haase (Sudeten Social Democrats), Bruno Kreisky and Josef Pleyl (Austria), Wilhelm Böhm (Hungary), Fritz Tarnow and Kurt Heinig (Germany), Stefan Szende, Ernesto Dethorey (Spain), Willi Smulowicz (Palestine) and Sigidur Thorarinsson (Iceland). On the Swedish side the following have taken part in one or more meetings: Gunnar Myrdal, Torsten Nilsson, Adolf Wallentheim, Richard Lindström, Torsten Sundström, Essen Lindahl, Ville Forsberg and Arne Björnberg.

(2)   The Norwegians took the initiative in the formation of the study group. Swedish party friends together with colleagues from a number of other countries were invited to a discussion on the peace aims of the socialist movement on 2 July 1942. Martin Tranmäl chaired the meeting and Willy Brandt reported on a working document for discussion which had been drafted by a group of Norwegian socialists in Stockholm. W.B. enlarged on these points among others:

Anti-Nazism and resurgent nationalism are progressive factors for as long as the war continues. But the nearer we come to the end of the war, the greater the conviction becomes that they can form no satisfactory basis for reconstruction ...

The conflict between democratic and revolutionary socialism need not arise again if we keep our minds on the actual problems before us.

The Russians should be drawn into international collaboration, but if such collaboration is to be successful it is absolutely essential that they should first give up the Comintern ...

The one part of the European socialist movement which still continues to have a voice in government, namely the British Labour party, has put forward a programme for reconstruction whose main points can profitably be accepted by the socialists of other countries.

As things have turned out, we must assume that demands for the disarmament of the Fascist states will be linked with a more or less comprehensive military occupation of these countries. Socialists and sincere democrats cannot support any kind of occupation policy as such.

On the other hand they must adopt a positive attitude to the changing realities of the situation and seek on the basis of the given circumstances to achieve a desirable outcome.

But we must be clear that the reactionaries in the victorious states will be more than anxious to intervene on the continent in order to check or even suppress those who do not rest content with the prevailing democratic framework, but who want to go further and grasp at the social roots of Fascism and the war.

I take the view that it ought to be possible for socialists even now—however embittered they may be about the actions of the Fascists—to unite in their resistance to such tendencies.

The demand that individual nations should have the right to live their own lives must also hold good for those nations which today are under Nazi domination, provided only that they have gone through a process of transformation which offers satisfactory guarantees for the future.

In addition, setbacks to the radical democratic and socialist revolutionary movement in certain parts of Europe would inevitably result in checks and weaknesses elsewhere.

... If we seek to establish an organisation for international justice which will not founder in the same way as did the League of Nations, then it must first be accepted that all nations should surrender a little of their national sovereignty in the cause of common security. In that case, there will be no room for neutrality. The delegation of the solution of military and economic problems to an international organisation does not necessarily imply the surrender of political independence.

It is not beyond the bounds of possibility that we shall see the day when Europe is united. But this will only come about if the victorious powers lay the proper organisational foundations. It is more probable that the formation of localised federations will constitute an intermediate step on the path from national separatism to a comprehensive community on a European and international scale.

Under the leadership of a working party made up of Hilding Färm, Ernst Paul, Inge Scheflo and Fritz Tarnow, nine evening discussions were held between September 1942 and May 1943.

In addition an international gathering took place on 1 May under the joint auspices of the Stockholm Social Democrats and the socialist refugee groups (the Polish Minister of Commerce Kvapinski was one of the speakers).

W.B. presented a resolution to this gathering on 1 May 1943 which ran :

Members of the socialist movement from fourteen countries, who are gathered here on 1 May 1943 in the Medborgarhuset in Stockholm, give their support to the work which has found its first expression in the working document 'Peace aims of democratic socialists'.

... Wherever freedom was lost, the socialist movement perished also. But the ideas of socialism have lived on and today leave their mark on a substantial part of the discussions on post-war reconstruction.

... The war must be won outright ... The new peace must become a peace for all socialist peoples ...

THE NEW PEACE

At the meeting in November 1942 it was resolved that a committee be set up to explore the possibility of working out a common basis for discussion on the peace aims of democratic socialists. Members of the committee were : Gunnar Myrdal, Ole Jödal, Martin Tranmäl, Tarnow, Böhm, Paul, Karniol, Kreisky, one friend from both Czechoslovakia and France, Szende and Brandt, the latter as secretary. Early in 1943 Richard Sterner was asked to join the committee. The 'Peace Aims' of March 1943 contained the following :

In accordance with the true aims of all nations, democratic socialists are working towards a just and lasting peace. The Allied victory over Hitler's Germany and her confederates is a necessary condition for a just and lasting peace.

The war can be won on the battlefield and yet still be lost by the politicians. Real victory will only be achieved when we sweep aside the social and international conditions which created the Fascist and Nazi threat. It will depend on the political and social changes which follow on the defeat of Nazism whether or not the war will ultimately be taken to its logical conclusion.

Responsible people on the Allied side have established principles which are broadly in agreement with the ideas put forward by the international socialist movement long before the war.

Democratic socialists unconditionally support the programme set out by Roosevelt, which is as straightforward as it is promising :

namely, freedom of opinion, freedom of conscience, freedom from want and freedom from fear.

The declaration of August 1941 which has the support of all Allied governments is based on the recognition of these four freedoms. They cannot be the last word for democracy but we take the view that the principles laid down there constitute a useful basis for further work.

Peace must be built upon reason. Hatred cannot form any viable basis for peace. Post-war policies must not be dominated by revenge, but borne along by the will towards common reconstruction.

The desire for national unity, which has risen up again to play an important part in the battle against Nazism, is not enough to fashion the new peace unaided. The problems which the war has thrown up and which must be solved when peace is concluded are not limited to national frontiers; they must be resolved on an international scale.

The Atlantic Declaration establishes that the Allies are not seeking territorial or other kinds of gain. Nor do they wish for any territorial changes to be carried through which are not in accordance with the freely expressed desires of the population concerned. . The right of self-determination for all nations, and the right of all peoples to lead their own lives accordingly number among the declared peace aims of the Allies.

We endorse these principles and regard it as the duty of democratic socialists to hold fast to them, in case they should be challenged in the future course of the war or during the conclusion of the peace.

Hitler's Germany, supported by Fascism and Fascist sympathisers in various countries, bears the direct responsibility for the war. Seen in a broader context it is nevertheless the case—as the British Labour party has shown in its post-war programme early in 1942— that the responsibility for the conditions which made the Second World War possible falls on the old system as a whole. Should guarantees be created for an enduring new peace there must be no way back to the world as it was in 1938.

A NEW LEAGUE OF NATIONS

The bankruptcy of the old League of Nations was a consequence of isolationism and narrow-minded capitalist policies based on commercial interests. They prevented the establishment of a collective security and the resolution of the economic causes of war. In order to bring into being a viable organisation of international justice, all nations must freely surrender a portion of their sovereignty for the sake of collective security. The age of isolationism is past.

Individual nations lose none of their real independence if they cede the execution of military, economic and other common tasks to an international organisation.

After this war a strong organisation for international justice with effective executive bodies must be set up to settle matters of dispute between nations and to put international lawbreakers out of harm's way.

A new League of Nations must be worldwide. It is natural that it should evolve from the collaboration among those nations which have come together during the war. After the shortest possible transitional period it must be made open to all nations, victors, neutrals, and vanquished alike.

We support the positive proposals of the British Labour party that a new League of Nations must have the necessary power to apply military and economic sanctions against every state which opposes the decisions taken by an international court.

In the spirit of the four freedoms, guarantees must be established for the basic rights of all people in every nation. International organisations must ensure that individual states do not infringe upon these rights.

A new League of Nations must give expression to the will of the people; it must not be allowed to degenerate into a mere diplomatic talking shop. The main constituent bodies of the League must be made up of representatives elected by the people. The big powers must not be allowed to rule the roost at the expense of smaller nations.

Supranational bodies must be established either as part of or in co-ordination with the League for the solution of special tasks in the economic sphere and other areas.

Efforts must be made within the framework of an international system of law towards the formation of federations between neighbouring countries with common interests.

It is of the utmost importance for future European co-operation that the smaller nations should group together in federations on a geographical basis. In this way they can the more easily hold their own against larger states. In the 1919 peace a number of European states gained independent nationhood. The new peace must restore their sovereignty but at the same time bolt the door on particularism. Federal systems in Europe are essential if peace is to be secured on the continent.

Through far-reaching trade, tariff and monetary treaties and with the aid of other measures, we must strive to transform these local political federations into economic units as well.

The establishment of an international order of justice and a viable League of Nations demands that there should be no break between the Soviet Union and the Anglo-Saxon democracies. If the present collaboration terminates in open conflict the danger of a new war threatens.

Democratic socialists must do their utmost to advance and extend collaboration among the Allies. They must make their own contribution to the removal of the mistrust which has existed between the Soviet Union and the democracies.

From an economic point of view the Atlantic Declaration promises that all states, whether large or small, victorious or defeated, should have equal access to world trade and raw materials. The Allies seek to broaden international co-operation in order to guarantee improved working conditions, economic progress and social security. One of the greatest dangers for the postwar period lies in the fact that the world economy has fossilised into national autarchies. This danger must be immediately removed by energetic measures to achieve a fair division of labour and exploitation of natural resources among the nations which are essential if living standards are to be raised and peace secured.

The economic collaboration which has developed among the Allies in the course of the war, one of whose present aims is the immediate provision of food and raw materials to the impoverished nations after the cessation of hostilities, must be carried further.

An international credit and guarantee system must be estabished to help countries confronted with serious problems of reconstruction which have to reform their monetary systems.

The International Labour Organisation must be extended and the influence of the workers strengthened; guarantees must be set up to ensure that the resolutions of individual countries are put into operation.

Alongside the Labour Organisation new bodies must be set up to deal with the problems of economic and social reconstruction in the short and long term, and also to tackle other economic and social issues which are ripe for international solution.

The socialist movement, in common with other progressive forces, demands a decisive change of policy towards colonies and dependencies. Democratic socialists associate themselves with national democratic movements in the colonies and are combating prejudice and discrimination against coloured peoples. The aim of future policy must be to assist colonial nations to achieve as rapidly as possible the conditions which will enable them to attain self-government.

All territories not in a position to govern themselves for the present must be placed under effective international control in order to protect the long-term interests of the local population.

Serious steps must be taken on a national level to raise the social and cultural level of the colonies. Raising the standard of living in the colonies will be a significant factor in the creation of a period of general progress after the war. This would decisively clear the way towards independence for the colonial nations. In order to prevent exploitation of the local population, the interests of private capital must be excluded from the colonies or at the very least severely limited by means of national or international controls.

In spite of the actions of the Nazis we must not lose sight of the fact that one of the essential positive aims of the war is the democratisation of Germany.

The Labour party and other circles in Britain have also given to understand that the Allies, both in their own interest and in order to secure peace for the future, must take a vital interest in assisting the establishment of a democratic government in Germany, Italy and other countries under dictatorship.

The destruction of all free organisations and the Nazi poisoning of youth—alongside the material consequences of war and defeat—do not constitute a favourable starting point for the construction of democracy in Germany. None the less this target must be achieved. It cannot be solved from outside. However, the democratic world must help to reshape social life in Germany by the appropriate measures in order to strengthen democratic forces and to help defeat the enemies of democracy.

A necessary condition for the achievement of this objective is close collaboration with German democrats and re-establishing links with the democratic traditions of Germany.

SOCIALIST INTERNATIONALE

Tranmäl, Böhm and Brandt were given the task of presenting a working document on the reconstruction of the Socialist Internationale. At the session on 28 June 1943 such a document was presented which included the following :

... The initiative for the reconstruction of the Socialist Internationale must come from the British socialist movement.

The British Labour party is the only one of the parties in the old Internationale capable of taking on such a task. The few authorised parties still in existence elsewhere in Europe (Sweden, Switzerland, Hungary, Denmark, Finland) are not capable of achieving this. By and large, the underground parties in the countries occupied by Hitler's Germany are represented in England and they will certainly go a long way in supporting the Labour party. This also holds good for the party groups, the spokesmen in exile from countries under Nazi and Fascist rule or the underground cells which are still in existence there.

The reconstruction of the Internationale must be instituted in such a way that the greatest possible unity is achieved and that it is not restricted to Europe as was previous international collaboration.

. . . As far as America is concerned, feelers should be put out with a view to establishing links with the trade union movement and the American socialist party which has begun to grow up there over the past few years. There is little value in having a representation such as in the last Internationale, which was limited to sectarian socialist parties.

Further, there should be a thorough exploration of the possibility of establishing strong ties with socialist parties in the British Dominions and the socialist movement in China, India, South America, the Near East and the African colonies.

A special committee should be set up to prepare a minimum programme for the Socialist Internationale and its findings should be distributed among all interested parties for discussion . . . If socialists take the view that states should surrender a little of their sovereignty in favour of supranational institutions, they should not make any less stringent demands on their own movement . . .

In conclusion : we propose the formation of a preparatory committee for the reconstitution of the Socialist Internationale. We request the British Labour party to take the initiative in this and to invite the co-operation of socialist movements in other countries.

On 28 June 1943, Tarnow was given the task of forming a circle for the discussion of economic and financial problems in the postwar period.

Paul undertook a parallel task for the discussion of cultural postwar questions (in which Alva Myrdal played a decisive part).

CONSEQUENCES OF DEFEAT (3)

The Germany which is to come after the Third Reich cannot escape the consequences of Nazi defeat. Among these consequences are the terms which will be imposed upon Germany at the time of armistice and in the peace treaty. The new government is entitled to seek to change and mitigate these conditions but it cannot simply dissociate itself from them. An intransigent attitude would lead to utter isolation, even from the natural allies of the new German democracy.

But much more important is the need for clear recognition of the fact that a radical break with traditional German policies lies in the interest not least of the German people themselves. The future of the German people cannot be secured by weapons, but only by peaceful economic and cultural collaboration. Taking this very special interest of the German people as a starting point, we turn to the conditions and tasks of German foreign policy for the future.

The German people do not bear the sole responsibilty for the war. We know that the war was a result of shortsighted capitalist policies based on commercial interest. We know that it could have been averted if the principle of collective security had been put into effect and we know too that the ruling circles in England and France at the time not only sacrificed Abyssinia, Spain, Austria, Czechoslovakia and part of China and condemned the League of Nations to impotence, but also raised no objections to German expansionism in the direction of the Soviet Union.

However, the fact is that Hitler's Germany started the war. It is a fact that the Hitler régime was able to count on the support of all too many of the German people in its rearmament and war policies; it is equally a fact that in the course of recent years the gravest crimes were committed by Germans in the name of the German people and that as a consequence massive hatred has built up against the entire German nation.

It will be the task of the foreign policy of a new democratic Germany, first, to sweep away the foundations of German imperialism; secondly, to make at least partial restitution for the Nazi crimes by special contributions to the reconstruction of Europe; thirdly, to offer proof of the peaceful nature of the measures of the new Germany by patient and disinterested efforts and gradually to build up a new situation based on trust. There are reactionary forces in the camp of the victorious powers which have a vested interest in preventing or at least hindering the reconstruction of democracy and socialism in Germany. We also must be clear about the fact that it will not be easy for the populations of the countries at present under occupation after all these years of the worst persecution to respond with automatic trust to a new German régime. Trust cannot be forced, it must be won. To the races and nations under the Nazi yoke which have suffered the greatest loss of human life in the struggle against Fascism, we can do no more than say : All we are asking for is a chance to prove through our actions that we have nothing to do with the Germany which you have come to know from its ugliest side, and that there is nothing more vital to our interests than to collaborate with you in the peaceful reconstruction of Europe.

We are naturally not fighting 'Vansittartism' because it denounces the crimes of the German Nazis, militarists and imperialists. We are fighting it because what it advocates is a kind of racialism in reverse, and because in terms of concrete political measures its express intention is the submission of the German working population whilst reactionary groups including big capital will be allowed to go scot free.

A realistic policy for post-Hitler Germany must begin by recognising that the reshaping of Germany cannot unfold *in vacuo*, independently of the international power situation. That holds good for every revolution of our age, but it will be doubly important in the present situation. We can assume that the main Allied powers will occupy Germany. The intentions of the Allies as far as the length of the occupation is concerned and the size of the military forces to be stationed on German territory are not so far known. There are many indications that it will come to a division into English, Russian and American zones of occupation. As a result, differences in policy among the occupation forces could well result in varying conditions for reconstruction. It will be the active concern of German democrats and socialists to join together even in a situation like that which would threaten the development of democracy and uniform progress, and to work against those trends which could lead to permanent partition.

This war is being won by a coalition which is far from united in itself. This has already become apparent in the course of the war; after the end of the war real and imagined clashes of interest will become even more evident. In addition, the differences within the individual powers will stand out more clearly after the war. But we do not believe that any realistic German policy can be based on the exploitation of conflicts within the camp of the victorious powers. In our view it would be disastrous to base future German policy on playing off one victorious power against another because this would distract attention from the social questions which socialists should be striving to resolve, imperil their own constructive policies and encourage extremist nationalists.

There are many signs that collaboration among the principal Allied partners will survive the end of the war. If this is so, then the main feature of the development of Europe in the short term will be determined by the understanding arrived at between England, the Soviet Union and America. This will also establish the framework within which future policy in Germany will have to operate. Concern for the creation of a secure peace demands that there should be no break in the Allied camp and that the anti-Hitler coalition will be further strengthened and extended by a genuine system of collective security. Any German policy which does not take this into consideration will not serve the work of securing the peace. Other nations will regard it as an attempt to sabotage peaceful reconstruction.

German democrats and socialists must work from the point that international power relationships will be radically changed by the outcome of the war. The present European states will no longer number among the leading great powers. Germany will play the part of a second-rate power. It must be the task of German democrats and socialists to speak out for the right of their people to self-determination within the framework of an international organisation and to secure the national existence of Germany. It cannot be their task to fight for a re-establishment of German supremacy on the continent. The democratic solution for Germany does not lie in the exploitation of the techniques of secret diplomacy and international intrigue but in conscious, honourable and determined efforts towards putting German interests into line with those of the European community of nations.

It is more than likely that the victorious powers will impose unjust demands on Germany. We do not at all take the view that a provisional democratic government should blithely put its signature to every bit of paper placed in front of it by foreign powers. Each individual case will require a scrupulous examination of the circumstances. Above all this government must be ruthlessly honest towards its own people. Supporters of a post-Hitler government should not be caught unawares by secret treaties but it must be made clear by press, radio and in meetings what the current demands of the victorious powers contain and what their acceptance on the one hand or rejection on the other would involve. There must be no concessions to nationalist tendencies. On the contrary, even when it is impossible in a specific situation willingly to fulfil a demand by the victorious powers, it must be clearly and unambiguously stated that it was the criminal policies of Nazism which brought Germany into this incredibly difficult position *vis à vis* the outside world.

If we do not accept an unconditional 'policy of compliance' we do however wish at the same time to make it clear beyond all doubt that a policy of 'clean hands' and of continuous protestation will not lead to any reasonable outcome. We shall have to take the situation as it exists and arrive at a *modus vivendi* with the outside world. The revolution will be stifled and the people starve if we do not succeed in normalising our relations with the victorious powers.

Letters on the 'Peace Aims' were before the study group on 10 August 1943 from Jaksch and Gillies (British Labour party) amongst others. Arthur Deakin (TUC and Labour) spoke on 16 August 1943 on the British socialist movement and postwar problems. I. H. Oldenbroek reported on international trade union activities.

Brandt reported on the reorganisation of the study group. He began with a greeting to the Italian socialists :

... We have seen the strength of tradition which the socialist organisations and democratic parties are able to draw upon—even after twenty years of Nazism.

This offers us hope for the future elsewhere on the shattered map of Europe. We have seen how some of the young people who were actually born under Fascism took part in the very first spontaneous demonstrations which accompanied the fall of Mussolini. Above all, we have seen the decisive and active part played by socialists in the democratic uprising. It is with great pleasure and enthusiasm that we greet the active involvement of our comrades, the Italian socialists and union members, in the battle for freedom and peace...

We take this opportunity to express the hope that the Allies will yet be able to arrive at a policy based on the simple recognition that their natural allies are not Victor Emanuel, Badoglio, newly-converted Fascists and old reactionaries, but the socialist and liberal forces in Milan, Turin and Genoa, if this war is to follow the course outlined by the Atlantic charter...

PERSECUTION OF THE JEWS

Stockholm, 21 April 1944

The international group of democratic socialists in Stockholm has discussed the questions arising in the context of the Nazi extermination campaign against European Jews, and have passed the following resolution :

The socialist movement must work together with all sincere democrats to ensure that no practical opportunity for saving the lives of Jews is wasted.

At the same time we must conduct the most energetic campaign against anti-Semitism and other forms of racial persecution and discrimination. Now that the Nazi mass murders have demonstrated the consequences of such ideologies, we must work energetically against anti-Semitism.

As democratic socialists, we have already indicated earlier that it is one of our peace aims that all nations should have the opportunity of leading their own lives and that equal status should be guaranteed to minority groups.

It is an inescapable demand of justice that citizens of Jewish origin in every country should be granted equality of civil rights, and of cultural, social and economic conditions.

At the same time we express our sympathy towards the work of reconstruction in the Jewish national home in Palestine, which has saved more Jews than any other country. Even after the war Palestine will still be in a position to take in a considerable number of European Jews.

We congratulate the workers of Palestine on their laudable initiative. It is our hope that the socialist movement together with other progressive forces will continue to do all in its power to arrive at a community of interest between the Arab and Jewish nations.

International steps must be taken to secure basic human rights in every country; to carry the fight against racial hatred over into future educational policies; to take into consideration the situation of the Jews on their return and in relation to the work of reconstruction; and to secure the further development of the Jewish national home in Palestine.

In this way we can make at least some restitution for the crimes Hitler's Germany has committed with the support of reactionary extremists in other countries . . .

THE APPROACHING PEACE

1 May 1944 :
International May day celebrations, together with the Stockholm Social Democrats.
Speakers : Minister Gustav Möller, Martin Tranmäl, Victor Sjaholm (USA).
Brandt presented the following resolution :

... Regardless of whether we come from nations involved in the armed struggle or from neutral countries, from democratic or Fascist lands, we regard ourselves as allies in the fight for the victory of freedom.

... We are more firmly convinced than ever that democracy and socialism offer the right guarantees for a complete victory over the instigators of terror and war, a victory which is not only military but also political and economic.

The meeting wishes to underline the importance of the reconstitution of democratic socialist organisations in the liberated countries at the earliest possible moment; of the broadening of international collaboration even before the end of the war; and of ensuring that the socialist movement through its international associations participates in new international institutions and can thus contribute to the creation of a just, realistic and honourable peace.

Meeting 24 May 1944 :
Brandt reported on the peace aims debate and the second front. Gösta Rehn reported on the postwar programme of the Swedish socialist movement.
(The invitation ran : Evening snack costs 2.25 Kroner. Please bring butter and bread coupons.)

Lunch 27 June 1944 :
Tranmäl's 65th birthday.
Myrdal delivered the speech in celebration. Kreisky also spoke.

Study group 29 August 1944 :
Greetings to French friends (on the liberation of Paris).
Report by Karniol on the battle of Warsaw.
Message of greeting to freedom fighters.
At Brandt's suggestion letter sent to Harold Laski (*re* the London declaration on the Atlantic charter).

Study group 19 September 1944 :
Report on Swedish initiative (introduced by Paul) on behalf of Léon Blum and others.
Written report from Paris.
Böhm reported on south-east Europe.

Resolution of 23 September 1944 :
'The international group of democratic socialists in Stockholm, in which twelve countries are represented, holds in its memory Wilhelm Leuschner, Ernst Thälmann, Rudolf Breitscheid and the many other members of the socialist movement who have fallen victim to the latest wave of terror by the Nazi régime in Germany. Their endeavours will never be forgotten nor will the freedom fighters in the occupied countries.'

Heinig as representative of the leadership of the SPD was against this, because Thälmann was named ...
May celebrations 1 May 1945 :
Introductory speech : Oscar Hansen.
Speakers : Sigurd Hoel; Wilhelm Böhm; Gunnar Myrdal.
Brandt presented the following resolution :

Socialist refugees and trade unionists from Denmark and Norway and a whole number of European countries ... wish to express their heartfelt gratitude to the Swedish socialist movement and the Swedish people for the hospitality they have found in this country and for the work which Sweden has carried out and still continues in giving assistance to the victims of war, most recently for the liberation and transportation to Sweden of over 15,000 people who have suffered innocently in German prisons and concentration camps.

... When we return to our own homelands we shall ensure that friendy international co-operation is continued so that we can all make our contribution towards ensuring peace for the future. (Towards the end of the meeting Brandt read out the agency report which stated that Hitler was dead.)

INDIVIDUAL PROBLEMS

Oslo, 20 September 1946

Dear Bruno Kreisky,[1]

A few days ago I returned from my latest trip to Germany, when I also spent a couple of days in Stockholm, but I was unfortunately unable to get in touch with you. You are a very busy man. If I am right in hearing that you are soon coming to Oslo, perhaps you could squeeze in a half hour for me?

I am also writing to ask if you could give me some assistance on a practical matter :

There is a Mr. . . . here, who was employed as ministerial adviser in the Reich commissariat during the war, and was indeed a 'card-carrying member', but had worked resolutely against the Nazis. He was also one of the principal witnesses against Quisling. And now the man is to go to Austria to take over control of a Norwegian factory there. The mayor concerned has already agreed that he should receive a residence permit. But it all depends on his being given status by the government, particularly because he is understandably anxious for his family to come along after him (they are still living in the eastern zone).

Would it be possible for you to draw up a favourable document for this man, whom I can commend to you as a reliable anti-Nazi and who has the most impeccable documents from the Norwegian authorities? If the answer is yes, please do so by return, because it is quite likely he will have to set off as soon as the end of next week.

Give my regards to your wife. And my own very best wishes to you.

Oslo, 27 July 1946

Dear friend Böhm,[2]

... I should like to thank you once more for the time we worked together in our modest international circle. Many things now appear considerably more complicated than they did at the time, but we should none the less not need to feel ashamed of the groundwork we did then.

A UNITED OR DIVIDED SOCIALISM   (4)

The discussions on the unification of German socialist and Communist youth organisations were somewhat pushed out of the public mind in the last year of the bloody war in Spain. But within the framework of the individual organisations they have continued to flourish, and pleasing progress on the path to unity has been made. In the various camps the conviction, desire and will towards unity are all growing. The reservations and real differences which have to be overcome are considerable but the task that brings us together is much greater : to win over the current younger generation in Germany. Setting out from the realities of the present situation, we must and surely shall arrive at the recognition that all youth organisations and groups are only one element of a movement which has the common task of assisting in the formation of a front which will be fighting for freedom and building on the basis of socialism ...

We consider it essential that the groups and individual members of the SAJ and SJV and the socialist youth wings of the various organisations should affiliate with one another. They should start by exchanging experiences, reports, and other material and discussing the tasks which confront socialist youth work in Germany today ...

In this way the collaboration of the socialist youth groups on the efforts towards the united front and on the efforts for the creation of a free German youth movement must be continued and strengthened.

Socialist youth will in the future have to urge that due account is taken of the necessity for youth work in the opposition movement as a whole and especially in the committees for the preparation of a German popular front. The socialist young will never give up their socialist objectives in their own work . . .

(5)   THE COMINTERN AND THE SOVIET UNION

. . . The organisational practice which the Comintern has evolved over the years contradicts the most elementary principles of the socialist movement. Persistent intervention from above, even in the smallest organisational questions, and the atmosphere of heresy created in the battle against 'deviations' from the party line had inhibited any healthy development of the individual Communist parties. But that was not the only aspect of the collapse of the Comintern. The complete dependence of the parties on Moscow, on the money and agents of the Soviets, demoralised what was left of the Communist movement. After they had 'purged' the Communist parties of all who did not wish for a complete break with the socialist movement and every opposition group on the 'left' and 'right', all that remained were the party functionaries, and their moral backbone had been broken. So the Comintern was turned into a bureaucratic apparatus which toed the party line and contained many bought and corrupt functionaries who blindly danced to Moscow's tune. But the purges and expulsions did not end there.

Disputes within the Communist camp have taken on a quite distinctive form. Anyone voicing criticism against the dogmas, demands or institutions of the Communist 'church' which is the sole path to salvation, is worse than the enemy himself. There is only ever one opinion which is right and that is dictated from above. If the line carried through by the Comintern, and that means by the Soviet leadership, has no success, the responsibility lies among the faithful of the national parties. These party faithful denounce one another as class traitors or worse. Discussions in a Communist party mostly have the task of establishing the ideological reasons for the purges carried out. Such discussions can degenerate into pure comedy.

This internal malaise of the Communist movement has the effect that no faith can be placed in the party faithful. One does not even know if they will still be there the next day or whether it will be their turn next to be branded as traitors and criminals. A movement which is carried on year after year on such principles will inevitably rot from within.

. . . Communists naturally have the same right as any other

citizens in a democratic society to represent their views, regardless of whether they are right or wrong. Hard facts and experiences must indeed be allowed to show which policy is the right one. But the Communists proclaim it as the first article of faith on which all must swear that their policy and their policy alone is right. All those who do not recognise this article of faith are heretics and traitors.

... The tactics of the Communists aim to cook the books in such a way that they brand political opponents inside the socialist movement as criminals in order to justify their ruthless persecution.

... The Comintern policy must be defeated. It has failed to measure up to its objectives. The battle against the European socialist movement has caused great damage. Its tactics have not led to great successes. Its methods have undermined the socialist movement and the principles of its organisation have proven disastrous.

The old Internationale collapsed in 1914 because the big socialist parties were unable to maintain their independence in the face of the bourgeois régimes which were conducting the war. The Comintern has created a new relationship of dependency.

The socialist movement must be independent, for only then can it also conduct a policy of federation, and it must above all be united, for only then can it win over the whole people and pursue a truly national policy which, far from denying the internationalism of the socialist movement, is the source of its greatest strength.

Although the Russian revolution of 1917 broke with the concept (6) of big power politics, it has latterly been readopted by the Soviet authorities, who are now employing precisely the same aggressive tactics as the other big powers. We do not know how far the Soviet authorities intend to go, but they have stated with greater force than ever before that self-interest is their only consideration.

The socialist movement in England and France based its attitude to the international crisis on the fact that it concerned the defence of democracy, the independence of nations and the struggle for the liberation of Europe from policies of war and dictatorship. The underground socialist movement in central Europe is heading the fight for a social upheaval which it hopes will gain new ground for the movement, for socialism and democracy, and will be in the forefront of a new European order. In neutral countries the fight for peace and freedom, for the independence of smaller nations and against the dictatorship of the big powers is the key task of the socialist movement. In all these countries the socialist movement felt itself betrayed by the policies of the Soviet Union. By entering into a pact with Nazi Germany, the Soviet régime opened up a wide gulf between herself and the European socialist movement. She has placed herself outside the ranks not only of the socialist movement but also of those opposed to Nazism. She has made it all too clear that she is exclusively concerned with her own national interests and will have no truck with anything not directly related to the narrow interests of her own country.

The Soviet Union has therefore excluded herself from the international socialist movement and also from the fighting front for peace, freedom and the independence of smaller nations.

... But what has happened in the Soviet Union is certainly no proof that socialism is a practical impossibility. Experience shows to the contrary that socialism has more to it than state takeover of the means of production. Socialism must be built upon freedom and democracy if it wants to be able to conduct a policy which really gives it the right of bearing the name.

... Because of her foreign policy line, the Soviet Union has thrown away every chance of exercising a positive influence in the task of shaping a new Europe after the horrors and shocks of war. If the socialist movement is unable to solve this problem, then no one can. The socialist movement, facing up to the great historical tasks of the future must, independently of the interests of the great powers, prepare the way for a new socialist and democratic order which will sweep the ground away from under any potential new imperialist conflicts and wars among the great powers.

(5)   Lenin, who stood at the head of the victorious Russian revolution, took the view that the European working classes were revolutionary in the Bolshevist sense, and that there was only a tiny minority—the party functionaries and the 'workers' aristocracy'—preventing them from putting their revolutionary sentiments into practice. Experience has shown that he was looking at Europe through Russian eyes. In Russia the rebellious but ignorant peasantry formed the mass basis for a resolute and tightly knit leadership. And what could be done in Russia should be equally possible in Europe. Accordingly, the top priority was given to building up a party in every country on the Bolshevist model and to the formation of a federation of these parties with the ultimate objective of one vast, centralised world party under the leadership of the Bolshevists.

The Russian establishment of a party and the Soviet state as the political manifestation of the revolution were to be the pattern for the socialist movement in other countries. It was not enough that a large proportion of the socialist organisations were sympathetic towards the Russians and prepared to collaborate with them. A new Bolshevist-cum-Communist political vanguard was to be established. All those unwilling to submit to the demands of the Bolshevists were to be challenged, defeated and cast out. For the revolution was just round the corner. At any rate the red flag was to be hoisted all the way from Vladivostok to the Rhine. As a result, the old organisations and their party faithful would be a mere dead weight if they were dragged along as well. Once the revolution has been victorious, then the new parties would easily be able to take the lead and reunite the working classes on a new basis.

From the outset, enthusiasm for the Russian organisational plans and demands was less than sympathy for the Russian revolution. As early as the autumn of 1918, when she was still in prison, Rosa Luxemburg had written a polemical pamphlet against Bolshevism. She warned principally against the suspension of democratic freedoms which would inevitably result in the establishment of a bureaucratic and party dictatorship. And, early in 1919, she joined other leaders of the German Spartacists (who became the KPD) in warning against the Russian plan for founding a new Internationale. Rosa Luxemburg's strongest argument was that it simply will not do to organise a single-party Internationale, especially as this party had arisen in such an untypical fashion as was the case with the Russians. Their organisational guidelines, their relationship to the working class, etc., had sprung from the underdevelopment of Russian society. An Internationale in which the Russian party holds the majority cannot help but get on to the wrong tack. One of the last resolutions which Rosa Luxemburg carried through the leadership a few days before her death, sent the German representative to the conference in Moscow with the task of voting *against* the foundation of a new Interationale.

In spite of this the Russian will prevailed. The conference in March 1919, at which only a few foreign representatives took part, resolved to regard itself as the first congress of the Communist Internationale...

Since the end of the First World War many negotiations—on (7) national and international levels—have taken place with a view to healing the split in the socialist movement. Frequently they were concerned only with questions of tactics. But one thing is clear beyond all doubt : during the negotiations in the summer of 1945 the Norwegian Labour party was inspired by the sincere desire to find common ground. Scarcely before has a socialist party shown such a great willingness to meet others half way in order to eliminate points of difference. No one side would have to give in, and no one side would come out on top . . .

This attitude of the Labour party did not rest on uncertainty and inner weaknesses. It sprang from the view that practical questions should not be allowed to stand in the way if there was to be agreement on the policies the united socialist parties were to conduct . . .

There can be no doubt that the vast majority of the members of the Communist party also sought unification. It was not they who destroyed the basis for discussion. This is made clear beyond all doubt in the documentation submitted through the federation of trade unions . . .

Resistance against the Nazi occupation forces and the Quisling régime was carried on by men and women from all walks of life. The socialist movement has played a very important part in this and made great sacrifices. But no one group has the right to exploit the work of the home front and the victims of the years of struggle for the purposes of political speculation.

This is precisely what the Communist leaders and their press are trying to do. They strike up their pose and declare that the Communists made the greatest effort during the occupation. They maintain that the Communists put forward the only correct programme and that their tactics had been infallible. That is not true. The Communists played their part. They made their sacrifices. Let no one dispute this, but let them not seek at the same time to claim a monopoly in the national resistance movement which lasted five long years and in which the majority of the Norwegian people were involved . . .

The Communist leadership has no right to set itself up as the ringmaster of national policies. For the fact is that it took some little while before the CP leadership decided in favour of participation in the national resistance movement . . .

. . . The Communist leaders also have no right to act as if they had won the Russian defensive war . . . The war was won through the combined efforts of the Allies. It was not won by the Communist parties.

The future

Nuremberg, 9 February 1946

Dear Irmgard and August,[3]

... The representatives of the Social Democrats should certainly stress that they can draw on a tradition of eighty years in their support of the programme characterised by 'Democracy and peace'. But they should also understand that what must be done—whilst taking over valuable traditional elements—is to form an essentially *new party* : a party which does not depend on the past for its constitution, its structure, and its direction, but rather takes account of the radically changed social conditions of the present day. Only such a party will also be in a position to ward off senescence and to become the party of the younger generation. And that is not their least important task ...

I cannot associate myself with Walter Ulbricht's view that anyone who is not for the unity party in the form recently proposed deserves the title of 'enemy of the people'. The issues are far too complex for that sort of thing. It does not *have* to be a misfortune if we do not achieve amalgamation. For this does depend in large measure on factors outside Germany. But we should do everything within our power to achieve the *greatest possible* common ground among socialist and democratic forces for the reconstruction of Germany. We must at least prevent a repetition of the 'fight to the knife' and support and further practical collaboration in the unions, factories, local areas, etc.

Oslo, 11 April 1946

Dear Erich,[4]

Concerning agreement on the way ahead : it all depends in my view on the fact that in addition to consolidating our organisations and influence in the west we never for a moment lose sight of Germany as a whole. It is from our side that the initiative should come for interzonal co-ordination in the trade union field. In so doing we should also be able to go some way towards overcoming the isolation of our comrades in the east. In any case we cannot consider them as 'traitors', even if they have decided on policies which in the present circumstances we regard as disastrous.

Oslo, 30 April 1946

Dear J.,[5]

... During the last few weeks all kinds of new material have come in which proves beyond dispute that what the SEP (=SED) regard as unity policy is something quite different from what we have been striving for in our own unity policy . . .

But the crucial factor is that the formation of the SEP has been hurried along by undemocratic methods and to some extent even by coercion. Where socialists—as in the western sectors of Berlin— were able to vote they turned against amalgamation by more than 80 per cent, whilst at the same time they took a stand in favour of collaboration between the two socialist parties. For the rest a general ballot was prevented, on the strange grounds that such 'primitive forms of democracy' were more appropriate to the infancy of the socialist movement and that since those days more appropriate methods had been evolved.

It must also be made clear that the manner in which the unity policy has been forced through in the eastern zone has reversed the desire for unity among the vast majority of Social Democrat workers. In all the western zones, and not only there, the Communist party is now regarded with a not unjustifiable mistrust which has already begun to turn into open emnity . . . Compulsory unification doubtless does little to make the zonal frontiers more flexible. The SEP can make as many proclamations as it likes, but the effect will remain the same. For the western powers, but also for the western socialist movement, SEP policy reveals itself as a function of Russian foreign policy. The result will be a deeper division instead of the greater degree of unity which is so necessary.

. . . For my part I draw the conclusion that today more than ever we must make the socialist party in the west as strong as possible and work within its framework towards the most progressive policies that we can achieve.

Notes

1. This letter to Dr. Kreisky is just one of the very many attempts Brandt made to help people in difficult circumstances.
2. Wilhelm Böhm, socialist Hungarian envoy to Stockholm.
3. Enderle.
4. Erich Ollenhauer.
5. Jacob Walcher.

VII

In Germany Again

VII

In Germany Again

A few days after the surrender of Germany I was in Norway once more. As a journalist I spent the summer months commuting between Stockholm and Oslo, and in October I had the opportunity of going to the war crimes tribunal in Nuremberg as a reporter for Scandinavian newspapers.

I landed in an English plane at Bremen airport. August and Irmgard Enderle had also settled there as collaborators of Felix von Eckardt on the Weser Kurier. *Senator Adolf Ehlers and other friends from Bremen numbered among the few who had risked maintaining contact with us throughout the war. At this time I also got to know the kind and wise figure of Mayor Kaisen.*

My Bremen friends took me to Lübeck in a service vehicle where I was reunited with my mother after ten years. She and my step-father had come through the war unscathed apart from a few minor irritations. My mother and I had met for the last time in Copenhagen in 1935, and my stepfather had visited me in Oslo in 1937. When I was living in Berlin in 1936 I was naturally unable to let myself be seen in Lübeck; that would have been dangerous for all concerned. Even during the war I could only very occasionally risk letting them know in Lübeck that I was still alive and well. Towards the end my half-brother had been called up as an anti-aircraft gunner at the age of seventeen, but he had survived the war.

I remained in Nuremberg—apart from a break around the end of the year—until February 1946, and in May I went there again. I made contact with friends in Germany and from abroad and got to know many young men and women who had striven under the most difficult conditions to get life going again and to found a new democracy. In Nuremberg I met up with the circle of Social Democrats round the old Reichstag deputy and trade union leader Josef Simon, who had survived Dachau; and I also met the Bavarian Prime Minister Wilhelm Högner. Arno Behrisch came from Hof: he had returned from Sweden and gave me shattering reports on the fate of the Sudeten Germans. In Frankfurt I met Willi Richter, later to be chairman of the DGB.

In January 1946 I had a first conversation with Kurt Schumacher. Erich Ollenhauer had come from London in order to take part in a conference of Social Democratic party faithful in the American zone with Schumacher. In Hamburg and Lübeck I discussed the situation with the people who had taken up the reins immediately after the war.

I had not yet gone to Berlin. But I met Annedore Leber in the west and Gustav Dahrendorf told me by letter how difficult dealings with the Communists were.

In May 1946 I took part in the first party conference of the reconstituted SPD as reporter for my Scandinavian newspapers, but also as guest delegate for German Social Democrats in Sweden and Norway. The whole conference was dominated by the personality of Schumacher. A few months later, in August, I visited him again in Hanover. I also reported on the founding congress of the DGB for the British zone in Bielefeld. There Max Brauer conveyed the greetings of the American trade unions. Together with Rudolf Katz, later to be vice-president of the Federal constitutional court, he had just returned from exile.

Finally, Theodor Steltzer, the first Prime Minister of Schleswig-Holstein, asked me in Kiel whether I was prepared to let myself be put forward for the office of mayor of Lübeck; he wanted mayor Otto Passarge to take on state office.

I had subsequently often asked myself whether it would not have been right for me to start up again in Lübeck. I hope it does not sound vain of me to say that I think things would rapidly have become too restricted for me there. On the other hand I must admit that the re-establishment of a free city of Lübeck was part and parcel of my own personal programme. Perhaps I would even have had some success which objectively would not have been a good thing. As an 'old citizen of Lübeck', it was difficult for me to accept that the city was to remain part of Schleswig-Holstein with which it had been merged by the Nazis.

On a visit in the late summer of 1946, during which I came across Herbert Wehner in the editorial offices of the Hamburger Echo, *I also met Fritz Heine, who had returned from London with Ollenhauer and was responsible for the press work with the party leadership in Hannover. He asked me to visit the men in Nauheim and Hamburg responsible for the news agencies in the American and British zones (DENA and DPD respectively). Both were in a state of transition to civil government, and people in Hanover took the view that this would be a useful field of work for me. And a tele-gramme actually came some weeks later from Hamburg with the request that I should accept this leading position.*

But whilst I was still waiting, quite a different proposal had been put to me. Foreign Minister Lange wanted to have me as his press attaché and for political reporting for his Foreign Ministry. First there was talk of Paris and then of Berlin, where the Norwegians like other Allies had established a military mission, that is to say representation accredited by the control commission. I did not take long to reply in the affirmative. But the formalities were not settled until towards the end of the year.

One of these formalities was the quasi-military status which had to be bestowed on me. Without ever having been a soldier, I now became an officer. The fact that I valued being a major rather than a captain had nothing to do with reasons of prestige, but simply because the salary scale was better. Besides, the appropriate docu-ment from the Oslo Defence Ministry made express mention of the fact that I should be accorded a semi-military rank. On the left arm of my uniform jacket, which I hardly wore except for the journey to Berlin, I bore the flash 'civilian officer'. . .

Another question—at the time a formality, later to become a problem—was that of my name. My diplomatic passport was issued only in the name of Willy Brandt. And my papers as journalist were also the same. I had written my books, been active in political life since I was nineteen, and become known outside Germany all under the same name. But it was not my 'proper' name, only a nom de plume which had come into use in Lübeck during the first days of the underground so that as early as the spring of 1933 I was made known to the Norwegian Labour party as Willy Brandt.

In dealings with officialdom in Norway and Sweden I had natur-ally always used the name I was born with, Herbert Ernst Karl Frahm. My Schleswig-Holstein certificate of citizenship from 1948 is made out as 'named Willy Brandt'. Official change of name did not come through until 1949 from the police chief in Berlin. As a consequence, I considered it right to let myself be known in every situation by the name which I had used since I was nineteen as a German refugee when living and writing abroad. The decision was made easier for me since the name I was given at birth did not mean a great deal to me. My mother no longer bore that name because she had since married . . .

In Berlin I soon met Ernst Reuter (who had taken the name of Ernst Friesland at one period in his political life). He had come

back from Turkey shortly before my return. Jacob Walcher re-
turned about the same time as myself to Berlin from America. I had
felt closely tied to him during the SAP years, but now our ways
parted because he decided in favour of the SED and work in east
Berlin.

One of my first Berlin acquaintances was Ernst Lemmer who at
that time was still working for the Christian Democrats in the
Russian zone.

My wife Rut came to Berlin shortly after I did, early in 1947.
We shared the difficult yet happy years after the war together. We
had both learned to love Berlin.

In the summer of 1947 Rut and I took part in the second postwar
party conference of the SPD in Berlin. Next we went to Prague,
still as Norwegians, and still before the Communists had silenced
their opponents. After the summer holidays the SPD party leader-
ship asked me whether I wished to take over the Berlin office. This
liaison post was first occupied by Erich Brost who had strongly
urged me to take over in succession to him; he himself went to the
Ruhr and started the Westdeutsche Allgemeine.

The months in Berlin caused me to take the final decision to
devote myself wholly to political work in Germany. Although a
difficult place to work in, Berlin suited me. My Norwegian friends
placed no obstacles in my way and showed great understanding for
my decision.

The tasks in Berlin were fascinating. Their significance for the
future of Germany and for the peace of the world could readily be
anticipated. I did not find it difficult to get used to working within
the party framework. In many respects my own development had
led to similar conclusions to those the SPD now made the basis of
their policies . . .

The impulses of my radical youth had not been shaken. But much
had grown on to them. Now I had also learned how not to pass
easy judgement on the men of the Weimar Republic, but to honour
Friedrich Ebert and his friends with their fitting place in history.

For me politics has always been a subject concerned not with
theory, but primarily with living people. Thus in the immediate
postwar period I tried to re-establish broken contacts, to help people
who had got into difficulties because of their participation in the
occupation régime in Norway, to point to the plight of refugees and
expellees, to send out parcels and to stimulate humanitarian aid. It
is no exaggeration for me to say that a whole younger generation
in Berlin owe their very survival of the period of greatest depriva-
tion to the Swedish soup kitchens. A helping hand was reached out

to refugees in Germany not only by neutral Sweden, but also by Norway and Denmark, where the wounds of the occupation period were only slowly healing over. And it was particularly pleasing to me that it was Norway which warmheartedly took in Berlin children in especially large numbers.

FIRST PROBLEMS OF PEACE

Stockholm, 23 August 1945

Dear friend Krebs,

Willi Seifert told me that you would perhaps be able to undertake research through the aid committee on people who have disappeared in German concentration camps. I should be most grateful to you if you would be able to do this in the following case:

My friend Hermann Ebeling, a teacher and youth official from Brunswick, who is now with the American army in the west as an ensign, has writen to me from there saying that he has lost track of his mother-in-law. She is Martha Fuchs, who was a well-known Social Democrat in Brunswick. When Ebeling was in Brunswick the last time his sister-in-law gave him the following information:
... Arrested August 1944. Taken to Ravensbrück, Mecklenburg in October. According to statements by prisoners, seems to have been transferred to Oranienburg in March. Alleged to have been in camp hospital there. It is possible that she was transported to Bergen-Belsen at the end of March. If this is not so, she may be an in-patient in a hospital in Mecklenburg. Please try to trace her through the Berlin radio.

My thanks in advance for your efforts.

Very best wishes.

Stockholm, 23 August 1945

Dear Ernst,[1]

You know I shall always feel bound to Norway by the closest ties. But I have never given up Germany. It would have been easier simply to remain in Norway. But I cannot make up my mind to do this.

What do I think about the situation in Germany? That is a subject for a pamphlet. I still believe that Germany will live on. Apart from its senseless far-reaching frontier changes, the Potsdam agreement represents from a political point of view an advance on the previous state of affairs.

Your present group is very lively. It is still under the inspired leadership of Bruno Kreisky. I have always worked well with him

during the war in the international group of democratic socialists
of which I was secretary. Now of course not much remains of the
group. The Norwegians and Danes have returned to their homes.
The well-known Allied representatives are no longer there either.
But friendly relations will continue to be maintained for the future.
Old Böhm has been quite ill more than once, but he is as cheerful
as ever although being completely cut off from home is depressing
for him. What is particularly tragic is the position of Ernst Paul
and his Sudeten German colleagues.

Stockholm, 26 August 1945

Dear mother,

I can't yet answer your question about when I am coming. The
return of political refugees is now proceeding more rapidly. The
American officials, and probably the English as well, are particularly
keen to have people back so they can enter the administration and
help in the reconstruction of the trade unions. So from this point
of view I should be able to get a chance of coming back without
any trouble. But there are a few things I still have to do here and
in Norway which I cannot just leave unfinished. But I shall be
turning up one day.

Oslo, 11 June 1946

Dear Schumacher,

Briefly this as well : a large number of gift parcels are being sent
out to Germany from Sweden. But the whole thing now seems to
be in jeopardy because they are not getting customs clearance in
Lübeck. Count Bernadotte has recently announced that there are
tens of thousands of parcels being held up in Lübeck and only 150
are getting cleared every day. This whole customs business is sheer
nonsense. Austria and Hungary let parcels in without any fuss. As
far as I know it is not just the Allied authorities who are responsible
for this situation but German officials as well (allegedly the Minister
of Finance in Kiel is behind this). This must be thoroughly looked
into. In the present state of emergency everything should surely be
done to give private acts of generosity a free hand. The least
demand that should be made is speedy clearance at the Lübeck end
so that the food there doesn't go off.

Oslo, 11 June 1946

I haven't yet come to a final decision about my work for the
future.[2] Various offers have come my way in Hanover. But if it is at
all possible I should like to be financially independent of the party.

In Lübeck where I spoke on 20 May for the first time in more than
thirteen years, I received a very heartfelt welcome and party friends
would very much like me to go there. Perhaps I might still do just
that, although I do feel that I would be far and away too restricted
there. The offer that I find most attractive is one which . . . some
friends have made, namely to take up a leading position in the press
agency.

Oslo, 3 October 1946

Dear friends in Lübeck,
I had hoped to be able to take up the invitation you sent me
and to be able to speak before your local elections. But for technical
reasons this is unfortunately not possible.

So I should like to use this opportunity to say to as many citizens
of Lübeck as possible that the elections which are to take place next
Sunday are of crucial importance, and not just for the internal
pattern of our old Hanseatic city. Mayor Passarge has rightly
stressed that Lübeck must be the future gateway to the Baltic. If
this is the case, then contact and co-operation with Scandinavia is
one of the most important conditions for the prosperity of Lübeck
which we should all be striving to achieve.

What must be done is to build the new Lübeck. What must be
done, together with all the democratically-minded forces of the
German people and with democratic north, is to work towards the
setting up of a European community. The representatives of democratic socialism offer the right guarantees for reconstruction, a
common endeavour, new avenues of political effectiveness, and a
dignified standard of living.

This is why it is my wish and hope that a strong majority of the
electorate of Lübeck will rally round the SPD candidates and vote
for work and bread, for peace and socialism.

PRESS ATTACHÉ IN BERLIN   (1)

'. . . During all those years of enforced absence I have never lost
contact with Germany and have always regarded myself as one of
those who have emerged from the German opposition movement.
I have come to feel very strongly that we can rebuild only on a
European basis and that a healthy love for the homeland and a
wholesome relationship with the movement in the country in which
one is living are in no way mutually contradictory . . .'

Re: appointment as press attaché in Berlin
Note from the end of October 1946

On 28 September I was at Halvard Lange's house. He said he had been given to understand that I had made up my mind to return to Germany. In case I had not yet come to a final decision he wanted me to know that I could take up a post in the Norwegian Foreign Service if I was so minded. Halvard Lange particularly had in mind an appointment as press attaché in Paris.

I now found myself faced with an extremely difficult choice.

My German friends were clearly expecting me to participate in one way or another in the reconstruction of Germany. The party leadership in Hamburg had let it be known that they would like me to take an editorial post in one of the zonal press agencies....

In May and September I had received several representations from Lübeck to the effect that I should return there. But I did have the feeling that things would be too 'confined' in Lübeck and that various leading friends in the party were somewhat worried about their position. So there would be conflicts (and there had already been some). Still I began to see this in a different light when I spoke to Th. Steltzer on 9 September in Kiel. He hinted at an arrangement (with reference to a previous conversation with Otto Passarge) whereby I could become mayor of Lübeck whilst Passarge would take over the post of chief of police (for the state).

When I saw Halvard Lange on 19 October again (he had just come back from Paris and was here for a few days before travelling on to the UN meeting in New York) I was really inclined to take up his Paris offer—in the hope that I would be able to make a reasonable contribution to European democratic socialism from there.

Halvard now confronted me with an entirely different situation. He said the Paris suggestion had not actually fallen through, but he would rather see me as press attaché in Berlin, not least so that I could keep an eye on the way the east-west problem was developing there. I accepted. Halvard telephoned Minister of State Gerhardsen who was in agreement with the arrangement which had been made. Press chief Schive was brought in and given the job of discussing practical questions with me. I had come to my decision.

Oslo, 22 November 1946

Dear Stefan,[3]

It was not an easy decision ...

A letter came from Lübeck saying that colleagues in the party were in Hamburg in order to secure my transfer to Lübeck. The letter closed with the moving words : 'As successor to Julius Leber you will be in an equal position to make a good start here . . . We must have you.'

. . . The Berlin suggestion was a compromise solution for me. Naturally I was causing great disappointment to my friends in Lübeck. But I want to maintain direct contact with developments in Germany as a whole and these I could follow better from Berlin than from a provincial city in the west, and there I hope I shall be able to be of assistance to my German as well as my Scandinavian friends in many ways. Since I only needed to contract myself for one year, I can decide after this time has elapsed whether to remain inside Germany or to follow an international or European course in all earnestness.

Do you agree with the decision which I have made? . . . I suppose I must put a letter together and explain to my colleagues in Lübeck why I am going to Berlin as one of the 'Allies'.

Oslo, 1 November 1946

Dear friends,[4]

I should like to inform you that I shall shortly be taking up a post in the Norwegian embassy in Berlin which is accredited by the control commission as the Norwegian military mission. The Foreign Minister here, Halvard M. Lange, and other friends, have urged me to work there as press attaché and political colleague. I have resolved to accept this post for one year.

It will perhaps strike some of you as odd that I am going to Berlin as one of the 'Allies', especially as I shall be obliged to wear a Norwegian uniform for some of the time. My status as an 'Ally' is however nothing new. I became a Norwegian citizen in 1940 after Hitler had deprived me of citizenship some years earlier. Up to now I have had no cause to seek for a reinstatement of my at present somewhat tenuous claim on German citizenship, and so relinquish Norwegian citizenship.

Questions of form cannot be decisive, nor can the disruption caused by the situation which Hitler's war has brought upon us. What matters is where the individual can be of most service in the rebirth of Europe and that means also of European democracy. For years, as you know, I have equally sought to further both 'German' and 'Scandinavian' interests. These were and still are in no way contradictory objectives. In the course of the last year I had tried in my travels as a journalist to help to enhance relations between the Scandinavian and the new German socialist movements and to arouse a sympathetic understanding for the socialist reconstruction of Germany.

Nothing has changed in my personal plans. I shall continue to strive to work for a broadening of knowledge and understanding on both sides. I shall aid the German press by the provision of material on the Scandinavian socialist movement. On the other side of the coin I shall keep the Norwegian government, the Scandinavian socialist movement and the press there up to date with developments in Germany. But what matters above all is to work within the situation as it exists towards the securing of peace and the development and stabilisation of European and international co-operation.

These are great objectives. I know that my friends in Lübeck, who had reckoned with the possibility of my return there, will be disappointed. At the same time I am certain that they will not close their minds to the considerations I have had to take into account. They should rest assured that I shall never forget the old Hanseatic city and what I have learned there, let alone desert it.

Members of the party leadership in Hanover have urged me to consider taking over the political editorship of one of the zonal press offices. The DPD in the British zone was probably at the front of their minds. Recently I was also asked to go to Hamburg to take up the work which for the time being was to be carried out under Allied leadership. I value this offer highly, but I can scarcely believe that I should have been able to do more useful work there than that which I am now about to take up. My independence as a European democratic socialist would not be stronger in Hamburg than in Berlin.

For many a year now I have made it the guiding principle of my political activities that I should not take on a position from a narrow national standpoint. Each one of you will understand that the fate of the Germany now struggling to find a new basis for existence will in large measure be decided on the international plane. I wish to take this opportunity to leave you in no doubt that my personal attitude to the German socialist movement is the same as it has always been. Today I can best serve that movement by acceding to the request of my Norwegian friends. Later the time will come for re-examining how and where I can be of most service in the common interest.

My loyalty and obligations to European democracy and international socialism far override secondary matters of form and questions of my own personal position. It is in this spirit that I remain

Yours,

Willy Brandt.

Re: work as press attaché.[5]
Berlin, 5 February 1948

I was appointed temporary press attaché to the Norwegian military mission in Berlin in December 1946 and took up the post on 17 January 1947.

The Ministry for Foreign Affairs had asked me to devote particular attention to reporting political matters... In 1947 I sent off 395 reports to the press offices, in January of this year 22 reports and documents, frequently with supplementary papers...

Apart from a few exceptions—particularly in connection with the issue of the size of the whaling fleet—I have been able to discover no malice or hostility in the attitude of the newspapers when they deal with Norwegian issues. But it is all too frequently the case that the rights and interests of smaller nations are neither understood nor sufficiently respected. Nor is the power struggle among the great powers in Germany particularly designed to advance 're-education' in this field. It must also be made clear that newspapers in the Russian zone are reliant on a very restricted range of information and articles, so that certain attacks or misunderstandings in the Russian press are so to speak automatically taken up in some of the German newspapers.

The only profitable means of disseminating knowledge of Norwegian affairs in Germany is to make people aware of the situation as it actually exists. We should not just 'forget' what has happened in the war, but the main stress should be placed on reconstruction and development in the fields of politics, economics, social welfare and cultural life. In so doing we shall be able to make our own small contribution from the Norwegian side to breaking down the isolation caused by Nazism and to creating a new awareness of conditions abroad on the part of interested Germans. But let there be no doubt either that future trade relations will best be served by factual information on economic problems.

A substantial part of the German press has been preoccupied with the prohibition against German whaling and the restrictions on German trawler fishing. On this matter there has been some sharp criticism of the Norwegian attitude.

A big Oslo newspaper has attacked the Berlin press attaché for allegedly having done nothing to get the Germans to understand the Norwegian views.

And I must be the first to admit that up to now we have reached only a section of the German public and we have not succeeded in convincing all those whom we have reached.

There must be no doubt that the extremely serious food situation in Germany after the war has placed many obstacles in the way of positive discussion. The significance of the questions discussed is displayed on far too broad a canvas, especially as far as the whaling question goes. Many have put the Norwegian view across in such a way as to give the impression that Norway has sought to exploit the German defeat in order to get rid of unwelcome competition. This notion is perhaps not all that absurd, particularly if it is seen against the background of German actions during the war and certain measures on the part of the Allies since.

No objections have been raised in the German press against Norwegian proposals for an agreement which aims at maintaining present fish stocks. But the restrictions on tonnage laid down by the control commission have been attacked, because, it has been claimed, this means a reduction in the capacity of the German trawler fleet. It is further asserted that Germany should not be prevented from increasing her own capacity for food production, and that the promises of the Atlantic Charter on the freedom of the high seas and free access to sources of raw material should be equally valid for those who have lost the war . . .

The question will perhaps fade more into the background when they have succeeded in improving the supply of fat. In addition I have gained the impression that the United States will accept the German demands to participate in the whaling fleet sooner or later —for that does not impinge upon any American interests.

. . . It cannot be the task of a press attaché to furnish daily papers and agencies with 'hot news'. But I have got a number of news-papers and a few agencies to the point at which they will ring up if they receive news from Norway which they either want verified or enlarged on. I also receive continual requests about Norwegian affairs in Germany (trade dealings, aid operations, etc.).

Collaboration with the agencies in the English and American zones leaves a satisfactory impression. The first-named (DPD) now has exchange facilities with the NTB. The news agency in the Russian zone has also distributed some of our announcements. On the other hand we have had no success in establishing firm contacts with the press office in the French zone.

In some cases material is accommodated by German radio . . .

The control commission has not yet been able to reach agreement on permitting the normal exchange of newspapers, periodicals and books between Germany and other countries. The western Allied authorities, as reported to the Foreign Ministry, made it known at the end of 1947 that they no longer wished to stand in the way of such a postal interchange within their zones as a whole. So it would now be possible—in any event, on a private, non-commercial basis—to exchange Norwegian and German publications.

But I should like to suggest that the attempt should be made to introduce a more normal procedure, for example by trading between Narvesen and a corresponding firm in Hamburg on an exchange basis.

A number of German specialist journals have come into existence again, and a start has been made on producing new publications which contain a wide variety of matter which is of interest to libraries, academic institutions and industrial organisations. On the other hand it is senseless for Germans to be cut off intellectually from the outside world or to be obliged to fall back on publications distributed by the four controlling powers... The attitude of the Norwegian press towards Germany can hardly be said to be satisfactory. On several occasions I have expressed the view that at the very least some of the largest newspapers should have a permanent reporter here in Berlin. It would be of importance and interest to follow events in Germany after the collapse of Nazism, but in addition there is the role of Berlin as one of the best vantage points for observing the power struggle between east and west. The British authorities are favourably disposed towards accrediting up to five permanent Norwegian correspondents. This would allow the establishment of fruitful collaboration between the press attaché and one or more correspondents in Berlin.

In connections with the travels of the new press attaché: every opportunity should, I feel, be taken to discuss press and information matters with the other Norwegian offices in Germany.

Among the various lesser matters in which I have been engaged, I should mention establishing contact between individual Norwegian and German publishers, provision of articles for theatrical journals, information for university and school circles, books and periodicals for the library of the Ministry of Foreign Affairs, the central office of statistics and the research centre for Norwegian industry.

I took part in the inspection of the archives of the Foreign Office and of the German embassy in Oslo in July 1947 together with the senior archivist Omang and in October and in November of the same year with Jakob Sverdrup and Gerhard Munthe.

At the beginning of 1947 a publishing house in Hamburg accepted a German manuscript of mine on the war years in Norway, which I based on my earlier brief commentaries, but it has not yet proved possible to obtain paper for printing the book...

At the beginning of November 1947 I informed the Ministry of Foreign Affairs that it was my intention to give up my post at the turn of the year. After discussions with the chief of the office here we agreed that I should work on until 1 February and I declared myself ready to help the military mission in tasks in the press and information services during any transitional period.

If I am asking to be allowed to cease working for you, this is because it has been my intention to accept the challenge to take part in the reconstruction of the country in which I was born... I have said to the Foreign Minister and I should like to take this opportunity to repeat that my new work and my future citizenship will alter nothing in my relationships towards Norway.

WORK FOR THE NEW PARTY

Berlin, 7 November 1947

Foreign Minister Halvard M. Lange
at present in New York
Dear Halvard,

During my visit in Oslo at the end of August you asked me if I might be toying with the idea of entering German politics. At that point in time that was still a hypothetical question.

Today the position has altered. The leadership of the German Social Democrats has pressed me to take over the task of representative of the party committee in Berlin and *vis à vis* the Allied authorities here.

I have given this a great deal of thought and as a result I have made up my mind to accept this position of trust. You can rest assured that it was not easy for me to make up my mind and I hope you will understand the motives which lie behind my decision.

It is not such a straightforward matter as choosing Germany instead of Norway. It seems to me that I can and must do something more active for the ideas to which I owe loyalty, and that such efforts are especially needed in this country.

I have already received similar invitations on an earlier occasion...

There are many reasons behind the fact that up to now I have neglected to react to such challenges. The most important was that I have found it difficult to 'give up' Norway.

I was very young when I came to Norway. Naturally I was involved in German anti-Nazi work. But I soon fitted into the Norwegian pattern of life and it meant a great deal more to me than a technical change of status when I was made a Norwegian citizen. Besides, that happened some years after I had been deprived of German citizenship, which at that time was rather something of an honour.

Norway has also moulded me as a man of politics and in many other ways. I am profoundly grateful for this, and it is not my intention to turn my back on what has happened.

It is a wrench to have to give up direct contact with a society which I feel a part of, and with a people whose good and bad sides I have come to love. Political work in Germany, on the other hand, means getting together with all manner of men with whom I do not feel so much in common. In addition there is the uncertainty over the way the future will turn out.

But it cannot be helped. I know that the solution of the German problem will be dependent on decisions taken on an international political level. But there is much to be done inside Germany in the interests of Europe, democracy and peace. And despite everything there are positive forces within the German people which will be able to make their mark on future developments.

You ought to know that I have no illusions. But I wish to try to help bring Germany back into Europe and as far as possible to make it part of that third force which is essential in order to avert the greatest catastrophe of all time. It is fairly certain that I shall suffer disappointment and perhaps more than that. I hope I shall face defeat if it comes with the feeling that I have done my duty.

I shall carry with me all the good things I have experienced in Norway. There was much that was not good, but in my thoughts there is no hint of bitterness, and no artificial lines of demarcation can prevent me from feeling that I am a part of Norway. You can continue to depend on me for the future.

I should like to have told you in good time before I gave in my notice from my present post. That was unfortunately impossible as my future job demanded a swift decision. For this reason I shall inform the Foreign Ministry in the next few days that I wish to resign with effect from next February.

When I was appointed, it was agreed that the appointment was to be for one year in the first instance. If it should turn out to be desirable, I can perhaps be able to accept specific tasks in the press and information services during a transitional period but it would be a good thing if my successor were to appear no later than 15 January.

Nothing would please me more than if I could maintain close contact with you and your representatives here after I have left, and if I could be of assistance wherever appropriate.

Gunnar Myrdal had asked me whether I would like to go to Geneva as a 'public relations man' if I did not continue in my present work. That will now fall through too, and I shall let Myrdal know in the next few days.

Many thanks for the trust which you have shown towards me in sending me to Berlin. I have done my best. I should be unhappy if you were to suffer any inconvenience on my account.

With very best wishes.

Berlin, 23 December 1947

Dear comrade Schumacher,

The information which Erich Brost gave me yesterday after his return from Hanover has worried me deeply. It causes me to fear that you have some grounds for mistrust which will prejudice our profitable work together.

I have been told that—because of renewed . . . scribblings against me—you should like to speak to me, but that such a discussion could not take place before 10 January. Naturally I shall be pleased to come to Hanover and put myself in your hands as far as fixing the exact time goes. But a renewed postponement of several weeks seems to me to be intolerable. It also puts me into an impossible position towards my Norwegian friends and colleagues and towards the Allied authorities which have been informed of the planned change of domicile.

So I have made up my mind to write to you in all openness about the intrigues which have been spun out against me by Scandinavian emigré circles. Erich Brost has promised me to transmit this letter to you with all despatch. I should be pleased to have your answer in my hands soon. It would be better to settle once and for all, rather than let a confused situation drag on.

First this : I had long been clear in my mind that it was my duty to take an active part in building the new Germany sooner or later. But I did not have the remotest idea that the party leadership would make me its representative. After the question had been discussed in Hanover, Erich Brost asked me in October if I would be disposed to take over the post as representative in Berlin. I thought it over for a few days and then gave an answer in the affirmative. At the beginning of November I was briefly in Hanover and informed you and General Heine of my final decision. On this occasion I also stated that as Berlin representative I should naturally have to express the views of the party, but that that would be all the easier for me if I was given the opportunity of presenting my personal view to the leading bodies of the party in the event of differences of opinion arising in one matter or another. At that time that was taken completely for granted. Nor was there any question of political or personal reservations against me.

I should like to make this position quite clear. I have resolved after mature consideration to give up my post and more besides. But I have not pushed for any particular office. Even today I should not wish to do that. There is only one thing I would ask, and that is that I should no longer be put off, but that I should be put fully in the picture . . .

I only needed some financial support to live in the first weeks of my years abroad. After that I was able to manage with my journalistic work and in the last few years even earn a decent living. It was fairly easy for me to find my feet in Scandinavia. In contrast to many other people I was not a complete outsider. I had success. A few people, in whose eyes I was far too young anyway, still have not forgiven me for this even now . . .

A number of Scandinavian friends and colleagues have written to me in the course of the past few weeks and expressed their sympathy with my intentions. As you perhaps know, Professor Gunnar Myrdal had asked me to take up a post with the UN commission in Geneva. After I had written off to him, he replied on 24 November : 'Alva and I read your letter of November 8 with the most cordial and respectful feelings of sympathy. We do not know all the circumstances, but we feel you are doing the right thing by starting work again for the one of your two countries which is the poorest and which is most in need of your assistance.'

As Franz Neumann said to me and Erich Ollenhauer later confirmed, I have been suspected in Stockholm emigré circles and probably too by a few gossip-mongers in Oslo as being an 'SED man in disguise' or the like. In this respect there has been talk of my relations with Jacob Walcher.

To take the last charge first : I have never concealed the fact, but expressly told Erich Brost at the beginning of the year that Walcher occasionally visits me. We have known each other since 1933 and were close friends in the years before the outbreak of war. From a political point of view we have gone more and more our own separate ways since 1939. The previous summer, when he was still in America, I wrote to him in no uncertain terms that I could not follow him along the path to the SED, but that I was and should remain a Social Democrat . . .

I have never kept silent about the fact that in my time I have been a supporter of a unified socialist party, which should be independent and rest on a democratic foundation. The disputes surrounding this question have been overtaken by events. I have changed my attitude to a number of other questions and have not the least grounds for making a secret of the fact nor of being ashamed, not even out of consideration for a Stockholm clique which does not need to examine itself because it never held firm opinions.

Let me declare to you unambiguously : I stand by the principles of democratic socialism in general and the policies of the German Social Democrats in particular. I reserve the right to work out my own views on any new issues that may arise. And I shall never agree in advance to every detailed formulation of policy, even if it is stamped by the leader of the party himself.

It seems to me that it also does not contradict the policy of the party if, while taking the most resolute stand against the régime of terror and lies, one should never give up trying to win over the more honourably minded German Communists. Further, I believe that neither Germany nor Europe will finally settle the development of a real strategy of the third force. We are faced with a much tougher tussle than before against Bolshevist aspirations for power on the one hand and the reactionaries of international politics on the other. In the struggle with Bolshevism I should perhaps make much more of an effort than some of our colleagues to examine the historical background to developments inside Russia. Also in judging the development in countries within the Russian sphere of influence I should be inclined to give central importance to the historical and social background to present events . . .

To return to Stockholm once more : you have certainly already heard a great deal of fuss being made about the heights of absurdity to which the emigré mentality could occasionally rise. That no longer particularly bothers me. And besides, I do not feel inclined any more to turn the other cheek.

In this respect I should none the less like to remind you that the group of German Social Democrats at the time who represented the vast majority of our colleagues in Sweden—and equally the small Oslo group—appointed me last year as guest delegate to the party conference in Hanover . . .

Let me assure you in conclusion that I have never been a simple yes-man, and hope I shall never be one. But for a long time I have learned to fit in and to work to the best of my ability for our cause in the position to which I have been allotted.

After many years of preparation and commentating from the sidelines I long for active involvement. It would be all the easier for me to take over responsible work for the party, as I am aware of your programmatic demand for a rejuvenated German Social Democratic party. Tradition means a great deal. But respect for what has been handed down should never go so far that the errors and mistakes of the past are not admitted. How else can a party grow from within? And how else can it be successful in winning over the younger generation?

Please do not be angry if this letter should sound somewhat heated. Basically what that means is nothing other than : I shall not push myself forward, I see no reason why I should defend myself, but I stand by the cause and by my word.

Yours,

Willy Brandt.

Notes

1. Ernst Winkler.
2. From a letter to Jacob Walcher.
3. Dr. Stefan Szende.
4. This is a duplicated circular letter sent out to personal and political friends.
5. Brandt worked as press attaché in Berlin from 17 January 1947 until 31 January 1948.

Postscript

'Where was Brandt in 1948?—In safety!' This was the slogan on the banners which two aeroplanes towed behind them when I was carrying on the Bundestag election campaign in September 1965. This was only one of many defamations in a far from pleasant election battle which drained a great deal of my resources during two big campaigns and in the years in between.

In safety in 1948—what was that supposed to mean exactly? I had exchanged my Norwegian passport for a German one, and in so doing had in no way improved my economic circumstances, and had changed from being a member of a diplomatic service to becoming an employee of a party. That did not happen at any old time, but *before* the currency reform, *before* the Berlin blockade and *before* the foundation of the Federal Republic of West Germany.

I have often asked myself if I should not show some consideration for those who evidently have found it so difficult to understand me, although they have not exactly handled me with kid gloves. Perhaps I find this a little easier since September 1965 which I regard as a dividing line. For the attitudes I met with then showed me that my opponents, who claim political power on the grounds that they are accustomed to it, are not just concerned to exclude me as an alternative. Their attitudes were also conditioned by the fact that my life has differed so much from that of the majority of my fellow countrymen. A new generation will see many causes to wonder at the kind of yardstick used in those years.

I was not against Germany but against her despoilers. I had not broken with Germany, and I was moved to act by concern for our nation. I did not choose the easy path but risked my neck on more than one occasion. It was definitely not the case that fleeing Germany after 1933 meant choosing the easy way out.

And yet I must appear to many as an extreme case : two changes of citizenship, not both willingly, but still two; a change of name—as a protection against persecution and then as a matter of conviction, but still a change; the resolution of a young radical leftwing socialist—who becomes chairman of the Social Democrats, perhaps the biggest change of all.

I should have been as unwilling to miss my youthful convictions as much as the experience I have gained since then. I know today that my hope for a 'third force', which still finds expression in the letter to Schumacher two days before Christmas 1947, will have to remain a vain hope in view of the cold war. Today I know even more about German history and the Prussian spirit. Today I no longer see things in terms of black and white, not even when it is a matter of explaining the victory of National Socialism in 1933. Today I should judge an event like the war in Spain with more discrimination and careful thought. Today I have long since overcome my anticlerical prejudices and have admitted 'that the churches in a free society not only have a claim to have their presence tolerated, but also they can count upon a secure place in our picture of society and on our support'.

Since long stretches of the path which led to this recognition have seemed to many to have lain half concealed, it was my intention to document my previous political development in book form. Anyone who wants to can now form a better picture of what I have experienced, thought and written 'outside Germany'.

Now this book lies before me. I have not read without some apprehension what Günther Struve has put together of my writings. On the strength of his responsibility as editor he presented a cross-section, which in his own conviction is objective and fair. I myself must declare myself biased. I have certainly offered him suggestions, but I did not have any part in the selection.

Instead I have asked myself the question whether such a book can lay claim to any interest. There are other questions besides : will anyone understand what was put on paper in 1933 by a nineteen-year-old or in 1937 by a twenty-three year-old? Will it be understood that this is not a matter of self-justification, but of an attempt to explain a man's thinking and to show what his point of departure was and how he became what he is today?

I have always striven to find clear and honourably appropriate answers to the open questions of our age. This is how I expressed it in my Dortmund speech to the SPD party conference on 1 July 1966 :

'Twenty years ago I should scarcely have thought it possible that an industrious and efficient nation would achieve since then what it has. Anyway, most people did not think it likely that twenty years on Germany would still be split in two, armed in its divided state against itself and with no practical prospect of a peace treaty.

At that time, twenty years ago, everyone knew that Germany had lost the war. Today many people would rather forget the fact. At that time there was a strong united resolve to open out new horizons. Over the years the inclination to retrenchment has become stronger. At that time, despite many inhibitions, there was considerable awareness of the common good, moral values and qualities of the spirit. Since then economic success has become the yardstick of success pure and simple.

'Many of the fundamental tasks of the Social Democrats still remain uncompleted. Broad masses of the people still feel themselves cut off from the affairs of state. The integration of the workers is far from being achieved. Equal opportunities, not least equal educational opportunities, and everything else which belongs to democratisation, and this means also the defeat of economic feudalism— these are the broad issues. For us the democratic and socialist Federal republic is a permanent task. Anyone who seeks to damn systematic thinking ahead as a heresy is turning progress itself into a heresy. We can only bring about what is necessary for our country with a new-style policy, a policy of honesty, of objectivity, of co-operation, of agreement. We must do everything to put into practice what we recognise to be right. That is the lesson of Weimar.

'We need have no *fear of Communism* as an ideology. We need no Chinese wall policies. Even in the Communist-ruled part of the world things are not standing still. We answer the decisive political questions in diametrically opposed ways. Whether we like it or not, the Communists are a big political force on German soil. But a fundamental as well as a practical political gulf divides us, one of which we are still very much conscious of twenty years after the forced unification in the other part of Germany.

'*Relations between politics and the national spirit* have been disturbed in the Federal Republic. In German territories there is widespread hypocrisy. Adult citizens should not be fed as if they were educationally subnormal. It is decisive for the further advance of a democratic Federal republic whether the population at large have a sense of commitment. The forces of the spirit have been stifled by material prosperity. Smugness, selfishness, lack of sense of responsibility have become widespread. But the nation as a whole is full of strength and healthy at heart.

'We must adopt *a positive attitude to our nation,* otherwise it cannot survive in the long term without losing internal stability, without losing footing in times of internal and external crisis. As Germans, we should never forget the past. But we cannot be weighed down all the time with the burden of guilt, the younger generation even less than its predecessors. A subservient citizen is not the best patriot. We are patriots if we secure in our own country the freedom of the individual, if we help to secure democracy in the economic and social spheres as well. We must do all in our power to save as much as possible of Germany for the Germans. Our patriotism recognises itself at the same time as a European and worldwide political responsibility. Measured against peace, the nation state is no longer the greatest of all possessions. If our Federal republic is to be more than the past put to rights then its social pattern must accommodate itself to change. Our nation can only survive with a modern, mobile and humane society. The political leadership must have the courage to speak the truth, even when it is unpleasant. Our people must be fully aware of the position of this country and on their guard against empty phrases and vain illusions.'

Willy Brandt.

List of sources

I AFTER THE WAR—WHAT NEXT?

1. *Stormaktenes krigsmål og det nye Europa* (War Aims of the Great Powers and the New Europe), Oslo, 1940.
2. *Krigs- og fredsmål* (War and Peace Aims), Stockholm, 1943. Written for the Information Service of the Norwegian Embassy.
3. *Efter segern—diskussionen om krigs- och fredsmålen* (After Victory—the Discussion on War and Peace Aims), Stockholm, 1944.
4. From an article on France, Stockholm, Sept. 1944.
5. *Der zweite Weltkrieg—ein kurzer Überblick* (The Second World War —a short Survey), Stockholm, 1945. Pamphlet issued by the SDU committee for democratic reconstruction.
6. *Tendenzen der alliierten Okkupationspolitik* (Tendencies of Allied Occupation Policies), Autumn 1945.
7. 'LFP-Gespräch mit Annedore Leber und Willy Brandt' (Lübeck Free Press in conversation with A.L. and W.B.), *Lübecker Freie Presse*, 7 September 1946.
8. *Forbrytere og andre tyskere* (Criminals and other Germans), Stockholm, 1946. Misrepresented by W.B.'s opponents as 'Germans and other Criminals'.

II THE OPPOSITION IN CONFLICT

1. *Hvorfor har Hitler seiret i Tyksland* (Why Hitler was victorious in Germany), Oslo, 1933. Short text for secondary school students.
2. Contribution to a Norwegian Labour Party pamphlet, Oslo, 1933.
3. From *Arbeider-Ungdommen* (Socialist Youth), Oslo, May 1933, July 1935.
4. Written during an illegal stay in Berlin, Autumn 1936.
5. From *Marxistische Tribüne* (Marxist Tribune), II, 7, Paris, March 1937.
6. 'Zu unserer Losung: Sozialistische Front der jungen Generation' (Notes on our Watchword: Socialist Front of the Younger Generation), *Kampfbereit*, 1936. Duplicated.
7. From a letter, 27 December 1937.

8. 'Fünf Jahre Hitler-Herrschaft' (Five Years of Hitler's Rule), *Arbeiderbladet* (Socialist News), Oslo, 29 January 1938.
9 'Deutschland vor und nach München' (Germany before and after Munich), *Det 20de århundre* (The 20th Century—Journal of the Socialist Party), December 1938.
10. Meeting of German Socialists in Norway shortly after the outbreak of war.
11. 'Deutscher Sozialismus und der Krieg' (German Socialism and the War), *Det 20de århundre*, December 1939.
12. 'Dem Ende der ersten Kriegsphase entgegen' (The Ending of the First Phase of the War), Oslo, 1940. Duplicated information sheet produced by the Oslo study group 1939–40.
13. 'Unsere Haltung in Rußland', *Det 20de århundre*, January 1940.
14. *Zur Lage* (Situation Report), Stockholm, November 1940.
15. Study on the German Resistance, Stockholm, September 1943.
16. *Kräfte der deutschen Revolution* (Forces of the German Revolution), April 1944.
17. *Forbrytere og andre tyskere.* (cf. I/8)

III FOR AND AGAINST 'THE OTHER GERMANY'

1. *Forbrytere og andre tyskere.* (cf. I/8)
2. *Efter segern.* (cf. I/3)
3. *Guerillakriget* (Guerilla Warfare), Stockholm, 1942.

IV SPAIN

1. *Bürgerkrieg oder Unabhängigkeitskrieg* (Civil War or War of Independence). Report for friends in exile. Barcelona, March 1937.
2. From an unpublished manuscript *Der Kampf der spanischen Jugend* (The Struggle of Spanish Youth), Oslo 1937.
3. *Briefe des Genossen Willy* (Letters of Comrade Willy), written in Spain in February to June 1939, distributed from Paris.
4. From address *Ein Jahr Krieg und Revolution in Spanien* (One Year of War and Revolution in Spain), Paris 1937.
5. *Det 20de århundre,* 1937.
6. *Arbeiderbladet,* 1939.

V NORWAY

1 *Norwegens Freiheitskampf 1940–1945* (Norway's Fight for Freedom 1940–1945), Hamburg, 1948.

2. *Oslo-universitetet i kamp* (Oslo University at War), Stockholm, 1943. Pamphlet issued by the Stockholm Institute for Foreign Affairs.
3. Article written in Berlin in 1947, after a visit to Norway.

VI INTERNATIONAL CONTACTS

1. From the Progress Report of the 'International Group of Democratic Socialists' for the year 1944, Stockholm 144.
2. Extracts from Notes, Protocols, Discussion points, etc.
3. *Zur Nachkriegspolitik deutscher Sozialisten* (Postwar Policies of German Socialists), Stockholm.
4. *Sozialistische Jugend* (Socialist Youth), November/December 1937.
5. *Splittelse eller samling* (Split or Unity), Oslo, 1939. Pamphlet for the Socialist press.
6. *Sovjets utenrikspolitikk 1917–1939* (Soviet Foreign Policy 1917–1939), Oslo, 1939. Pamphlet for the Socialist press.
7. *Kjensgjerninger om kommunistenes politikk* (Facts on Communist Policy), Oslo, 1945. Pamphlet for Norwegian Labour party.

VII IN GERMANY AGAIN

1. 'LFP-Gespräch mit Annedore Leber und Willy Brandt'. See List of sources to Chapter I (7).

ABBREVIATIONS

CNT	(Confederación Nacional del Trabajo) Spanish Anarcho-Syndicalist Trades Union
CP	Communist Party
DENA	Deutsche Nachrichten-Agentur (U.S. Zone)
DGB	Deutscher Gewerkschaftsbund (German TUC)
ECE	Economic Council for Europe
FAI	(Federación Anarquista Ibérica) Anarchist Secret Society
FET	(Falange Española Tradicionalista) Spanish Teachers' Union
ILO	International Labour Organization
ILP	Independent Labour Party
KPD	Kommunistische Partei Deutschlands
NAP	Norwegian Labour Party
NSDAP	(Nationalsozialistische Deutsche Arbeiter-Partei) National Socialist German Workers' Party
NTB	Norwegisches Telegrafenbüro
POUM	(Partido Obrero de Unificación Marxista) Spanish Trotskyists
PSUC	(Partido Socialista Unificado de Cataluña) United Catalan Socialist-Communist Party
SAJ	Sozialistische Arbeiter-Jugend (Youth organization of the SPD before 1933)
SAP	Sozialistische Arbeiter-Partei (radical splinter group from SPD)
SD	Sicherheitsdienst (The Security Service)
SED	(Sozialistische Einheitspartei Deutschlands) Socialist Unity Party (merger between SPD and KPD)
SHAEF	Supreme Headquarters Allied Expeditionary Force
SJV	Sozialistischer Jugendverband
SOPADE	Sozialdemokratische Partei Deutschlands (SPD in exile)
SPD	Sozialdemokratische Partei Deutschlands
SS	Schutzstaffeln (Nazi élite force)
TUC	Trades Union Council
UGT	(Unión General de Trabajadores) Socialist Trade Union
UNO	United Nations Organization
Waffen-SS	Military units of the SS

Index